The World's Greatest Unsolved Mysteries

This book is dedicated with grateful thanks to our many friends all over the world who have so generously given their time, energy and hospitality to help us during our long years of research into these unsolved mysteries.

Lionel and Patricia Fanthorpe
Cardiff, Wales, UK 1997

Lionel & Patricia Fanthorpe

The World's Greatest Unsolved Mysteries

HOUNSLOW PRESS
A MEMBER OF THE DUNDURN GROUP
TORONTO · OXFORD

Hounslow Press
A member of the Dundurn Group

Publisher: Anthony Hawke
Interior photographs: Lionel & Patricia Fanthorpe
Printer: Webcom

Canadian Cataloguing in Publication Data

Fanthorpe, R. Lionel
    The world's greatest unsolved mysteries

ISBN 0-88882-194-8

1. Curiosities and wonders.   I. Fanthorpe, Patricia.
II. Title.

AG243.F36 1997   001.94   C97-931145-4

2 3 4 5 BJ 01 00 99

The publisher wishes to acknowledge the generous assistance of the **Canada Council**, the **Book Publishing Industry Development Program** of the **Department of Canadian Heritage**, and the **Ontario Arts Council**.

Care has been taken to trace the ownership of copyright material used in this book. The authors and the publisher welcome any information enabling them to rectify any references or credit in subsequent editions.

Printed and bound in Canada.

 Printed on recycled paper.

Second printing: January 1999

Hounslow Press
8 Market Street
Suite 200
Toronto, Ontario, Canada
M5E 1M6

Hounslow Press
73 Lime Walk
Headington, Oxford
England
OX3 7AD

Hounslow Press
2250 Military Road
Tonawanda, NY
U.S.A. 14150

CONTENTS

FOREWORD

Everyone loves a good mystery and those capable of writing one, and writing it well, will always be assured of many readers. The list of such writers is long and stretches from Wilkie Collins, to Arthur Conan Doyle, Dorothy L. Sayers, and the prolific Agatha Christie. The best of them are skilled at weaving a story which leaves the average reader puzzled about its ending until the very last pages of their books. Their ingenuity in creating a mystery, and then solving it, knows no bounds.

What all these writers give us is fiction. They offer us imagined situations and invented characters. The book we have here, incredible as it may seem, is not fictional at all. It is fact. It is hard to believe a lot of it. Much of it defies common sense, seemingly remote both from human experience and reality. All of what we read here actually happened. None of it is from imagination; everything is from life.

The Reverend Lionel Fanthorpe, with the help of his wife Patricia, has achieved three things in this book of his, one of many he has written in his very busy life:

First, he has highlighted for us a selection of the most bizarre happenings that have occurred over the years, some of them taken from the natural world, and some from human character and behaviour. He has identified for us twenty such 'mysteries' and could have shared with us many more had space allowed. Of course he is not the only researcher who has looked at these strange stories over the years. Many others have been fascinated by them and there will be others yet to come. We owe them much, these researchers, with their enquiring minds, for, left to ourselves, we, more average, ordinary mortals, would never have made the effort. We would have been content to believe everyone and everything as normal and ordinary as we are ourselves.

We may, for example, have a friend who is a parish priest. We see him at work, visiting the sick, preaching in his Church, burying the dead. He will be one of many thousands living the ordinary life of any such parish priest. Here, in this book, we meet one who was very different. A poor priest, inexperienced, coming new to a run down parish, with a dilapidated Church, in a remote area of France, suddenly becomes wealthy, able to fund grandiose schemes and costly works. Where did his sudden riches come from? During his life time it was a mystery and it remains so. He took his secret with him to the grave.

We are aware of children being abandoned by their parents. It happens sadly all over the world. Dr Barnardo, a few generations ago, found many such rejected youngsters and gathered them into his homes. But what would even Dr Barnardo have made of the young Kaspar Hauser you will read of in the book, who appeared suddenly in Nuremberg, sixteen or so years old, oddly dressed, unable to speak but able to write his name, never able to explain where he had been during the early years of his life and the only food he could bear to eat bread, washed down with water.

In this book, run of the mill people like us, come face to face with the extraordinary. The normal, every day behaviour we are used to is challenged with much that seems totally "out of this world." Whether our lives are enriched or troubled by meeting unusual people and strange events we cannot tell. At least this book makes us aware of them.

The author has not only introduced to us certain strange happenings he has carefully researched them. Here, no doubt, his wife, as in so many other ways has been his greatest asset. For many years of his life he has written and lectured on the strange, the paranormal leading him in recent weeks to front a series of programmes on TV which have fascinated a large company of viewers. His understanding of the strange things of life is considerable but, of course, it did not come of itself. He had to work at it. He and his wife have visited, talked to people, read widely, verified everything as closely as they could. In this book, for example, we read of the Money Pit of Nova Scotia. It's vividly described for us, but not merely from books. He has been to Oak Island, where the pit is, several times and talked to those who are still longing to find what treasure if any lies at the foot of it. He gives one the impression of longing to have a dig at it himself.

Even without this book, most people would know something of the *Mary Celeste*. It remains one of the great unsolved mysteries of the sea. Here the ship is brought alive for us — its building, its size, its captain, its crew, its cargo, the course it was taking at the time of its abandonment. The fate of the ship becomes ever more poignant for us for he helps us know the people who were on board on that fateful day.

In fact long years of research have gone into the making of this work and the authors can be proud of it.

Finally they seek to do for us what all the greatest of our mystery fiction writers do. They set out to explain why and how much of it may have happened. The average among us needs this help. We are part of an ordered world and we feel there must be a logical answer for everything. Where there is an effect there must surely be a cause for it. Lionel and Patricia do their best for us. They set out reasons for these strange mysteries, often not merely one but many possible reasons for the same phenomenon. We are left to choose our own or to reject all or everyone of them, and substitute our own.

No doubt many over the years will enjoy reading this book. Indeed the careful work that has gone into it deserves a large and thoughtful readership. Enigmas, puzzles, riddles are here in plenty. Fiction of many kinds has over the years kept readers enthralled and libraries busy. Of such books, as the Bible says, "there will be no end." This book is different. It is fact not fiction and there is nothing in fiction to touch it. Mark Twain was right and the last word will be left to him:

"Truth is stranger than fiction. Fiction is obliged to stick to possibilities. Truth is not."

Stanley Mogford, MA
Cardiff, Wales, UK 1997

---

*Footnote: The authors are very grateful indeed to Canon Stanley Mogford, one of the greatest and most deservedly respected scholars in Wales, for his kindness in writing this Foreword. It is always an honour and a privilege for any author to have his support.

INTRODUCTION

One of the deepest and most profound instincts in every human being is the need to find out. When the first hunter-gatherers came down from their trees, or peered around the entrances of their caves, they wanted to know what was on the other side of the river, what was behind the waterfall and what lay beyond the mountain.

Today we wander the Web and navigate the Net for the same reason that they did their exploring millennia ago — *because it's there.*

If someone produces an impossibly accurate ancient map of a coastline he cannot have seen because it's underneath a mile of ice — *we want to know how he did it.*

When honest and reliable witnesses come down from a trip in the Rockies and tell us they've seen *something* like a human being — but eight feet tall and weighing 500 pounds — *we want to know what it is.*

When some invisible psychic force wrenches off the door of an iron oven and hurls it into the air — *we want to know about it.*

When lead-lined coffins weighing a ton each move inside a sealed tomb like leaves blowing around in the fall — *we want to investigate.*

We've had the privilege of researching scores of unsolved mysteries for over forty years — and we're still looking for answers. We can thoroughly recommend it: it's *fun* as well as being challenging and exciting — and occasionally downright *dangerous.* In the pages that follow, we extend the reader a hearty invitation to come and join us in the quest.

Lionel and Patricia Fanthorpe
Cardiff, Wales, UK
1997

ANTARCTICA AND THE ANCIENT MAPS

Did an advanced civilisation flourish on Antarctica 15000 years ago?

Every so often strange things — Fortean things — turn up and smudge the elaborate picture which most of us are busily painting on the flimsy canvas of commonsense reality (which screens us from the *Ultimate Reality* which we know is waiting out there somewhere).

They may be anachronistic fossils, odd drawings or carvings that have survived for thousands of years, huge lines carved across a flat plain so that they make much more sense from the air than from ground level, or semi-legendary, semi-mythical accounts of angels and demons, monsters and demi-gods, who could by a slight tweak of the text be better understood as extra-terrestrials, or as the weird, vestigial survivors of strange pre-human civilisations.

There are ancient buildings and subterranean labyrinths that the best modern machinery would be hard pressed to construct: and there are very old maps, copies of even older maps, which show the detail of coastlines and geographical features that have been totally inaccessible for millennia because of a thick covering of ice.

In July 1960, USAF Lt Colonel Harold Z. Ohlmeyer of the 8th Reconnaissance Technical Squadron, Westover, Massachusetts, wrote a devastatingly important letter to Professor Charles H. Hapgood. Hapgood had asked Ohlmeyer to study the Piri Reis map drawn by that famous old Turkish Admiral in 1513, and Ohlmeyer's answer was that the seismic work of the 1949 Anglo-Swedish Expedition showed that Reis's coastline, far below the present Antarctic ice sheet, *was accurate*. Ohlmeyer concluded that the coastline in question had been mapped *before* the ice covered it.

Who was Piri Reis, and how did he get that accurate geographical information in the early sixteenth century? He was a high ranking officer in the Ottoman Turkish Empire, and, as far as can be judged, a particularly honest and open character. He made no claim to have compiled his map by his own unaided efforts or his own practical cartographic expeditions, although he was an excellent sailor who travelled far and wide, and had written a text book on sailing. Notes in his own handwriting tell how he compiled his map from many sources — some of them as recent as Christopher Columbus, others going back to at least 400 BC. Somehow or another he clashed with the Ottoman High Command and was beheaded circa 1555. His precious map drawn on gazelle skin was rediscovered in the old Imperial Palace in Constantinople in 1929.

Hapgood's work in 1963 envisaged Reis working away among the ancient documents preserved at Constantinople, which were themselves based on far older sources, compiled in turn from older sources still . . . and going way back beyond 4000 BC. This argument implied that a very advanced technological civilisation had existed at a far more distant date than was generally accepted by most pre-historians. Hapgood traced this channel of geographical and navigational information through the Minoan and Phoenician cultures, through ancient Egypt and way back beyond that.

One map alone, however interesting its history, and however accurate its details of the Antarctic coastline, could be regarded as nothing more than a strange coincidence. If *another* old map turned up *independently*, that would be much more significant. Such a map did appear: it's known as the Oronteus Finaeus map and was drawn in 1531-2. It shows carefully drawn mountain ranges as well as a surprisingly accurate Antarctic coastline, and realistic rivers draining down from the mountains. It is also significant that the central area nearest to the South Pole itself has been left blank — as though the accurate and honest cartographer who drew it has acknowledged that this central region is heavily shrouded in ice so that no details of mountains or rivers can be surveyed or measured.

A major discrepancy on the Oronteus Finaeus map is that the Antarctic Peninsula goes a long way too far north. It almost touches Cape Horn. But a closer scrutiny of the *whole* of Oronteus's representation of the Antarctic continent shows that *all* of it extends too far from the centre, too far north, in fact, in every direction. It is not *inaccurate* — it's simply drawn to the *wrong scale* for the rest of the Finaeus map. Whoever first made the scaling error, it was made in the distant past and copied by a succession of cartographers including Piri Reis himself.

The very old portolanos on which the medieval navigators depended did not carry regular grid lines like our modern lines of latitude and longitude. Instead they tended to use central points — located at various positions on the map — from which lines radiated like the closely fitting spokes of a bicycle wheel. The centres may have been meant to reproduce the directions of a primitive mariner's compass, and navigation would probably have proceeded by attempting to recognize the ship's location by the position of various landmarks, islands, cliffs, bays and headlands. Having established its present position, the navigator would possibly have tried to line up the ship's course along the grid line which would have taken it nearest to his intended destination.

A.E. Nordenskiöld, who was an acknowledged world authority in this area, compiled an atlas from the many portolanos he studied, and concluded that they were based on much older and far more accurate maps. The Dulcert Portolano of 1339 was, in particular, he argued, accurate beyond the capabilities of typical fourteenth century navigators and cartographers. His next point was that there was no observable *development* in the maps and charts which appeared from the fourteenth to the sixteenth centuries. Two

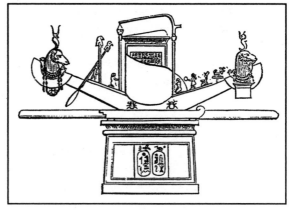

This strange old Egyptian Ark pre-dates the Exodus. Did its weird design and mysterious contents reach Egypt from a lost Civilization which flourished on Antarctica before the Ice Age destroyed it?

hundred years of sailing, exploration and discovery was not reflected in the maps. He concluded that this was because someone in the early 1300s had discovered an exceptionally accurate map, which was destined not to be surpassed for the next two centuries at least. It also seemed to Nordenskiöld that there was only one such excellent original and that all the good and reliable portolanos had been copied from it.

His measurements revealed that as far as the Mediterranean and the Black Sea were concerned, all the portolanos were practically identical, and the same scale was used on them all.

Nordenskiöld was intrigued to find that the scale used was not obviously linked with the customary Mediterranean units of measurement, except for those found in Catalonia. He suggested that the historical link between Catalan and the ancient Phoenicians and Carthaginians could well account for this. If the units of measurement and the scale were Carthaginian, then there was a strong possibility that the original, accurate map from which the good portolanos had been copied, had also been known to the Carthaginians — even if it had not originated with them.

Nordenskiöld then examined the rôle of Marinus of Tyre, a navigator who lived during the second century AD and was the predecessor of the famous Ptolemy.

Theodorus Meliteniota of Byzantium, from whom most of the information about the great scholar's life is derived, suggests that Claudius Ptolemaus, popularly known as Ptolemy, was born in the Greek city of Ptolemais Hermii, and did most of his scientific, astronomical and mathematical work in Alexandria. He was certainly making astronomical observations between the years 127 and 151 AD, and may still have been working as late as 155. There is also an Arabian tradition that Ptolemy died at the age of seventy-eight.

From his studies of the portolanos, Nordenskiöld felt that their units of measurement could not have been any later than the time of Marinus of Tyre, and were probably far earlier. Comparing them with Ptolemy's work, he saw clearly that the original source from which the portolanos had been copied was greatly superior.

To give Ptolemy the credit he richly deserves, he was the most famous geographer of his time. He had access to the greatest library of the ancient world, and all its geographical documents and records. He was a fine mathematician and he had a modern, scientific attitude to the phenomena he observed and studied. As Hapgood so rightly argues in *Maps of the Ancient Sea-Kings*, it is very unlikely that medieval sailors during the fourteenth century *without* the advantages of Ptolemy's reference library and high mathematical skills could have produced charts superior to his.

Assuming that it was the Carthaginians and Phoenicians who had access to much older and more accurate charts than Ptolemy was able to produce, and assuming again that these reappeared after an interval of well over a thousand years to form the basis of the portolanos, why did they vanish, and where might they have been hidden? The answer could lie in the grim and chronic struggle between Rome and Carthage known as the Punic Wars.

To understand the hatred and rivalry between these two great ancient powers, it is necessary to look briefly at their respective histories.

The first legend of the foundation of Rome relates how Aeneas, the Trojan prince, escaped from the ruin of Troy, married a Latin princess and founded the city of Rome and the Julian Dynasty. The second legend concerns Romulus and Remus, descendants of Aeneas on their mother's side, and, in the myth, the sons of Mars, god of war. Thrown into the Tiber by an unfriendly King of Latium, they drifted to Capitol Hill, were raised by a she-wolf and founded Rome in 753 BC — a date from which all Roman history traditionally begins.

The most likely historical origin is that clusters of settlements on Rome's seven hills got together to form a city state round about 1000 BC.

Having been involved in various battles with fierce Celtic neighbours and Gauls, "Rome conquered the world in self-defence!"

The Roman Empire was a great trading organisation, and freedom of the seas was vitally important to her both commercially and militarily. The Carthaginians were the major maritime problem for Roman ships in the Mediterranean. It was inevitable that one power or the other would have to go down.

The history of Carthage begins with Phoenician colonists from Lebanon and Syria 1000 miles to the east. Lacking the manpower to establish large settlements, they set up a few coastal cities as trading posts. The silver and tin of southern Spain were a great attraction to them. Phoenicians looked for places easily accessible from the sea but not open to hostile tribes from the hinterland:

they liked offshore islands, rocky peninsulas, and sandy bays to facilitate beaching their ships. Carthage conformed to this pattern. It was also in a good position to expand into the fertile areas around it. The name itself derives from two Phoenician words *kart hadasht* which means "new city."

The implacable attitude separating the two great Mediterranean powers is clearly illustrated by the bitter words of the grim old Roman Senator Marcus Porcius Cato (234 - 149 BC) " *Delenda est Carthago*" — " Carthage must be destroyed."

The first Punic War (264 - 261 BC) started because of problems in Sicily. The second (218 - 201 BC) ended with Scipio Africanus's triumph over Hannibal the Carthaginian general at the epoch making Battle of Zama in what is now Tunisia. The third and final round (149 - 146 BC) ended with the total destruction of Carthage and her people.

Did the precious old maps survive the destruction of Carthage, or were they safely on board a Carthaginian ship which somehow evaded the Roman blockade and made its way east, back towards the old Phoenician homelands from which the ill-fated colony at Carthage had originally sprung?

It is interesting to speculate that *if* the precious and highly accurate old map did find its way back to the Middle East before the final destruction of Carthage, it could well have surfaced again during the Crusades, the period prior to 1307 during which the indomitable Templars were in the ascendancy. They were great sailors as well as great soldiers: were their successes at sea due in part to their possession of superior maps and charts, copied from highly accurate originals which pre-dated the maritime Phoenicians and Carthaginians?

So one possible scenario suggests that some very ancient but unknown source produced maps of high quality which came into the hands of the Phoenicians, and passed from them — indirectly — to the Templars, and so to European navigators in the thirteenth and fourteenth centuries.

Where could the advanced technical knowledge behind those maps have come from in the first place? Assuming that Graham Hancock's thoroughly researched and well reasoned theories have the sound basis in fact that they certainly appear to have, then Antarctica would be as good a starting place as any.

If Hapgood's deductions about the ability of continental land masses to slide over the earth's surface — that is, if the crust is able to move independently of the core beneath it — are correct, then areas which once occupied warm or temperate zones, may find themselves relatively quickly inside polar circles, and vice versa.

Hapgood and his colleague, James Campbell, put forward the theory that the earth's crust rests on a very weak layer below — a layer that is virtually liquid. Following an idea suggested to them by Hugh Auchincloss Brown, the engineer, they investigated the possibility that a force powerful enough to move the entire crust of the earth over this weak, quasi-liquid layer, could be generated by the mass of the polar ice-caps themselves, and their centrifugal effects arising from the earth's own rotation.

The centre of gravity of the Antarctic ice-cap, for example, is approximately 300 miles from the South Pole. "As the earth rotates," suggests Hapgood, "the eccentricity creates a centrifugal effect that works horizontally on the crust, tending to displace it towards the equator."

Einstein himself supported this theory: in the introduction to Hapgood's *Earth's Shifting Crust,* Einstein wrote:— "His (Hapgood's) idea is original, of great simplicity, and — if it continues to prove itself — of great importance to everything that is related to the history of the Earth's surface."

Following Hapgood's hypothesis, if there was an advanced civilisation living on the continent which is now Antarctica before it moved into a polar position where it would rapidly become ice-locked, what would such people do to save themselves, their children and their culture?

Such cataclysmic shifting of the Earth's crust would inevitably be accompanied by dynamic geological and meteorological phenomena. There would be earthquakes, volcanic disturbances, fierce storms, destructive winds and tidal waves. Those who could — those who had ships strong and buoyant enough to survive the devastation and the accelerating onset of the paralysing cold — would head north towards warmer zones. Where might those fortunate few refugees and survivors have landed?

Heading north from all sides of the ice-doomed Antarctic continent would bring the desperate travellers to: Cape Horn, the Cape of Good Hope, New Zealand's South Island, the southern coast of Australia, and — if anyone had travelled far enough due north along the 109 degrees west longitude — to the remote mysteries of Easter Island.

Is there the faintest possibility that the indecipherable *rongo-rongo* script and the inexplicable stone heads of Easter Island are thousands of years older than is generally thought to be the case?

Just suppose that a highly advanced civilisation once flourished on the land that is now buried under thousands of feet of Antarctic ice. Those of their refugees who travelled up the East African coast could eventually have reached Egypt. Was it their skill, perhaps, that designed and constructed the Sphinx and many of the other massive structures that are still defying time?

Did another group of them reach South America and leave indelible traces of their architectural knowledge and structural expertise there as well?

When the oldest indigenous Australians talk of the *Dream Time* does their mysticism go right back to another half-remembered place from which they came millennia ago, and will paintings one day be discovered under the ice of Antarctica which bear an uncanny resemblance to the oldest Australian rock and cave art?

Puzzling legends of lost civilisations persist all over the world. The vanishing of a once great Antarctic civilisation below the ice of the present South Pole might reveal the history behind those legends.

THE CANADIAN SASQUATCH AND OTHER STRANGE ANTHROPOIDS

Something lives on the highest and loneliest peaks — could it have an extra-terrestrial origin?

There is a subtle difference between asking whether Bigfoot or Sasquatch is real and asking whether the phenomenon associated with that name is real. The phenomenon is certainly real. New reports of sightings, or of footprints, come in almost daily. Someone or something — psychic entity, mental aberration, extra-terrestrial being, unknown physical life-form, you name it — is causing the sightings. Someone or something is leaving the footprints. An enormous amount of Sasquatch evidence is accumulating in the Pacific North-west of Canada and the USA.

On October 20th, 1967, at just after 1:00 PM, Bob Gimlin and Roger Patterson managed to take 953 frames of 16mm cine film of *something* that looked like a very big, hair-covered humanoid. The existence of their film eliminates two theories: whatever they saw was not an hallucination, nor was it the result of auto-suggestion, self-hypnosis, or any sort of psycho-sociological mind trick that they'd accidentally played on themselves. As far as is known, cameras can't record images that exist only in the camera-user's mind.

The film wasn't perfect, but it was good enough to dispose of another theory: whatever's on the Gimlin-Patterson film is not some normal, commonly known, but misidentified zoological species. This thing wasn't any kind of bear or anthropoid ape seen in strange conditions or from an odd perspective. It could have been one of two things: a hoax, or an unknown creature of some sort, which possessed a type of objective reality capable of leaving a photographic record.

The indigenous people of Canada and North America have cultural and traditional histories of Bigfoot which go back several centuries. The oldest written records go back nearly 200 years, and the sightings are by no means culture specific. Indigenous people as well as European, African and Asian immigrants have all been involved in Bigfoot episodes.

Statistical analysis produces interesting correlations. There are, for example over 600 place names in the North Western States of the USA which are thought to have associations with the Bigfoot or Sasquatch legends. These place names are not positively linked to population density. If hoaxers had been responsible, it would have seemed probable that the more people there were around, the greater the chance of a hoaxer working the area — but not so. What the sightings and place names *do* seem to correlate with positively is mountain ridges and mountain crests: in other words, if there really are such things as Sasquatch or Bigfoot, then they are closely associated with high and inaccessible places — just as the Yeti is in Tibet and Nepal.

Taking one of thousands of typical reports, just as an example, two hunters from Stewart, British Columbia were travelling at an altitude of over 4000 feet along an old mine access road. As daylight faded they turned a corner and jumped from their truck thinking that they'd seen a bear moving ahead of them. Setting off in pursuit of it, they saw that it was walking upright. It became aware of them at the same moment and turned to look directly at them. It turned its shoulders and the whole of its upper body as it didn't seem to have a neck.

They described a dark face, with a small beard and a flattish nose. It seemed as surprised to see them, as they were surprised to see it. The last glimpse they had of it, the Sasquatch was vanishing among the trees. The hunters noted particularly that it was very big — over seven feet tall — and heavily built, and there was a powerfully unpleasant smell around it. They also noticed that the hands swung lower than the knees.

Albert Ostman had a much closer encounter than the Stewart hunters. He reported how in 1924 he was prospecting in Toba Inlet in British Columbia when an eight foot Sasquatch picked him up like a rucksack and carted him along inside his sleeping bag for about three hours. When dawn broke he found he was in a Sasquatch 'homestead' of some description and that it was occupied by the adult male that had kidnapped him, an adult female and two young ones. Although they prevented his escape for several days, Ostman was unwilling to use his gun on them because they had done him no harm, and clearly intended no harm. He finally escaped by tricking the adult male with some snuff from his pack, and while it was rushing to find water to sooth the irritation, Ostman made a dash for freedom.

Dr W. Henner Farenbach performed another interesting piece of statistical analysis on a large sample of Sasquatch footprints. The print size of any natural animal species including human beings tends to follow a normal bell curve of distribution. Most human beings for example have British shoe sizes greater than 4 but smaller than 11. The great majority — the apex of that normal distribution bell curve — being from 6 to 9. A few very small footed people have sizes 2 and 3, and an equally low number of large footed people wear sizes 11 and 12.

When Dr Farenbach made the calculations he discovered that the Sasquatch prints adhered well to this normal, natural pattern. If hoaxers were responsible it seems highly improbable that they could have colluded over such wide distances and over so many years to produce such a realistic sample range.

In addition to footprints and occasional hair samples, there are sound recordings in existence. Some of the most interesting of these were made by Al Berry and Ron Morehead in the Sierra Nevada. They can actually be contacted through the Internet at their web site "Sierra Sounds," and a CD plus tapes are available from them.

Another question frequently asked by serious Sasquatch researchers is why prominent, orthodox scientists haven't joined their ranks in any perceptible strength. It may be argued that they have, but that the traditionalist and rather cautious academic official media are still reluctant to give much space or weight to Sasquatch research.

The well balanced information available over the Internet and World Wide Web via the Virtual Bigfoot Conference Site organized by Henry Franzoni suggests that part of the problem is to be found in the suspicion among a number of researchers that Bigfoot seems to possess a kind of paranormal sixth sense, and perhaps some additional, ultra-human abilities. How else, one might sensibly ask, has it managed to avoid contact with *homo sapiens* for so long?

Once the question of a sixth sense arises, Franzoni warns, orthodox scientists begin to shy away from delving into a phenomenon. This is probably because of the heavy bias in favour of the mechanistic philosophy of science which appears to have been a dominant influence since the seventeenth century, and the lasting impact of René Descartes.

Dr Rupert Sheldrake's profound and highly readable work entitled *Why Puzzling Powers of Animals Have Been Neglected* makes the point that academic biology has inherited from seventeenth century science a strong faith in reductionism — a technique for explaining complex systems in terms of smaller and simpler parts. For example, it was once believed that atoms formed the fundamental bedrock for all physical explanations, but recent subatomic research has shown that the atoms themselves can be thought of as patterns of vibrations within fields: which more or less dissolves the foundations of the old style materialistic science.

Karl Popper, the great philosopher of science, has said: "Through modern physics, materialism has transcended itself." What seems to have revolutionised the philosophy of science as far as physics is concerned has not yet conquered the stubborn materialism that still persists in some areas of biology. As Dr Sheldrake says, "Fields of enquiry that are inherently holistic have a low status in the hierarchy of science."

There is, however, another biological philosophy of science known as *vitalism* which suggests that living organisms are *truly* alive, whereas mechanistic and materialistic theories regard them as merely inanimate and soulless.

Because vitalism admits the existence of unknown vital principles, its adherents tended to be open minded about the possibilities of phenomena which were not vulnerable to explanation in mechanistic terms. Vitalists were interested in studying the psychic powers of human beings and uncanny powers in animals — such as the apparent sixth sense of the Sasquatch.

J.W. Burns worked for many years as a teacher among the indigenous Chehalis people of Harrison River, close to Harrison Hot Springs. From his Chehalis friends he heard many accounts of the Sasquatch, not as huge, ape-like semi-humans, but as a magically gifted giant race: they had clothes, fire, weapons and basic technology and lived in villages. They also had paranormal abilities.

Such beings would have been in line with the report from Union Town in Pennsylvania, published in a paper by Stan Gordon for the 1974 UFO Symposium. A woman was sitting at home watching TV when she got up to investigate a strange noise from her porch. Thinking that something dangerous might be out there, she picked up a loaded shotgun first. As she turned on the porch light and stepped out to look, she saw a seven foot tall creature, covered in hair and barely six feet away from her. It raised its arms above its head, but she thought it was about to attack and fired her shot gun into its body at point blank range. There was a flash of light and the thing simply vanished: no blood, no carcase, no nothing.

It may be unkind to suggest that perhaps mechanists are mechanists *because* they are afraid of vitalism and its implications, but it often seems as though they are. As Dr Sheldrake argues again, for them to admit the reality of anything mysterious or mystical in life would mean abandoning their faith in the hard won certainties of science.

Some embarrassing phenomena are then either attacked or ignored, not because they are unorthodox, illogical, fallacious or ridiculous, but simply because they don't conform to the comforting mechanistic theory which sets out to explain the universe and all it contains.

Sheldrake maintains that a broader alternative to the mechanistic theory of life has grown up in the form of a holistic or organismic philosophy of nature. The whole is *more* than the sum of its parts. Nature is made up of organisms not machines.

Against this more liberal philosophical-biological background, Sasquatch and his Himalayan cousin the Yeti, have much more opportunity of emerging into the light.

An amazing encounter was reported by nineteen-year-old Lakpa Sherpani in 1974. She said that her yak herd was attacked by a a short but immensely powerful yeti, which killed five of them by twisting their horns and then knocked her unconscious. The incident occurred at an altitude of 14000 feet in the vicinity of Mount Everest.

In 1957 Professor V.K. Leontiev was in the Caucasus Mountains near the source of the River Jurmut, when he saw strange tracks in the snow. That night he heard inexplicable sounds, and saw a weird, unknown creature the following day. He described it as over seven feet tall and very broad. The body was covered in hair and it walked upright, not touching the ground with its hands. The professor referred to it as a Kaptar, the name by which it was known locally. He examined its footprints carefully after it had gone, and described them as unlike the prints of any animal he had ever come across previously.

In July of 1924 a party of miners was attacked by a group of Sasquatch in the Mount St Helen's/Lewis River district in Washington State. The miners had heard strange, frightening sounds for over a week before the Sasquatch actually attacked them. They saw a weird, seven foot tall creature and fired at it, then ran to their cabin and barricaded themselves in. All through the night the Sasquatch hurled rocks at the cabin and attempted to break in the door — despite their massive strength, it held. Press men from the *Portland Oregonian* came to investigate and found giant footprints all around the miners' cabin. After the attack, the place was renamed Ape Canyon — a name by which it is still known today.

Ivan Wally of Vancouver was driving his pick-up along the Trans-Canada Highway above the River Thompson, three or four miles east of Lytton. It was the evening of November 20th, 1969. As his vehicle climbed the hill he saw a creature ahead of him on the road. It was approximately seven feet tall; the legs looked long in proportion to the body, and Ivan guessed that it probably weighed over 300 pounds. The creature had short greyish-brown hair all over it. As the truck approached, the creature turned to look at it, and raised both arms. Ivan said later that its face reminded him of a wizened old man. Something about the thing sent Ivan's dog — which was on the seat beside him — half crazy with either fear or anger, maybe a combination of both. At that point the creature loped away on its long legs. Ivan turned around and drove back to Lytton where he reported the incident to the RCMP, who took him seriously and searched for footprints. Unfortunately, the roadside gravel was not conducive to taking impressions, and they found none.

Volumes could easily be filled with similar incidents: hundreds, perhaps thousands, of sensible, truthful and reliable witnesses from Canada, the USA, Tibet, Nepal, China and Russia have reported sighting after sighting of strange creatures resembling very large men, covered with hair. So what might they be? A significant number of the reports suggest that there is something paranormal about them. Are they simply some unknown but perfectly normal and natural anthropoid? If so, why do we never find their bodies? Perhaps they bury their dead. Perhaps they go off to find a lonely and desolate place — maybe a hidden mountain cave — where they can die with dignity, privacy and secrecy when they feel that their end is near. The strangest theory of all is that they enjoy enormous longevity.

In the Hunza valley, high in the Himalayas, the normal human inhabitants enjoy exceptionally good health and extremely long life-spans — possibly attributable to their pollution free air and a diet rich in apricots and apricot oil. If the Sasquatch and Yeti and their cousins around the world's other mountain ranges also benefit from the pollution free air available at those altitudes, perhaps their life-spans are many times ours.

Some researchers suggest that they may have had an extra-terrestrial origin: the jury's still out on that one.

It seems highly unlikely that the Sasquatch and his close relatives are merely myth, legend, hoax or imagination. There have been so many reports of these enigmatical hairy giants that there simply *has* to be someone or something up there in the mountains — the great unsolved mystery is *what*.

THE MYSTERY OF SINCLAIR'S TEMPLARS

There is a strong probability that refugee Templar Knights brought an ancient and mysterious treasure to Nova Scotia

The Sinclairs of Orkney have long deserved their reputation as a noble, courageous and hospitable family. The central character of this particular Sinclair adventure is one of the best of them all: Henry Sinclair the Navigator, friend of the Venetian Zeno brothers, and the most likely candidate for the role of Glooscap, the legendary Micmac hero of Nova Scotia.

Henry was the eldest son of Sir William Sinclair, also rendered St Clair, and derived from a Latin phrase meaning *the Holy Light*. Their earlier ancestors had been of Norse descent and known as Møre. They had controlled land around the coast of Norway, the Orcadian Islands and Caithness in Scotland. The famous Earl Rognvald was one of them, and from him had come Rolf, Duke of Normandy, a fore-runner of William the Conqueror.

At the time of Henry the Navigator's birth his parents were living by the banks of the River Esk in Roslin Castle, which had been built in 1304. The mysterious Rosslyn Chapel, which contains some of the most complex Templar and Masonic symbolism in the world, was built by another Earl William Sinclair in the middle of the fifteenth century. In the sealed vaults below it, Sinclair Knights, still dressed in their armour, lie as though only asleep.

Henry Sinclair the Navigator was born in 1345, and became the first Sinclair Earl of Orkney through his mother, Isabel, daughter of Malise, Earl of Strathearn, Caithness and Orkney. On May 28th, 1344, her father, as he died, had sealed a document declaring her to be the rightful heir of his Earldom of Orkney, unless there were any male heirs — there weren't. This vitally important document made young Henry Earl of many islands, subject to his acceptance by the King of Norway.

A man who was heir to such an earldom would have to rule it by sail, and the skills of the sea would be as important to him as using his sword or riding his horse.

Chaucer's famous *Canterbury Tales* contain an excellent contemporary description of a typical knight of this period:

> *A Knyght ther was, and that a worthy man,*
> *That fro the tyme that he first bigan*
> *To riden out, he loved chivalrie,*
> *Trouthe and honour, fredom and curteisie.*
> *Ful worthy was he in his lordes werre,*
> *And therto hadde he riden, no man ferre . . .*
> *. . . Aboven alle nacions in Pruce . . .*
> *He nevere yet no vileynye ne sayde*
> *In al his lyf unto no maner wight*
> *He was a verray, parfit gentil knyght*

> There was a Knight, and he was a worthy man,
> And from the first day that he rode out
> He was chivalrous,
> Truthful and honourable. He was courteous to all, and a
> defender of their freedom.
> He fought well in his Lord's wars,
> And had ridden farther than any other soldier in his service . . .
> Above all other nations he had fought in Prussia . . .
> He had never spoken an evil word, nor done an evil deed
> To any many throughout the whole of his life.
> He was a perfect example of what a knight should be.

Henry's father, Sir William, died fighting bravely alongside his Prussian allies in 1358, and it is more than possible that he met Chaucer while travelling through London to take ship to Prussia. Did the great fourteenth century poet model the Knight in the *Canterbury Tales* on Sir William Sinclair? He could scarcely have found a better pattern.

As a result of his father's early death in battle, young Henry, although still barely into his teens, found himself carrying great responsibilities. But responsibilities have always rested well on the Sinclairs. His grandfather, another Sir William, was the loyal friend and comrade of Sir James Douglas and died fighting alongside him while attempting to keep their promise to bury the heart of Robert the Bruce in its silver casket in the Holy Land.

There were also very strong and persistent links between the Sinclair family and the indomitable Knights Templar.

In Latin, the Templars' full name was *pauperes commilitones Christi templique Salomonici:* the Poor Knights of Christ and of the Temple of Solomon. Godfroi de St Omer and Hugues de Payns from Burgundy went to Jerusalem in 1119 with the stated purpose of abandoning the world and living like a monastic order in poverty, chastity and obedience. They also declared that they intended to guard the roads so that pilgrims could travel to the various shrines and holy places in safety. The King of Jerusalem from 1118-1131 was Baldwin II, and he gave the Templars permission to use part of his palace. Their headquarters were very close to the al-Haksa Mosque, which was commonly referred to as Solomon's Temple, and it was from here that the Templars took their title.

Graham Hancock's superb study *The Sign and the Seal* suggests that Godfroi, Hugues and their fellow warriors had other motives for establishing their base where they did. He argues that a handful of knights — however great their prowess in battle — would have been a hopelessly small task force to guard any length

The mysterious Apprentice Pillar in the Templars' Rosslyn Chapel, said to have been carved by a craftsman from Sinclair's Orkney Islands.

of pilgrim road. In Graham's view, Hugues and company were secretly excavating the supposed site of Solomon's Temple in the hope of finding lost secrets or concealed treasure.

One of the most probable theories concerning Rennes-le-Château is that Father Bérenger Saunière had deliberately acquired the living of that remote and obscure mountain top village in order to be in the best position to search for the lost treasure which he believed was concealed there — just as the Templars had gained access to whatever might be buried under their Jerusalem headquarters.

Whatever strange and esoteric discoveries the Templars actually made, there is no doubt that they also acquired vast wealth during their period of ascendancy.

However, disaster struck their great Order in 1307 when the greedy and vicious Philip IV — ironically called *Philip le Bel* — moved treacherously against them. Not all of the Templars succumbed, however. Over the years, a few handfuls of their doughtiest warriors cut their way through Philip's minions

Roslin, or Rosslyn Chapel, below which Templar Knights lie buried in a sealed vault.

and eventually reached Orkney, where they were warmly welcomed and generously assisted by Henry Sinclair.

In addition to their military and ecclesiastical building skills, and their great feats of arms, the Templars were also expert sailors and navigators. Henry was therefore able to combine three great nautical traditions when he consulted with them as well as with his colleagues from Venice, the Zeno brothers.

This Zen family, known variously as Zenone, or Zeno in Italian, and as Geno or Genus in Latin, had been in Venice since the foundation of the city. They had been in Byzantium long before that and it was their ancestor, the great Zeno of Alexandria, who had constructed the famous mathematical paradox of the mythical race between Achilles and the tortoise.

The tortoise is given 100 paces start. During the measured count of 10, Achilles covers this distance easily, but the tortoise has managed to travel on 5 paces while he did 100. The paradox goes on to argue that each time Achilles reaches the spot where the tortoise *was* the tortoise has covered one twentieth of the distance Achilles has covered, and so remains permanently ahead of him, though the distance between them eventually grows immeasurably small. That kind of mathematical problem setting was an ideal family background for Zeno descendants who were destined to become some of the best navigators of the fourteenth century.

Until the Templars and other military orders built their own fleets, the pilgrims and soldiers heading for the eastern Mediterranean were glad to hire strong Venetian ships and skillful Venetian sailors.

Carlo Zen was a very prominent and powerful Venetian statesman towards the close of the fourteenth century, and he had two brothers — both expert captains and skilled navigators. It was these two — Nicolò and Antonio — who left the Mediterranean and sailed to Sinclair's cold, northern waters. A huge

Stone sarcophagus of a Templar Knight from the 13th century in Rosslyn Chapel near Edinburgh, Scotland.

question mark is raised over why two such important captains could be spared to sail north in such turbulent times when every able bodied Venetian sailor was needed in home waters. It is a daunting question which casts its shadow over the whole of the controversial *Zeno Narrative* and the *Zeno Map*, both of which remained upublished until the sixteenth century. Yet there is a reasonable answer.

Templars, crusaders and pilgrims knew that the Kingdom of Jerusalem and Christian access to the holiest of the shrines were now lost to the Muslims for the foreseeable future. The dedication and idealism of the warrior priests in the military orders — and especially among the Templars — began to turn to the dream of a New Jerusalem, a New Holy Land away to the north and west. Shadowy accounts of such a land abounded, and tended to be exaggerated and sensationalised each time they were retold.

The dream of the Christian Kingdom of Jerusalem was slowly but surely being replaced by the dream of a New Jerusalem far away to the north-west, out beyond the Pillars of Hercules and across the vast and dangerous waters of the Atlantic Ocean.

The three strands now weave tightly together: Henry the Navigator, Earl of Orkney, is fully sympathetic to the hopes and aspirations of his Templar protégés. They have salvaged something infinitely precious from the pillaged treasures of their Order and wish to conceal it in a new land far beyond the reach of the successors of Philip le Bel and their other European enemies. The Zeno brothers are happy to share their Venetian navigational knowledge, and to acquire other navigational knowledge from Sinclair and his Templars. They also want to find this New Jerusalem across the Atlantic. They wish to expand their present knowledge of the world's sea routes. Venice survived by trading: so among other things, the Zenos were hoping to find new trading opportunities among the inhabitants of whatever strange lands they might discover in the far west.

The Templars went on a mission to hide *something* of immense value and importance, which had once been a central component of their treasure. Sinclair went to increase his knowledge of navigation and to assist his Templar friends. The Zenos went to find what the New Jerusalem might hold in the way of additional trading potential for their beloved Venice.

The expedition sailed, crossed the Atlantic successfully, landed in Nova Scotia, and remained there for a year or so. During that fateful year, the fascinating Micmac cultural traditions about their great and good hero, Glooscap, came into being.

In general terms Glooscap is something of a Hiawatha figure — a wise and benign teacher who shows his people how to improve the physical qualities of the lives by improving their diet, and how to improve the cultural and spiritual qualities of their lives by behaving ethically towards one another.

Some archaeological evidence exists that there was a sudden and significant dietary change for the Micmacs round about the end of the fourteenth century. Prior to then, fish had been a relatively small fraction of their diet. Suddenly it became a major input. The Micmac account of Glooscap tells how he taught the people to make nets and to use them to catch fish in greater quantities than they had achieved before.

Among the maxims and aphorisms which Glooscap left were:

Never speak in your own praise.
Listen carefully and think hard
about everything that is said to you.
Control your temper.
The heart of the Law is to concern yourself only with controlling
your own life: do not interfere with the lives and happiness of
others.

Those who met him made favourable comments about him. Some described him as "sober, grave and good." Others felt that he could "look into the hearts and minds of men and read their thoughts."

The Micmac said of Glooscap that he was a great King or Prince in his own land, one who had often sailed the seas. His home, he had told them, was in a town on an island far away, and he had reached their country by way of Newfoundland.

The Micmac traditions tell that Glooscap encountered them for the first time at Pictou. His weapon was " a sharp sword" which seems to suggest that he reached Nova Scotia before firearms were common or effective. In answer to Micmac questions about his family, Glooscap told them that he had three daughters. Admiring him as they did, the young local chiefs were much more interested in finding out about his daughters than his sons, as they hoped to marry into his family. The legends tell that Glooscap was an enthusiastic explorer and that he stayed in Nova Scotia only for one long winter season, sailing away again when the weather improved.

This Micmac history and folklore concerning Glooscap tie in closely with what is known about Henry Sinclair's voyage of 1398. Sinclair had three daughters: Elizabeth, Mary and Jean. Sinclair came by way of Newfoundland and landed at Pictou. His home was in a town in the Orkneys. Glooscap told the Micmac that he would return one day. Sinclair was a man of his word, but Glooscap failed to return. What happened?

In the summer of 1400, Henry IV invaded Scotland, and some of his fleet attacked the Orkneys. Using Scapa Flow as a natural shelter, King Henry's ships came close to Kirkwall and his men disembarked under cover of darkness. News reached Henry Sinclair, who was furious to think that his Earldom was being invaded. Impetuously, he decided to counter attack at once, instead of waiting prudently for the English attack to falter and fail against his rugged castle walls. A contemporary account tells how Sinclair was beaten to the ground and killed by overwhelming odds. So Glooscap never had an opportunity to keep his promise and return to his Micmac friends.

There is a poignant comment in one of the Glooscap stories in which he helps Mi'kmwesu. After the young man and his friend have undergone many adventures in a special "canoe like an island" which Glooscap lends them, they return it to him and thank him for his help. He smiles and says that he has already followed all their adventures because he has a special power of *seeing*. Then he says, at the end of their story: "*If you ever need me, think of me and I will come.*"

Assuming that Henry Sinclair, the navigator and friend of the Templars, was Glooscap, and that he sailed home again after his short stay in Nova Scotia, what became of the Templar refugees whom he had brought with him? Some may have returned with him, of course, but others may have stayed behind to accomplish another task. Sinclair/Glooscap's goodness and charismatic powers of leadership had made a strong and positive impression on the Micmac.

His friends the Templars would have been welcomed among them in his name. What might have persuaded the Templars to stay in Nova Scotia? Suppose that they had intended to work on their great concealment project, hiding their priceless treasure so securely that no enemy would ever be able to recover it? Sinclair was trusted by those Templars who stayed on and worked in Nova Scotia. If Henry the Navigator said he was coming back for them in a year or two, then Henry would come — or like his gallant ancestor with Robert the Bruce's heart — he would die in the attempt. Their hopes of rescue died with

Henry at Kirkwall. What was the great work of concealment that those dedicated and indomitable Templars carried out ? Could it possibly have been the Oak Island Money Pit with its impregnable flood-tunnel defences? And what became of them afterwards? The Micmac are an attractive and friendly people: did the Templars, having completed their great mission, and with no hope of ever returning to Scotland, abandon their vows of chastity and marry into the Micmac Nation? Does a little of their proud old Scottish Templar blood still run in Nova Scotian veins today?

THE RIDDLE OF RENNES-LE-CHÂTEAU

A century ago, an impoverished French priest apparently discovered an amazing secret which made him immensely rich.

Rennes-le-Château is a tiny hilltop village in south-western France, resting among the foothills of the Pyrenees. Today, there are a few shops and restaurants; a small museum; the ruined Château Hautpoul owned by Monsieur Fatin, the sculptor, and his sister; the mysterious old Church of St Mary Magdalen, where many lost secrets could still lie buried; a gaunt watchtower with a steel door; and the stately Villa Bethania — once owned by Bérenger Saunière and his housekeeper, Marie Dénarnaud.

Renne-le-Château poses three challenging questions: first, *where* did Bérenger and Marie find the money to do all that they did in the village between 1885 and 1917 — when Saunière died in what were alleged to be sinister circumstances? A second, and greater, riddle is the unknown *source* of whatever mysterious wealth they uncovered. The third and greatest question is: *where is it now?*

There are at least ten major theories concerning the origins of Saunière's sudden wealth. Some researchers believe that it can all be accounted for by anonymous donations, by selling masses, and simply by collecting money from grateful visitors, pilgrims and local parishioners. But when every last account book has been audited and every legal record of Saunière's spirited battles with the querulous and obsessively bureaucratic Bishop Beauséjour has been scrutinised, there still appears to be a significant credibility gap. To put the counter argument at its most basic: *Saunière seems to have spent a lot more money than the supposed gifts and paid masses could ever have brought in.* So if that first, basic, common sense "explanation" of Saunière's wealth and conspicuous spending isn't quite adequate, what else might account for his undeniably conspicuous spending power? Ever since New Testament times, the opponents of Christianity have tried — so far with singular lack of success — to discredit Christ's resurrection. Two thousand years ago, the High Priest and his minions even attempted to bribe the Roman guards to testify that Christ's disciples had stolen his body from the rock tomb while they, the soldiers, were sleeping on duty.

This ancient and badly decayed red herring has been revived, disguised with southern French mustard; camouflaged with Oriental curry; hidden under a veneer of contemporary, pseudo-scientific, synthetic spices, E-numbers and aromatic flavourings: then exported with alacrity to Rennes-le-Château.

There are several quaint variants of this totally untenable hypothesis, but in essence it proposes that Jesus was secretly married to Mary Magdalen, and eventually fled with her and their children to the south of France, where their descendants became part of the Merovingian Dynasty. It is alleged that Christ either recovered after the crucifixion, or allowed someone else to die in his place — Simon of Cyrene being the favourite candidate for this altruistic but unenviable rôle.

It is then further proposed that two millennia later Saunière found some damning, anti-resurrection "evidence" hidden in or near Rennes. Proponents of this idea seem to be suggesting that it was Christ's mummified body: neatly labelled, of course, and duly signed and verified as authentic by a conscientious first century Frankish government embalmer. How about Christ's birth, wedding and death certificates — while they're at it — witnessed by Peter, James and John, of course, and then countersigned by the local Rabbi and a respectable Roman Notary Public?

The ruined Chateau Hautpoul in Rennes-le-Château. One tower is called "The Tower of Alchemy".

The theory then goes on to suggest that Saunière promptly used whatever he'd found to blackmail the Church. The whole idea goes down faster than the Titanic once it collides with the inconvenient iceberg of fact.

The historical evidence then dismantles even the sunken wreckage. If the disciples and the early church had had the slightest doubt about whether Jesus really was who he said he was, and that he had in fact risen from the dead, they would never have faced persecution and death for their faith. A brave man or woman is willing to die for the truth, or a greatly loved person. Nobody knowingly dies for a lie.

Then there is the *personality* of Jesus himself: it shines radiantly but realistically through all the contemporary accounts in the Gospels, the Acts and the Epistles. This totally unselfish and dedicated God-Man had immense courage and the highest moral principles. He would never have quit. He would never have let someone else die in his place while he escaped ignominiously to France.

It is historically possible (but perhaps unlikely) that Mary Magdalene, Mary of Bethany and "the woman who was a sinner" who anointed Christ's feet with perfume and tears, and then dried them with her hair, were really one and the same person — and that *that woman was married to Jesus.* She might also have been "the woman taken in adultery" and brought to Jesus by his enemies to see whether he would condone the ancient Mosaic Law about stoning her to death, or choose instead to obey the current Roman Law which prohibited the death penalty except with Roman permission. It was an impossible situation for him. Either answer was a decisive socio-political loser. Yet how much worse for him if it had been *his own deeply loved wife* whom his enemies had just caught in the act, and cynically brought to him for judgement?

Christ's intensely busy public mission would have left him little or no time to be a loving and attentive home maker, husband and father — which is the strongest argument (and the only acceptable one) for his never having married. But what if it had been his beloved wife, Mary Magdalen alias Mary of Bethany, who was now in the hands of these hostile, hypocritical puritans, and waiting at his feet for life or death judgement? Just suppose for an instant that her understandable, human feelings of loneliness and neglect had led her into an almost fatally disastrous, adulterous relationship?

Christ's total understanding and ready forgiveness — his skill in turning her would-be executioners aside with the unforgettable "*Let him who is without sin cast the first stone at her*" — all these factors would make poignant sense of her subsequent anointing of his feet, and her grateful tears.

And again, if they *had* been married, was it at Christ's earlier instigation — his thoughtful provision for his family's future — that she later took their children to the relative safety of south-western France following his crucifixion and resurrection? After all, Mary *was* the first person to see him alive again in the garden. Was that genuinely miraculous reassurance and earthly farewell a special, unique privilege for a loving wife?

Another moment's reflection raises several deep questions about the *nature* of this supposed " Saunière-blackmailed-the-Church" *evidence* which the boldly adventurous village Priest was thought to have found.

It would have been incredibly easy for the opponents of Christianity to proclaim that almost any crucified male body of approximately the right height and age was the body of Jesus. If Saunière had merely turned up some imperfectly preserved mortal remains *purporting* to be Christ's that would constitute no proof at all. Insurance investigators' records contain numerous records of fraudulent claims based on the criminals' hope that the body in question would prove unidentifiable. Saunière could not have found incontrovertible "proof" that Christ's resurrection never took place *simply because no such proof could exist.*

The obnoxious Bishop Beauséjour and his superiors had their faults — but they weren't fools. It would have been a thousand times easier and a million times cheaper for the Church authorities to challenge Saunière's hopelessly insubstantial claims than to submit to his blackmail. On the scale of probabilities, it is infinitely more likely that the mummified body of Donald Duck will be discovered at Rennes rather than that the body of Jesus is hidden there.

That Saunière was a blackmailer is yet another theory put forward from time to time. Some researchers suggest that he betrayed the Seal of the Confessional and made certain wealthy — but indiscreet — penitents pay exorbitantly for their past misdemeanours. Admittedly, it's a possibility, but it doesn't fit with what we know of Saunière's *character* after twenty years research. The profile is all wrong.

Saunière emerges as a bold, extravagant, ambitious and resolute man. He was physically and mentally powerful, independent, unafraid and unconventional. If sufficiently provoked, or threatened, he might well have killed an opponent on the spur of the moment — just as Moses "smote" the Egyptian taskmaster who was ill-treating a Hebrew slave.

Saunière was also romantic and red-blooded: he could easily have succumbed to the attractions of his nubile young housekeeper, Marie Dénarnaud, or indulged in a passionate fling with the glamorous and sophisticated opera star, Emma Calvé — as some researchers have suggested. But Saunière's characteristic sins would have been those impetuous and understandable sins of the flesh — not the mean, cruel, calculating and premeditated sins of a heartless, professional blackmailer.

A far stronger possibility is that Bérenger found either a treasure — or some strange, ancient secret that made it possible for him to *create* wealth. Although only a tiny hilltop village today, there is viable evidence that Rennes was once a significant Visigothic citadel, defended by a garrison of 2,000 men.

There are plenty of possible sources for such a treasure. The Visigoths

Mysterious faces set into the wall of an ancient dwelling in Rennes-le-Château. Does their strange coded symbolism provide a clue to the treasure?

sacked Rome in 410. Where better to hide the cream of their precious Roman spoils than in their own easily defended citadel of Rennes? The Templars had strongholds in the area, and when their gallant Order was decimated by the odious King Philip le Bel in 1307, it is possible, even probable, that some Templar treasure would have been hidden in or near Rennes — perhaps even in or under Saunière's ancient Church of St Mary Magdalen.

The almost impregnable Cathar fortress of Montségur was overrun by the Catholic Crusaders in 1244, but, just before the final disaster overwhelmed the defenders, four of their best mountaineers descended the precipitous crag below the fortress carrying with them "the treasures of their faith" — described in the Latin records of the Inquisition as "pecuniam infinitam" — literally *infinite or unlimited money*. Did those same fearless and fanatical mountaineers conceal their priceless secret somewhere in the vicinity of Rennes? Was that what Saunière found six centuries later?

There were ancient gold mines near Rennes; and strange, medieval legends — with at least *some* factual basis — told of parties of workmen labouring for *something* in part of the subterranean limestone labyrinth near the village.

There is also the persistent, and semi-historical, legend of the unfortunate shepherd boy, Ignace Paris. Searching for a lost sheep, Ignace climbed down after it into a crevice in the limestone and found a tunnel. He followed the tunnel and discovered a cave where armoured skeletons lay around great chests filled with gold coins. Hardly believing his good fortune, Ignace put as much gold as he could carry into his robes and went back to Rennes to tell his friends and neighbours what he'd discovered. Within minutes the local Seigneur was there. He descended on the boy in fury, brushed aside all explanations and hanged him as a thief *before he could disclose the exact whereabouts of the treasure*. The buried treasure theory certainly has much to commend it.

Another aspect of the hidden treasure hypothesis is concerned with certain mysterious parchments which Saunière is believed to have found. There are two contradictory versions of their discovery. In the first account, a wealthy benefactress had called at Rennes shortly after Saunière was appointed as Parish Priest. She offered to pay for a little restoration work. The old church had been neglected for centuries. Windows were missing. The roof leaked. The altar had slipped sideways. Bérenger asked her for a few francs to have the altar straightened. According to this version, a hollow Visigothic altar pillar held some mysterious coded parchments in Latin and Greek. The masons who discovered them took them straight to the Priest. Within minutes he was in the church telling them to cease work, and that he would send for the masons again when he needed them. The first, short manuscript was very easy to decode: certain letters were raised slightly. They spelled out the message: *"A Dagobert II roi et a Sion est ce tresor et il est la mort."* (Literally translated as: To Dagobert II King and to Sion is this treasure and he is there dead.) What did it mean? Sion was once the Citadel of King David in Jerusalem, or the code might refer to a supposed secret society known as *The Priory of Sion*. Dagobert II was allegedly an early French King of the ancient Merovingian line. Was something valuable buried with him — or in a secret hiding place in Jerusalem, below Solomon's Temple, perhaps, where the original Knights Templar had had their headquarters in King Baldwin's time? Perhaps the mysterious Priory of Sion had hidden it in the Rennes area? Or did " *il est la mort"* mean "It is death?" Did the parchment indicate not so much that the treasure was in the royal tomb of Dagobert II, but that like the legendary treasure of Tutankhamen it would bring death and destruction to any who tried to take it? Was it the curse on the treasure that had killed Ignace Paris?

The most intriguing theory of all, however, takes the Rennes mystery far back into the mists of time. Graham Hancock's brilliant research and his convincing arguments in *Fingerprints of the Gods* and his other excellent books and articles about such mysteries as the location of the lost Ark of the Covenant provide substantial evidence for the existence of a highly cultured and technologically competent civilisation which may have flourished some 15000 years ago on what is now the ice-shrouded, continent of Antarctica. Traces of them may well lie waiting to be rediscovered below that formidable ice. As it encroached remorselessly, we can imagine a party of well equipped colonists moving north towards the warmth and safety of the East African coast, Egypt and the Gulf.

If Hancock is right, the technology they brought with them could well have been responsible for creating the Sphinx — millennia before the rise of the Pharaohs to whom traditional Egyptologists give the credit.

Time passes. The *Mysterious-People-from-the-Far-South* gradually intermarry and blend in with the peoples of Egypt and North-east Africa. Some of their great cultural and technological secrets are carefully preserved by the inner hierarchy of Egyptian priests and courtiers, whose ranks Moses is eventually destined to join. Under his leadership, the great Hebrew Exodus gets under way. When Moses leaves, he takes some great and vitally important *thing* with him.

Glad at first to be rid of the troublesome nation-within-a-nation, Pharaoh suddenly becomes aware that this vital *thing* has gone with Moses. Does this traumatic discovery explain why he launched the flower of his charioteers to recover the mysterious and infinitely precious *thing* at all costs, risking military disaster to cross the perilous sea-bed in pursuit of it?

The unknown *thing* accompanies the Hebrews on their wanderings. It is, perhaps, even housed in their Sacred Ark alongside the Tablets of the Sinai Law. It is protected in their Tabernacle, then in Solomon's Temple. Centuries pass. Invaders come and go. Do the Romans carry it away, and do Alaric's conquering Visigoths take it from them to the remote safety of their citadel at Rennes-le-Château? Or is it in two or more parts, at least one of which stays concealed in a secret repository below the ruins of Solomon's Temple? Was that what the Knights Templar found when they dug there? Did they bring it to one of the Templar commanderies near Rennes? And did Saunière succeed in finding and reuniting those pieces again after so many centuries of separation? Was that the secret that he learnt from the manuscripts?

So what did the longer and far more complicated coded manuscript reveal? It's currently surrounded by fierce controversy, but we'll start with the *assumption* that it's old and genuine for the sake of clarifying the basic story. The decoding process alone is an unsolved mystery in its own right. The cryptographer must begin by finding 128 letters which don't belong to the rest of the text. These have to be spread out symmetrically on two chess boards. The next step is to use the letters *mort epée* (translated as "death sword" or "sword of death") as a key to another decoding process called the Tableau Vigenère. Here alphabets — each beginning at a different letter — are arranged in a square, and one or another is selected by using the letters of the key words *mort epée*. To solve the labyrinthine codes on the longer parchment, further alphabetical shifts are needed, and finally a message emerges, lacking all accents and punctuation because of the decoding process:

Bergere pas de tentation que poussin teniers gardent la clef pax
dclxxxi par la croix et ce cheval de dieux j'acheve ce daemon de
gardien a midi pommes bleues.

One literal translation reads:

"Shepherdess without temptation to which Poussin and Teniers guard the key peace 681 by the cross and this horseman of God I have conquered the demon guardian at midday blue apples."

Dozens of possibilities now confront the researcher. There is a shepherdess in the centre of a famous painting by Nicholas Poussin, the seventeenth century artist. She stands with three shepherds beside a tomb in a strange landscape, a landscape which just *might* be close to Renne-le-Château. A curious bas-relief replica of that same tomb and the characters surrounding it stands in the grounds of Shugborough Hall in Staffordshire in the UK, where it is referred to in the guide books as the Shepherd Monument. A curious inscription is cut into the stone below the carving. The letters are: D. O. U. O. S. V. A. V. V. M. The first and last letters are below the rest, and there is a centrally placed dot — like a decimal point — between each letter. Various suggestions as to their meaning have been put forward over the years, but so far there has been no definitive solution to the Shugborough riddle.

The great Staffordshire mansion was once owned by the Ansons, one of the earliest of whom was a contemporary of the mysterious Francis Bacon — sometimes credited with being the real author of the works attributed to Shakespeare. Francis Bacon had a brother Anthony who was engaged on the

The house where Bérenger Saunière the treasure-hunting priest was born in Couiza Montazels, just across the valley from Rennes-le-Château.

Elizabethan equivalent of CIA work in France. The Bacon brothers were very close. They were also, apparently, on the fringe of one or two seventeenth century continental secret societies. Was the mysterious Priory of Sion around in those days? Did it know something vital about the Rennes treasure, and did the Bacon brothers latch on to it?

The mysterious and adventurous Admiral George Anson (1697 - 1762) was also frequently at the family home at Shugborough. He sailed around the world and came back with enough gold to have paid off the national debt had he been so inclined. Did that gold really come from pillaging the Spaniards, or did George have another, older and more sinister source for his enormous wealth? There are links between the Rennes mystery and the equally intriguing riddle of Oak Island in Nova Scotia. Did coded information from Rennes via his Anson ancestors and their friends the Bacons enable George to exploit *something* of enormous value that was hidden on Oak Island?

The continental intrigues that involved the Bacon brothers are reminiscent of two other famous brothers, the Fouquets, who were similarly occupied. Nicholas, the elder, was Minister of Finance to the exceptionally powerful and successful Louis XIV, "The Sun King" of France. At the height of his immense power, there seemed to be almost nothing that Louis could not accomplish, yet it was said by many that Nicholas Fouquet was the *real* power in France at that time.

A letter written to Fouquet senior by his younger brother tells how he has met Nicholas Poussin, the painter, in Rome, and that Poussin has a truly remarkable secret, which he is willing to share with the Fouquets. Shortly afterwards, Fouquet senior falls from power, and is replaced by the odious Colbert. Louis XIV acquires Poussin's strange, coded painting of The Shepherds of Arcadia, which he keeps securely in the royal apartments at Versailles. Is it remotely possible that it was Fouquet senior who became the hapless Man in the Iron Mask? It is hard to understand why Louis kept the notorious masked prisoner alive at all — unless whoever it was had some vital secret which Louis desperately wanted. Suppose that Iron Mask *was* Fouquet. Louis dared not risk letting him go, nor dare he take the chance of his communicating with his many powerful friends. If Louis believed that the secret Fouquet had learned from Poussin would have provided enough power to threaten Louis and his throne, it would naturally be safest to kill him, of course. Yet if he did, Louis knew he would never gain access to the secret he coveted so much. Hence the otherwise inexplicable, long-running standoff with the King and his trusted prison governor, Monsieur St Mars, on one side — and the mysterious masked prisoner (Fouquet?) on the other. The politically astute prisoner knows that once he has given the King the information he wants, death is his only reward. Louis knows that the masked prisoner is his only route to some great secret that he desperately desires to control. Kill the masked man, and you sacrifice all chance of ever gaining the secret.

The stranger and wilder the Rennes theories are, the more intriguing they seem to become. One tower of the ruined Château Hautpoul — which gives Rennes its name — is called *The Tower of Alchemy*. The Fatins who live there now kindly showed us around their crumbling, historic home. Monsieur Fatin, a talented sculptor, has a theory that the whole of Rennes-le-Château is one vast memorial to a long-dead king or some great, ancient war leader. His skilfully drawn diagrams of the village certainly show the outlines of what could well be a classical *Ship of the Dead*. Elizabeth van Buren, a descendant of President van Buren of the USA, has lived in the area and studied the Rennes mystery for many years. Psychically sensitive and very perceptive herself, she regards the mysterious village and its environs as a "gateway to the invisible" — and she could well be right. Her theories include the idea that there is a vast ground zodiac below Rennes and its environs. It seems possible, according to her researches, that King Arthur of the Britons himself may lie beneath this enigmatic old French village.

Other theories involve the idea that a 'magical' pentagon — formed naturally by several Rennes landmarks — may have rendered the area especially potent for 'spells' to be worked.

Bremna Howells, who writes excellent and erudite books as Rosie Malone, is an acknowledged expert on magic, paganism and ancient religions. She has carefully researched the hypothesis that Saunière and Marie Dénarnaud were secretly practising the sex-magic divination ritual known as *The Convocation of Venus* which its protagonists claim is capable of remarkably accurate forecasts of the future.

Assuming for a moment that Bremna's theory is on the right lines, then Saunière's wealth may have come from selling accurate prophecies — rather like those uttered by Mother Shipton, the Wise Woman of Yorkshire, or Nostradamus.

Our own Rennes research goes back a quarter of a century and new information still continues to surface. Like any other research team, we could, of course, be wrong, but with the evidence currently available — and with due attention to all the rival theories — the best and most exciting of the probabilities seems to lean in the direction of Graham Hancock's bold Antarctic hypothesis. Is it possible that the Rennes treasure — *whatever it finally turns out to be* — is a mysterious, almost magically powerful, artifact which originated in that pre-Ice Age culture? From Antarctica to Africa ... From ancient Egypt to Israel ... From Israel to Rome ... From Rome to Rennes-le-Château ... From Rennes to Oak Island off the coast of Nova Scotia ... And have its equally mysterious guardians — sometimes calling themselves the Priory of Sion — been hovering around it for centuries?

The so-called Treasure of Rennes-le-Château is probably very much older and stranger than most of us can imagine.

THE MYSTERY OF THE OAK ISLAND MONEY PIT

Centuries ago an unknown engineering genius hid something priceless in the labyrinth below Oak Island, Nova Scotia.

The modern end of the Oak Island story began innocuously enough one summer day in 1795. Three teenagers — Daniel McGinnis, John Smith and Anthony Vaughan — had been given a day's holiday from the heavy manual work of Nova Scotian pioneers: fishing, farming and lumbering. Life was tough for those eighteenth century Canadians — but they had the will, the strength and the tenacity to cope with it. When a brief opportunity to get away from their arduous labour came along, they enjoyed it all the more. The three young men spent that fateful day exploring Oak Island — one of hundreds of islands scattered around in Mahone Bay on the Atlantic seaboard. This particular peanut-shaped island was about a mile long and a quarter of a mile wide at its narrowest. The two broad ends stood forty feet above sea level, but the narrower central portion was low and covered by swamp. Clearly, as the centuries roll, Oak Island is destined to become two smaller ones.

The first thing that attracted their attention was a clearing towards the Atlantic end. In the middle of this clearing a saucer shaped depression suggested strongly that someone had once dug there, and the earth had subsequently settled. Beside the sunken earth stood a large, sturdy oak tree. One thick branch — its end deliberately lopped — extended across the low circle of ground. From that branch hung an old ship's block and tackle. Swiftly the boys drew an exciting conclusion: pirates or privateers must have buried their treasure there.

Oak Island was only a few hundred yards from the mainland, yet its prolific red-oak forest would have concealed anything suspicious from those who lived in the little fishing village of Chester. Besides, the island had a sinister, inhospitable reputation. The older members of the local community remembered a grim episode many years before: a party of fishermen had rowed

One of the many exploratory pits and shafts now riddling Oak Island in Mahone Bay, Nova Scotia. Something of great age and value is almost certainly hidden deep in the labyrinth here.

across to investigate some mysterious lights seen on the island one night: those fishermen had never returned.

The Nova Scotian coast was rich with stories of pirates and smugglers. The very name Mahone Bay came from the *mahone*, a type of ship which privateers had traditionally favoured. The undeservedly notorious William Kidd was alleged to have buried his treasure there — but detailed research would seem to indicate that he had had little or nothing of any real value to bury. In 1795, however, stories of the fabulous wealth supposedly accumulated by pirate captains like Kidd, Blackbeard and Morgan, or bold adventurers such as Anson and Drake, were very much in the minds of young Nova Scotians like Smith, Vaughan and McGinnis. The hope of discovering buried treasure was one of the counter-balances to an arduous life of hard work for subsistence returns. Digging up pirate gold meant a swift, almost miraculous escape from drudgery into luxury, comfort and ease.

Eagerly, the boys began to excavate the circle of fallen earth below the oak tree.

The first thing that encouraged them was the ease with which the soil came out: it was clearly soft backfill. As they cleared it away, the lads could see the original sides of the shaft: impervious, brick hard clay which still bore the pick marks of the original diggers. Whatever else they had found, it was not just some natural shaft or blow-hole: someone in the past had undoubtedly excavated it deliberately. Two or three feet down they hit a layer of flat stones, similar to paving stones, but the stone was not of a type found on Oak Island. It looked as if it had been brought there from Gold River, a couple of miles away. Was that a clue to suggest that gold from Gold River had been buried on Oak Island? Encouraged by finding the stones, the boys dug on. Eight feet below the flat stone layer, they hit a serious obstacle: a layer of horizontal oak logs had been let into the sides of the shaft. It was a struggle to get them out, but the young Nova Scotians were strong and keenly motivated: eventually the oak platform came away — but the expected treasure was nowhere to be seen. The soil had settled and fallen eighteen inches or so below the oak obstacle, but that was all. Disappointed, they continued to shovel out the loose backfill, consoling themselves with the thought that whoever had gone to the trouble of going this deep — and putting an oak platform across the shaft as well — must have buried something *very valuable indeed*. Mentally, they re-evaluated the hoped-for treasure: hundreds of thousands? *Millions even*? Thus encouraged they dug on until at the twenty foot level they hit a second oak platform and removed it. Still no treasure chests — only more backfill. We can imagine them looking at one another grimly and accepting that this was more than the three of them could handle by themselves. They reluctantly accepted that it would need several men with special equipment and — above all — enough financial resources to pay for the digging time spent away from their essential regular work.

They marked the spot carefully and left the island. The demands of daily life meant that years rather than months passed before the first full assault was made on the Oak Island Money Pit. Simeon Lynds from Truro, or nearby Onslow, organised it. While visiting the Mahone Bay area, Simeon heard about the mysterious shaft from the three young men, and visited the island with them. An article on Oak Island from *The Colonist* dated January 2nd, 1864, more than half a century later, refers to him as "... the late Simeon Lynds ..." and describes him as a relative of Anthony Vaughan's who was let into the secret because of those family connections. Lynds organised an effective consortium of business and professional men into The Onslow Company. They included Sheriff Tom Harris and Colonel Archibald, the Town Clerk and a Justice of the Peace.

The Onslow men worked hard and effectively. As the shaft grew ever deeper, they encountered not only platform after platform of oak logs at regular ten foot intervals but inexplicable layers of ship's putty, coconut fibre and charcoal. Hiram Walker, a ship's carpenter who lived in Chester at the time and worked with the Onslow Company, told his grand-daughter, Mrs Cottnam Smith, that he had seen bushel after bushel of coconut fibre being brought up. Another eye-witness account referred to enough ship's putty being recovered from the shaft to glaze the windows of twenty local houses.

Close to the ninety foot level, the Onslow men unearthed a strange inscribed stone, made of an unusual, hard, olive-grey rock — a form of porphyry unlike anything local. No-one at the time was able to decipher the strange alphabet in which the inscription was written. Many years later, however, Professor Barry Fell suggested that it was a form of ancient Coptic script, and that the message was of a religious nature: this led to the theory that the Oak Island shaft and its ancillary workings had been created by a party of religious refugees from the eastern Mediterranean area. Another cryptographer deciphered the marks to mean "forty feet below two million pounds are buried." The suspicion was, however, that those markings had been superimposed over the original inscription after the stone had been in the hands of a later treasure hunting company. Unfortunately, the stone has now disappeared.

As the Onslow team removed the stone from the ninety foot level, they noticed something else: the shaft was becoming uncomfortably wet. They were sending up one barrel of water for every two barrels of earth, and that was causing serious concern among the diggers at the foot of the shaft. Water was a great problem for early nineteenth century miners and tunnel builders. It was decided to stop work for the night and start again at first light. Just before finishing, however, one of the workmen probed the muddy floor with a long crowbar and reported striking something hard. Was it just another oak platform, or could it possibly be the lid of a treasure chest? It gave them all something to think about optimistically until sunrise.

First light brought a very unwelcome surprise: the pit was flooded to a depth of sixty feet. The water was rising and falling gently with the tide. One unconfirmed account says that a workman leaned over too far and fell in. When his companions hauled him out again, his first words were: "Hey, it's salt water down there!" That was the first clue to the amazing flood tunnels which were discovered many years later. The lower levels of the Oak Island Money Pit were cunningly connected to at least two potentially lethal flood tunnels. Whoever had built the system had also created an artificial beach at Smith's Cove, at the far end of the island. Below that beach lay a fan-shaped pattern of drains that fed the first flood tunnel. Ingeniously packed with large stones and boulders to prevent collapse or blockage, while still allowing water to pass easily, the two flood tunnels led the mighty hydraulic power of the Atlantic itself down into the Money Pit.

The Onslow men tried baling and pumping, but as one of them reputedly said at the time: " . . . it was like trying to eat soup with a fork . . . " Money ran out. Work had to be done back home. They were forced to give up for the time being — but they were more convinced than ever that there was some great treasure down there, if only some way of beating the flood water could be discovered. The following year they tried again. Their plan this time was to dig a parallel shaft and then cut across horizontally and try to extract the treasure from below the flooded part. It was a desperate plan, but it worked up to a point. They got down to the 115 foot level and began tunnelling across. Almost

Mysterious Gold River near Oak Island, Chester, Nova Scotia. Was it local gold from a secret mine in this area that now lies deep below the sinister Money Pit?

at once the flood water burst into their new workings and nearly drowned the diggers. That was the end as far as the Onslow Company was concerned. The Oak Island treasure and its watery guardian were abandoned for the time being.

Daniel McGinnis was dead and Smith and Vaughan were both over seventy before another Oak Island expedition was organised. This was the Truro Company, which began work on the Money Pit in 1849. Both Smith and Vaughan were involved in the work, as was Dr David Barnes Lynds, the son, or perhaps the grandson, of the Simeon Lynds who had led the Onslow men nearly half a century earlier. This continuity factor is an important one. The new Oak Island treasure hunting companies that were formed over the years almost invariably included veterans from earlier attempts on the Money Pit. This was vital for such basic essentials as confirming the precise location of the site — not the easiest task in the world when so much digging, pumping and baling had been done all around it.

Under the leadership of Jotham McCully, a drill with a pod-auger was used to explore the flooded depths of the Money Pit. Some amazing discoveries were made. At the ninety-eight foot level — just where the Onslow men had thought it was years before — the drill went through layers of oak and then loose pieces of *something* (metal or jewels?) which stubbornly refused to come up through the pod-auger. The Truro men were convinced that they had drilled through two treasure boxes piled one on top of the other.

Not long afterwards, thinking he was unobserved, James Pitblado, a drilling foreman, took *something* from the drill tip, examined it carefully and put it in his pocket. But John Gammell, a major shareholder in the Truro adventure, *had* seen him — and immediately challenged him about it. Pitblado stubbornly refused to show it to him, saying that it was so important he would show it only to a meeting of all the shareholders together.

∞

He never did. He left the island that night and failed to return. He and his partner, Charles Archibald of the Acadia Ironworks, tried very hard to obtain an appropriate Government treasure hunting licence and even attempted to buy the whole island — but with no success. Shortly after this fiasco, Archibald left Nova Scotia to settle in the UK and Pitblado was killed in an industrial accident, taking the secret of the drill tip fragment with him. Whatever it was had been enough to convince him and Archibald that there was something very valuable down there.

When the Truro men ran out of cash, further exploration passed into the hands of a new company called The Oak Island Association, which was set up in April of 1861. Jotham McCully and other members of the 1849-50 group provided continuity yet again. John Smith, last survivor of the three original discoverers, had passed his Oak Island land to his sons before he died. They had sold it to Henry Stevens, and he in turn had sold it to Anthony Graves, who was now the principal landowner on Oak Island. Graves made a good deal with the Oak Island Association, which entitled him to a third of anything they discovered on his land.

George Mitchell was now foreman on the island, and the Association's plan was to cut off the flood water before attempting anything else. With nearly 100 horses and men to do the job, Mitchell and his team tried to intercept and block the flood tunnel. They failed. Unbelievably, Mitchell then went for an option which had proved repeatedly disastrous with past expeditions: he attempted to sink a parallel shaft alongside the Money Pit and then cut across for the treasure horizontally. Abbot and Costello, the Three Stooges or Laurel and Hardy would have known better than to try that approach again.

Two of Mitchell's intrepid tunnellers were digging horizontally towards the flooded Money Pit from the foot of their new parallel shaft when all hell broke loose in the deeply flooded shaft they were approaching. Eye witnesses described the noise from the Money Pit as being " . . . like an earthquake or a bomb exploding . . . " A great surge of fast-moving mud hurled the two men back and almost cost them their lives. Something, which was probably the treasure chamber previously detected by the pod-auger, collapsed and crashed into the unknown depths of the Money Pit. It was followed by thousands of feet of cribbing timber which had once lined the shaft. The water foamed and boiled madly: the lower levels were now a chaotic ruin. Among fragments retrieved later from this cataclysmic mess there were a few pieces of oak, blackened with age, and definitely far older than the recent cribbing timbers which had collapsed so dramatically. Had this ancient wood been part of the original treasure chamber? Other very old, pre-nineteenth century pieces were found. These contained clear drill and tool marks which also helped to confirm the conclusions drawn from the pod-auger samples.

For nearly a quarter of a century after this very little treasure hunting work was done on the island, but there was a curious and significant accident. Sophia Sellers, daughter of Anthony Graves, was ploughing with a team of oxen barely 100 yards from the Money Pit, when the poor beasts and the plough crashed down into a large hole and nearly dragged Sophia down with them. The animals and equipment were later recovered — miraculously safe and uninjured — but the mysterious hole (referred to ever after as The Cave-in Pit) posed another intriguing problem for Oak Island researchers. Sophia's husband, Henry, filled it with boulders as a safety precaution, and nothing much was done about it until tireless and determined Fred Blair came on the scene in 1893.

Fred was one of the most dedicated and effective explorers to tackle the Oak Island mystery, and he worked there from 1893 until his death in 1951. At one point he dynamited the flood tunnels in an attempt to stop the water — but even that was only a partial and temporary success, and it probably achieved nothing except to scatter the remains of the contents of the supposed treasure chamber which had collapsed in 1861.

Blair drilled for samples as the McCully team had done fifty years before. His drill hit what seems to have been a cement treasure vault with impenetrable iron reinforcement at the 170 foot level. Somewhere inside this mysterious space the drill's behaviour suggested that there were more boxes of the tantalising loose metal which had failed to come up on the McCully drill.

Another strange discovery was a fragment of ancient parchment that came up in the core samples: it bore only two letters "VI" but had evidently been torn from some larger document. The existence of this parchment opened up a whole new field of speculation.

As the years went on Franklin D. Roosevelt, the future USA President, became interested in the work, and was one of the shareholders in Captain Bowdoin's company — which made a brief and conspicuously unsuccessful assault on the Money Pit in 1909. A disappointed and disgruntled Bowdoin later wrote that there was no treasure down there and never had been.

A far more diligent and persistent later researcher was Mel Chappell, whose father had been a member of the expedition during which the parchment had been discovered. Mel and Blair worked together in 1931. A big new shaft was dug, but nothing significant was discovered. Had the constant dynamiting, flooding and pumping dispersed the treasure beyond reasonable hope of recovery?

Gilbert Hedden also deserves honourable mention among the heroes in the Oak Island Hall of Fame. He had excellent management and engineering experience, and he was a thoughtful planner. He hired Sprague and Henwood of Pennsylvania to do the drilling and clearing work and they made an excellent job of it. At the 150 level and below, the drill encountered pieces of oak of various sizes strongly suggesting that the remains of the old treasure chamber and its supports were down there somewhere. Hedden's team also discovered the remains of an ancient sea-ramp, jetty, or coffer dam, in Smith's Cove — where the artificial drainage beach and flood tunnels were also located. These old timbers which Hedden discovered were massive. They were also notched, and labelled with Roman numerals. They have never yet been satisfactorily explained.

Unhappily, like so many others before him, Hedden ran into financial difficulties which curtailed his Oak Island work.

The next major player was Professor Hamilton, an Engineering teacher from New York University. He made meticulous explorations of many of the old shafts and tunnels, and drilled down to limestone bedrock 200 feet below the island, where oak chips continued to come up on the drill. There was, however, no other sign of the elusive treasure.

George Greene, a tough, cigar chewing Texas oil man, made an attempt in 1955, but the skill and determination that had succeeded in the oil business didn't succeed on Oak island.

Robert and Mildred Restall were daring and exciting show business personalities. Robert was a motorcycle stunt-rider and Mildred a beautiful seventeen-year-old ballerina when they married in 1931. With a little capital put up by loyal show business friends, the Restalls came to work on Oak Island in 1959. Robert and his son, Rob Junior, died in a tragic accident in 1965, when some mysterious gas poisoning caused Robert to fall into a flooded shaft where they were working. His son died trying to rescue him. Two of their loyal friends also died trying to get them out.

With earlier accidents, that brought the total death toll to six — but the sinister legend of Oak Island prophesied that *seven* men would die and the last oak tree would fall before the mysterious treasure was recovered. The last oak has already fallen . . .

Bob Dunfield was next to attack the Money Pit, and he went at it like Hannibal's elephants charging the Roman army at the Battle of Zama — with as little success as Hannibal had against Rome! With massive financial resources and ruthless directness, Dunfield built a causeway to carry his huge clam digger across to rip the heart out of Oak Island. As of October 17th, 1965, Oak Island became part of the mainland of Nova Scotia. Dunfield's machine tore a hole 100 feet wide and 150 deep where the Money Pit had once been. He created something that looked like a miniature Somme battlefield — or the site of tank warfare during a monsoon: he destroyed priceless clues and archaeological

The causeway built by treasure hunter Bob Dunfield in 1965 which still links Oak Island to Crandall's Point on the Nova Scotian mainland.

evidence which later researchers would have found invaluable. All his investment and all his energy achieved absolutely nothing. In the spring of 1966, he gave up and left the island. He died in Encino in 1980.

Fred Nolan, a skilful and talented surveyor, has worked on the island for many years, and has discovered numerous strange marker stones — some of which form a distinct Templar Cross of very large proportions. He believes that the treasure is more likely to be hidden under the swamp than in the depths of the Money Pit. Fred's hypothesis is that those who sank the shaft tunnelled upwards again at various angles, and concealed the treasure in several separate locations which could easily be reached from the surface if the diggers had the right directions. He thinks that his mysterious marker stones, together with an ancient stone triangle which was destroyed as a result of Dunfield's work with the clam digger, may hold the clues to these sites.

Next on the scene came a formidable combination of experts working as Triton Alliance — and the toughest and most formidable of them all was our good friend Dan Blankenship, former 1939-45 war hero. If any combination of courage, imagination, initiative and engineering skills will ever solve the Oak Island Money Pit mystery, Dan has that profile.

He, himself, almost became the seventh victim of the Oak Island curse when the steel shaft inside which he was working collapsed under the colossal weight and pressure of the mud surrounding it. His son's strength and determination — as he worked the cable winch that hauled Dan to safety with only seconds to spare — were the vital factors in the rescue. Even that hair's breadth escape failed to deter Dan and his team.

Their work still goes on: and when the Oak Island secret is eventually revealed, it may well turn out to be the eighth wonder of the world. What might it be, and who could have put it down there in the first place?

One of the best theories comes from another of our close Nova Scotian friends, George Young, a retired surveyor and Royal Canadian Navy Officer. With his unique combination of professional knowledge of both sea and land, coupled with his linguistic skills in ancient Ogham, and an interest in unexplained phenomena in general, George's theories are always well worth considering. He wonders whether the Money Pit and its formidable defences were intended not as a treasure cache but as a securely protected burial place. If Professor Barry Fell was right and the ancient stone found at the ninety foot level contained a religious inscription, is it possible that a community of religious refugees from the eastern Mediterranean found their way through the straights of Gibraltar and across to the Nova Scotian coast long ago?

George's studies of prevailing winds, tides and currents make this a feasible conclusion. Theoretically, at least, such a journey was possible.

The sturdy oak platforms at ten foot intervals are than explained as shields to prevent the weight of earth from crushing the body of the *arif*, the revered leader of the community whom his followers buried there. The artificial beach with its drains and flood tunnels can also be seen as precautions against grave robbers and desecrators. What the drill went through was not a treasure chamber containing chests of coins and jewels — but a burial vault containing coffins.

In the fascinating museum at Yarmouth, Nova Scotia, lies the famous Yarmouth Stone, discovered on the shore by a local doctor in 1812. It has what appear to be runic inscriptions engraved on it which suggest that an early Viking expedition made its way successfully to Nova Scotia centuries before Columbus reached America. So is it Viking treasure in the depths of the Money Pit? Did some ancient Norse sea-king once rest there: complete with his armour, his weapons and his treasure?

The problem in trying to decide who originally excavated the pit and its associated flood tunnels and artificial beach drainage system is that it must have taken a large group of strong, intelligent and disciplined people a long time to complete the work. Whatever else it is, the pit is not the quick, casual, haphazard work of swashbuckling pirates: a six foot hole under a tree and a few crude measurements on a rough sketch map are much more in keeping with traditional pirate style.

Another fascinating theory concerns the refugee Knights Templar. They left France after the treacherous Philip IV attempted to destroy their great and valiant Order in 1307. There is evidence that the noble and hospitable Henry

Sinclair, ruler of Orkney, took them in and subsequently provided transport for them across the north Atlantic. He enlisted the help of the Venetian Zeno brothers, who were among the greatest navigators of their day.

The Templars were as famous for their building skills — some of their medieval fortifications are among the greatest military architecture of all time — as for their courage and prowess in war. They would have had the engineering knowledge, the time, dedication and discipline to construct the Money Pit. They would also have had priceless treasure and holy relics from Palestine, and the Saracen lands, to conceal there. In the fourteenth century, a voyage across the Atlantic was as rare and daunting an enterprise as a trip to the moon today. Did the indomitable Templars conclude that the safest place for their treasure — the farthest possible hiding place from the avaricious Philip le Bel and his successors — would be on the far side of the Atlantic?

Or was it the work of Francis Bacon? Did that enigmatic Elizabethan statesman and scholar conceal secret manuscripts there, with the intention that posterity would ultimately re-discover them, and give him what he considered to be his rightful place in history? Bacon — a pioneering scientist as well as a man of many other talents — had a theory about preserving documents in mercury. Among the strange things found on Oak Island of recent years were many old earthenware flasks which still held traces of the mercury they had once contained. Was that tiny scrap of parchment bearing the letters "Vi" (recovered from the Money Pit in 1893) a fragment of one of Bacon's manuscripts?

Another tenable theory concerns King George III. Before his sanity left him, he was an intelligent and ambitious man. He wanted to reign supreme, as a real, decision-making monarch, not a democratised and constitutionally restrained figure head. He had learnt the lessons of Charles I. George knew well enough that to take power you had to take money first. Enough cash would buy enough mercenaries to subdue a kingdom. There is some evidence that with the help of a powerful secret cabal of statesmen — including the mysterious and incalculably wealthy Admiral Anson of Shugborough — George III had arranged for his War Chest to be kept safely on Oak Island, to be drawn on as necessary when the power struggle against parliament began, and the mercenaries were needed. The insanity struck first: various vitally important plotters died, or withdrew their support. Everything ended in ignominious failure: but does George's treasure still lie concealed below the Money Pit?

A closely associated theory suggests that either French or British military engineers constructed the great subterranean "safe" with its flood-tunnel "locks" to keep an army payroll out of reach of their enemies during the American Wars of the mid-eighteenth century. Military engineers certainly fit the profile as far as skill and discipline are concerned.

Exciting theories abound. The most breathtaking of all is the possibility that some part of the ancient, secret Arcadian treasure that was once concealed at Rennes-le-Château was smuggled across to Canada, and buried below Oak Island.

This would link in with the curious geographical fact that there are *two* Oak Islands attached to the Nova Scotian peninsula: one on the Fundy side, the other on the Atlantic side. It has been suggested that those who knew about the secret over the centuries had deliberately planted oaks to mark the island for later travellers in their arcane organisation. Near each of the two Oak Islands is a river which flows down from the centre of the peninsula. There is some archaeological evidence — albeit controversial — that a settlement or fortress once existed there in that central region. Some curious remnants of it still remain.

The theory then goes on to suggest that something of immense value and importance — something which, perhaps, came originally from the ancient pre-ice-age culture which once supposedly flourished below the ice of what is now Antarctica, and which Graham Hancock has argued for so logically in "*Fingerprints of the Gods*" — made its way first to Egypt, then to Palestine with Moses, later to Rome and from there to the Visigothic stronghold at Rennes-le-Château. Templars, or the successors of other more ancient guardians, were later responsible for secreting part of it below Oak Island. There are hints and suggestions that it was something so powerful that it was considered safer to have it in two separate locations: rather like keeping a gun in one steel cabinet and the ammunition for it in another. Were the oaks planted deliberately, long ago, on those two Nova Scotian islands both of which are now firmly attached to the mainland? Were those trees intended to show travellers from the Old World that they were in the right spot, and that they had only to sail up the adjacent river to find the settlement where other members of the group would welcome and protect them?

The final solution to the Oak Island mystery has yet to be revealed: there can be little doubt that it will be something truly momentous.

THE AMHERST POLTERGEIST
What paranormal horror almost destroyed
Esther Cox and her family?

During the evening of September 4th, 1878, Esther Cox leapt from her bed screaming that there was a mouse in the mattress: a trivial, almost humorous beginning for one of the most sinister and spectacular poltergeist cases ever recorded. She shared a bedroom with her elder sister Jennie, who was twenty-two; Esther herself was nineteen. The two girls were paying guests in the Princess Street, Amherst home of their married sister, Olive. Her husband, Daniel Teed was a foreman at the local shoe factory, and they had two young sons, five year old William and little George, an eighteen-month-old toddler. To help to make ends meet there were two other family members staying with the Teeds as paying guests.

The first was Daniel's brother John Teed; the other was William Cox, brother of Olive, Jennie and Esther. On that fateful September 4th, Jennie helped Esther to search for the supposed mouse. They failed to find it, gave up the fruitless search and climbed back into bed. The following night, Esther again felt certain that *something* was creeping around inside her mattress. As the girls made another search, a cardboard box under the bed seemed to move of its own accord. Convinced that they now had the elusive mouse cornered, Jennie and Esther crouched beside the box ready to catch it. To their amazement, the box rose up into the air and then fell over sideways. Despite their fright and surprise they searched it thoroughly: *no mouse.* Strangely disturbed by these relatively minor but nevertheless totally inexplicable events, the sisters agreed not to mention them to anyone else.

It was on the following night, September 6th, that things really began to get serious. Esther who was already in bed, started to scream in agony. Jennie woke up with a start and tried to help her, but there was nothing she could do. Esther's body was swelling up visibly and turning brick red.

Footnote: In 1957, when the authors were living in a bungalow on the edge of a large common called the Neatherd Moor in Dereham, Norfolk, England, Lionel was having a course of injections for hay fever. The contemporary medical theory was that if a patient had a course of injections of whatever it was that was causing the allergy reaction, an immunity to that allergy would be developed. In Lionel's case the problem was caused by mixed grass pollen. Instead of the hoped-for immunity to hay fever, he had a systemic reaction to the pollen injection, turned brick red and began to swell spectacularly until he was almost unrecognizable. Needless to say, that line of treatment was abandoned! The point of that reminiscence is that the human body can — and sometimes does — react to certain stimuli by swelling suddenly and dramatically. What made Esther Cox do it ?

There was a sharp explosive sound as though a cannon had been fired somewhere very close to the girls' bedroom. Three more very loud bangs followed and then Esther's swelling went down almost as suddenly as it had erupted. She stopped crying out in pain and went peacefully to sleep.

On September 10th another bout of swelling started but did not reach the same terrifying proportions. Esther's bedclothes were torn away as if by powerful, invisible hands and landed in a muddled heap in the farthest corner of the room. At that point, aroused by her sisters' cries of alarm, Olive Teed rushed into the room and tried to remake their bed. She had no sooner re-arranged the sheets and blankets than they were hurled off again.

John Teed came to help. The pillow which had been below Esther's head slid out sideways from under her, flew through the air of its own accord and struck him full in the face. Immediately after this two or three more of the strange explosive sounds came from the floor, or, perhaps, from under the bed. Then everything went quiet again and the entire atmosphere of the room seemed to change: it was almost as though some sort of psychic storm had blown itself out for the time being.

Not knowing what to do next, or where to turn for help, the Teeds sent for Dr Carritte, their family doctor. When he arrived on the evening of September 11th, Esther had already gone to bed. As Carritte watched, her pillow slid out sideways, almost like a drawer being pulled open. Then it slid in again of its own accord. The doctor was completely amazed, but there was more to come. The pillow again slid out horizontally, and this time John Teed made a grab for it. Something much stronger than he was pulled it back again and replaced it under Esther's head. Explosions sounded all over the room and seemed to be pursuing Dr Carritte.

The bedclothes leapt up into the air as they had done previously, and there was a sinister, metallic scratching noise — as if someone was using the point of a knife to carve out a message on the wall. The instrument making the noise was not visible, but the letters on the wall were: "Esther Cox, you are mine to kill!"

Footnote: King Belshazzar ruler of Babylon (Daniel 5) saw a mysterious disembodied hand writing the words: "Mene, mene, tekel upharsin" on his palace wall. The prophet Daniel translated them to mean: "You have been weighed in the balance and found wanting. Your Kingdom is to be divided between the Medes and Persians." *That same night King Belshazzar was dead.*

~

Dr Carritte continued to give the Teed family all the help he could over the traumatic days which followed. On one occasion he recorded seeing a bucket of cold water which was standing on their kitchen table start to boil although there was no heat source anywhere near it!

Shortly after this, the poltergeist — or *whatever* was hounding Esther — began to speak to her. Its language was foul and its menaces terrifying. One of its most persistent threats was to burn down the house and kill everyone inside it — and this was no empty intimidation: lighted matches began to fall as though from nowhere. Small fires started everywhere from the cellar up to the attic. Only constant vigilance and quick action prevented a major disaster.

Then their tormentor made himself visible — but only to Esther. He again threatened to set light to the house and burn everyone to death unless she left. For the sake of her family, Esther very reluctantly agreed to go.

John White was a staunch friend of the Teeds. He ran a busy tavern-restaurant in Amherst, and willingly offered shelter and protection to Esther. Things seemed to settle down for a month or so, and then a pocket knife that belonged to White's son flew through the air and stuck in Esther's back. Terrified in case he got blamed for throwing it — which he manifestly had not done — young White pulled it gently out of the injured girl. Something immensely powerful — but totally invisible — wrenched it from the boy's hand and thrust it back into the same wound. Esther's screams of pain brought the rest of the family running and the knife was removed.

Whether her poltergeist persecutor was responsible, or whether it was just the normal process of infection, Esther went down with a near fatal attack of diphtheria in December. It was almost three weeks before she was well enough to get out of bed. Strangely enough, during the days that she was severely debilitated by the illness *there were no poltergeist manifestations of any kind.*

After recovering enough to travel, Esther was sent convalescing to another of her married sisters, Mrs John Snowden, who lived in Sackville in New Brunswick. There was no poltergeist activity during the time she was there.

After returning to Amherst, Esther was allocated a different room in the hope that this would somehow prevent or inhibit the poltergeist's activities: it didn't. Lighted matches fell again, and the weird explosive noises also resumed. This gave Daniel Teed an idea. In an attempt to find out whether the poltergeist was an intelligent entity of some sort which could understand and respond to a question, he asked it to knock once for every person in the room. There were six people present and the poltergeist gave six loud knocks. Unlike the traditional séance procedure of one knock for yes and two knocks for no, or vice versa, the Amherst poltergeist gave one knock for no, two when it did not know the answer, and three knocks for yes. Daniel was particularly anxious about the possibility of the house being set ablaze. When he asked the poltergeist if their home would be burnt down, he received two knocks for an answer. One of Olive's dresses was tugged from its hook by some invisible power and bundled up under the bed. Next moment it was burning briskly. Daniel just managed to retrieve it from under the bed and smother the flames before any serious damage was done.

Esther was also physically hurt, embarrassed and humiliated when to use one investigator's words " . . . the ghost got inside her abdomen and moved around . . ." This produced a recurrence of the abnormal and very painful swelling which she had experienced earlier.

John White came to her rescue again, and took her to his tavern-restaurant once more. The poltergeist followed her there and its weird, inexplicable powers were soon manifested again. One morning, in broad daylight, the heavy, cast iron door of the large old Victorian oven rose from its hinges and flew across the kitchen. Defiantly, White replaced it and wedged it shut with an axe handle. The door flew up again and took the axe handle with it across the room. White tried again — and once more door and handle sprang away from the cooker. John ran outside to try to find a reliable, independent witness. He saw W.H.Rogers, a Government Fisheries Inspector, walking down the road outside his restaurant. Rogers obligingly came in — intrigued by the strange account John had just given him. The door was re-hung and securely wedged with the axe handle: in full view of Rogers, it flew through the air once more, complete with axe handle.

Some time later Esther was sitting in the restaurant when some heavy iron spikes more or less materialised from nowhere and laid themselves in her lap. Within minutes they were growing warm, and then too hot to hold. Seconds later they were glowing, red hot. Even before the terrified Esther could leap up and drop them from her smouldering apron, they flew across the restaurant of their own accord and landed over twenty feet away. Witnesses in the dining room at the time included: Robert Hutchinson, J. Albert Black, Editor of the *Amherst Gazette*, Daniel Morrison and William Hillson — all well-known, sober and respectable Amherst residents.

Walter Hubbell was a moderately well-known actor, conjuror, and general, all-round showman-entertainer during the closing quarter of the nineteenth century. He guessed that there might be money to be made out of the Amherst poltergeist, and he was undoubtedly familiar with the fortune that P.T.Barnum had made with "The Greatest Show on Earth." Hubbell guessed rightly that crowds would flock to watch a genuine poltergeist performing supernatural antics live on stage. It would have all the attractions of a great conjuring show *without being an illusion.*

His first thoughts, however, were that the Amherst phenomena were hoaxes, and he went to the house in Princes Street with every intention of debunking Esther and her supposed accomplices. A week's research was enough to convince Hubbell that Esther and her poltergeist were both absolutely genuine.

Working with Esther and John White, Hubbell set up the first stage of what he hoped was a theatre tour that would make them all very rich. It was a disaster: poltergeists stubbornly refuse to perform to order. Hubbell had other problems, too. Another showman had tried to persuade Esther to go on tour under his aegis, but she had declined. This frustrated and embittered rival was determined to do everything possible to sabotage the Hubbell Tour. When Esther and her two escorts left Amherst for their first show in Moncton, it is highly likely that the saboteur was surreptitiously aboard the same train, intent on trouble.

When Hubbell, White and Esther booked into the American House Hotel, the poltergeist got to work on an empty rocking chair. It was a good sign, they thought. It looked as though the phenomena were going to be with them on stage.

The *Moncton Despatch* of June 18, 1879, carried the whole amazing story: frustratingly quiet when they wanted it to perform on stage, the poltergeist knocked so violently while they were in the Baptist Church on Sunday evening that Esther and her two friends had to leave.

When they got back to the house in Wesley Street where they were staying, the poltergeist made another physical attack on Esther. A local doctor who was called in said that she appeared to be suffering from some kind of heart trouble, brought on by shock, or nervous excitement. She hiccoughed uncontrollably, and her body swelled up as it had done on previous occasions. Her heartbeat was dangerously rapid, and at one point her lungs seemed congested. Before the attack was over, Esther was vomiting blood.

A day's rest brought her back to something resembling normal health, and as she sat beside her open bedroom window, the small fan she was holding slipped from her hand and fell to the pavement below. Esther went down to recover it, but when she returned to her bedroom a moment later a heavy armchair was upside down beside the door — according to the *Moncton Despatch* it was almost as though the chair had tried to follow her. The *Despatch* added cautiously, however, that Esther was the only witness to this event.

Another interesting aspect of the case was that Esther was able to produce automatic writing in a style very different from her own. She was actually able to look away from the pen and paper while words appeared. A witness asked the "psychic writer" for its identity and the pen claimed to be under the control of a dead girl named Maggie Fisher who had been educated at the same school which Esther had once attended, the old red school house on the hill at Upper Stewiacke.

Reports in the Halifax *Presbyterian Witness* (June 1879) were scathing, criticising Hubbell for exhibiting Esther's " . . . infirmities to the public . . . " and the show's reception in Chatham, New Brunswick, was grim. It seems likely that Hubbell's vindictive rival showman had somehow stirred up the audience in advance: in any event an old man in the audience stood up, waved his walking cane at Hubbell who was delivering his speech and shouted, "Young man, beware!"

Esther took her bow. The curtain came down and loud, angry noises echoed around the audience. Esther and her two friends tried to slip out of the theatre quietly, but a dangerously excited mob chased them through the streets, shouting abuse and hurling stones. They managed to reach their hotel without injury, but once there a friend warned them that another and much larger hostile demonstration was being set up. They abandoned the tour and retreated ignominiously on the next train for Amherst. It's interesting to speculate about the factors which contributed to the debacle. Was the audience just disappointed because nothing paranormal had happened in the theatre? Did Hubbell's rival stir up most of the trouble? Or was the poltergeist itself somehow to blame? But the hostile crowds in Chatham were not Esther's only danger. The sternly puritanical, Dr Nathan Tupper — whose ideas were similar to those of the sadistic Matthew Hopkins, England's self-appointed "Witch finder General" — had already recommended flogging her to "drive out the evil."

Back in Amherst, the phenomena began again. Potted plants and buckets of water sailed from window ledges to the middle of the floor. One of the "ghosts" who were claiming to be present slapped Esther's face painfully hard. The most dangerous and malevolent of the "spirits" claimed to be a former Amherst shoemaker named Bob Nickle. He was accompanied by Eliza MacNeal, Maggie Fisher (who had been involved in the automatic writing episode), Peter Teed and John Nickle.

The phenomena continued with movements of the loft trapdoor, the lifting and dropping of the terrified family cat, the tearing of Esther and Jennie's night-clothes, and a hail of knives being thrown around. Bob Nickle, apparently the sinister ringleader of these attacks then stuck pins into Esther. Hubbell records that there were so many that he spent hours pulling them out!

The phenomena over-reached themselves to a point where familiarity was breeding contempt rather than fear. On one occasion Hubbell filled his pipe and jokingly called out: "Bob, fetch me a light!" According to Hubbell's account a shower of lighted matches fell around him almost at once!

Finally, Mr Bliss, the landlord of the Teed home, insisted that Esther must leave because he could no longer tolerate the risk of his house burning down. Esther then went to work as a domestic help for Arthur Davison, Clerk of the Amherst County Court, and his wife. She had been there only a few months when their barn burnt down. Esther was given a four month prison sentence for arson as the judge wasn't impressed by the psychic phenomena explanation. Public sympathy was with Esther, however, and she was freed after serving only a month.

Arthur Davison wrote an account of the time that Esther was with them. He testified that she was a good hard-working girl, but with only a very limited education. He was particularly intrigued by the strange way she seemed to glide or fly down the stairs. He didn't believe in ghosts or poltergeists as such, but he was convinced that there was something genuinely paranormal about Esther. His account included eye-witness reports by his wife that scrubbing brushes and mops moved of their own accord in Esther's presence, and he himself had once had to dodge a curry comb that was " . . . running along the stable floor . . ." towards him when Esther was nearby. On another occasion he was soaked by a milk dipper full of water which moved unaccountably while he was standing near Esther.

In commenting on Hubbell's book about her, Davison acknowledged that the actor might have sensationalised — "painted up" to use Davison's exact words — one or two events for the sake of stimulating sales, but on the whole Arthur strongly reinforced almost everything that Hubbell had written about her: "The facts were there," he said.

The poltergeist activities gradually subsided, and Esther moved away and married. Her first husband was a man named Adams who came from Springdale, Nova Scotia. After his death a few years later, she took a second husband named Shanahan. Her final home was in Brockton, Massachusetts, where she lived until her death in 1912 at the age of fifty-two.

In attempting to analyse the mystery, Walter Hubbell felt that Esther's troubles had somehow been triggered by a traumatic experience on August 28th, 1878 — just a week before the onset of the poltergeist phenomena. At that time she was going out with Bob MacNeal, a young Amherst shoemaker who had a somewhat unsavoury reputation in the area. He was taking her for a drive in his buggy, and suggested that they should get out at a secluded spot. Esther said no, and MacNeal became furiously angry with her. Drawing a revolver, he threatened to kill her unless she came into the woods with him. Interrupted by a passing carriage, Bob changed his mind and drove back to Princess Street at full speed. Despite the torrential rain, he angrily refused to raise the hood. He half-pushed Esther out of the buggy and abandoned her near the Teed house, soaked through and crying bitterly.

Hubbell's further enquiries and investigations led him to conclude that young MacNeal was seriously mentally disturbed. He was, for example, strongly suspected of being responsible for the agonising deaths of several Amherst cats. Both MacNeal and the late Bob Nickle (whose ghost was allegedly chiefly responsible for tormenting Esther) had been shoemakers. Hubbell's theory centred around the idea that the evil ghost of Bob Nickle had found it relatively easy to take over the disturbed personality of MacNeal and so induce him to try to assault Esther on that fateful evening of August 28th, 1879. Hubbell expanded his theory by suggesting that once Esther had been shocked and weakened by MacNeal's attempted rape, she herself would have been vulnerable to invasion by the evil psychic force which had once been Bob Nickle.

There's some mileage in Hubbell's theory, but the whole poltergeist experience needs to be assessed very carefully before suggesting any explanations to account for the persistent and widely reported poltergeist phenomena.

Poltergeists are rarely seen: it is their activities which are visible. They are almost invariably associated with girls and young women — much more rarely boys — going through puberty, or experiencing sexual trauma, chronic sexual frustration, or both. Hubbell detected a twenty-eigth day cycle in his observations of Esther's poltergeist problems. He attributed this to phases of the moon: other investigators might wonder if her menstrual cycle produced important psychosomatic changes some of which made her more able to act as an activity centre for the poltergeist. Almost nothing is known, even by the most up-to-date neurological researchers, of the potential power of mind over matter — especially at a subconscious level. There is a mountain of reputable evidence for ESP, for telepathy and for psychokinesis. It is *possible* that Esther (without wishing to do it deliberately) created all the strange poltergeist phenomena of 1878 and 1879 within her own unhappy and traumatised mind. It is equally possible that some invisible force, or psychic entity — which we call a poltergeist because we have no better name for it — was hovering in another dimension, some neighbouring psychic realm, just waiting for its chance to occupy a weakened human being.

At one point in the contemporary narrative it was recorded that a wise old Amerindian healer, probably a member of the Nova Scotian Micmac Nation, was called in to help Esther. According to this account, he succeeded in driving out the evil psychic presence of Bob Nickle, and making it promise never to return to trouble Esther. It was also rumoured that after she had been healed the mentally ill Bob MacNeal — who no longer lived in Amherst — became very much worse: it was almost as if the evil entity exorcised from Esther had somehow found its way into him.

Psychic problems and paranormal difficulties are by no means mutually exclusive — any more than physical ones are: chronic rheumatism doesn't prevent the patient from catching 'flu'. Was Esther the victim of several distinct but simultaneous paranormal experiences? Were a poltergeist and a group of hostile spirits acting against her at the same time that her own deep psycho-sexual traumas were creating PK phenomena around her by the power in her own subconscious? It may be significant that all the paranormal occurrences ceased after Esther was married.

There are two interesting sequels to the unsolved mystery of the Amherst poltergeist. Walter Hubbell went back to Amherst thirty years later and spoke to sixteen prominent and reliable citizens who all remembered the events of 1878-9.

They had each read Hubbell's book carefully, and they willingly signed a formal statement for him to the effect that every fact he had recorded about Esther Cox and the paranormal events surrounding her was true.

The second sequel concerned Frederick L. Blair, one of the most prominent and determined participants in the long Oak Island treasure hunt. Fred was a friend of author Edward Rowe Snow and once told Snow that he had been a witness to some of the Amherst phenomena. "I know the Amherst mystery to be true," testified Blair.

BORLEY RECTORY AND OTHER HAUNTINGS

Borley Rectory was once described as "the most haunted house in England" . . .

Borley Rectory once stood on the north bank of the River Stour in that area of East Anglia where Suffolk meets Essex. The Rectory, which was a red brick building, had some twenty-three rooms and was built in 1863 for the Reverend Henry Dawson Ellis Bull. Almost as soon as he and his family moved in, the notorious strange disturbances were said to have begun. So many alleged phenomena were reported that it would take many volumes to list them all in detail. In fact, Vincent O'Neill, who has an excellent site on the Internet called *Son of Borley,* has compiled a well researched definitive bibliography which already runs to several pages and will undoubtedly continue to grow.

Footsteps were heard. Tapping sounds occurred at night. Bells rang as they did at Bealings half a century earlier. Strange voices were heard . . . and so on . . . and so on.

The first Reverend Harry Bull and his wife Caroline Sarah (neé Foyster) had a large family — fourteen children — and they too claimed to have experienced these curious and inexplicable phenomena. One of the children, for example, was woken in the night by a sharp slap on the face — apparently delivered by a non-human assailant. Another child reported seeing a man in old-fashioned clothes standing over her bed. Numerous other witnesses over the years have reported that they have seen a headless phantom, a spectral coach and horses, a nun and a woman in white.

The site on which the Rectory was built was reputed to have been the site of a medieval monastery — although historical and archaeological evidence for the existence of such a monastery is not strong.

The original Harry Bull who died in 1892 was succeeded by his son, also called Harry, who took over the Rectory in that same year. He remained there until his death in 1927. Persistent reports of psychic phenomena continued under his incumbency as well. The dark figure of an old man in a high hat was seen. Four of the Bull sisters together said that they saw the form of a ghostly nun, and on several occasions a cook reported that a carefully locked door had apparently opened of its own accord during the night — at any rate she often found it open in the early mornings.

Poltergeist phenomena began to be recorded shortly before there was a change of incumbency.

The Reverend G. Eric Smith came to Borley in 1928 and wrote to the *Daily Mirror* about paranormal events at the Rectory. They sent V.C.Wall to investigate and also got in touch with Harry Price. He visited Borley on two or three occasions prior to 1930. In July of 1929, for example, he was there with his secretary Miss Kaye and Lord Charles Hope, while various phenomena were reported.

The Smiths left to take up a quieter and safer living in Norfolk, and in 1930 the late Harry Bull's cousin, the Reverend Lionel Algernon Foyster and his wife, Marianne, moved in. They reported that they too had had many disturbing experiences in the strange old building. Messages asking Marianne to get help appeared on the walls.

Harry Price and his team of investigators told how they had witnessed numerous strange phenomena: fires that started inexplicably, falling flintstones, and thermometers that recorded temperatures falling by as much as ten degrees.

Distinguished visiting investigators included Dr C.E.M.Joad, the broadcaster and philosopher, and Commander A.B.Campbell of the BBC's "Brains Trust" programme.

After some five years of enduring these curious psychic phenomena, the Foysters and their adopted daughter, Adelaide, were glad to leave. The Rectory was then bought by Captain Gregson. It burnt down in 1939 and the ghostly figure of a young girl was said to have been seen at an upper window, while other inexplicable cloaked figures were reported to have left the conflagration as unharmed as Shadrach, Meshach and Abednego in the biblical fiery furnace. No-one human was thought to have been there at the time except the owner.

During World War II wardens often had to investigate reports of mysterious lights seen among the ruins of Borley Rectory. In 1943, those ruins were excavated and human bones were found below the floor of what Harry Price called an ancient cellar, along with some items of religious jewellery. Messages at séances purported to supply the information that a young French nun named Marie Lairre had been persuaded to leave her convent near Le Havre to marry one of the Waldegrave family, who were landowners in the Borley area during the seventeenth century. According to the evidence obtained at the séance, Marie had been murdered by her fiancé on May 17th, 1667, in a building which had once stood on the site which Borley Rectory occupied two centuries later.

Historically, the village name, Borley, is taken from the Anglo-Saxon *Borlea* which means the clearing or pasture of the boar. The first wooden church probably stood on the site when William's Normans arrived, and the Manor of

Borley was given to William's half-sister. The twelfth century remains of the flint and rubble Norman church are still visible in the south wall of the present building.

The Waldegrave family — one of whom featured prominently in the seance story about the murder of Marie Lairre — held the manor of Borley from the sixteenth to the nineteenth centuries, and were also patrons of the living. Sir Edward Waldegrave was the M.P. for Essex at one time, but was imprisoned in the Tower of London along with his family because he had dared to have Mass celebrated in his home. He had also refused to take the Oath of Supremacy which acknowledged Elizabeth I as head of the Church of England. Sir Edward died in 1561, but his wife survived for a further thirty-eight years. Her second husband, and daughter, Magdala, are commemorated on the ornate Waldegrave Tomb inside the church. Researcher and author Frank Usher, who wrote an excellent and well-balanced article on Borley in "*Fifty Great Ghost Stories*" edited by John Canning, refers to a report that the coffins in the Waldegrave Tomb were said to have been found disarranged like the ones in the Chase Vault at Oistin, Barbados.

There are at least eight distinct legends attached to the alleged phenomena centred on Borley, which are worth summarising.

The first relates that during the thirteenth century a monk from Borley Monastery ran away with a nun from Bures Convent — about eight miles away. Their coach was pursued and overtaken by the authorities and they were brought back and executed: the boy was either hanged or beheaded and the girl was bricked up alive in her own Convent. There are, it must be said, a number of major historical problems with this account. Coaches of a design that would travel fast enough to elope in — with any reasonable hope of evading pursuit — were not really typical thirteenth century vehicles. The kind of fast mail coach that Dick Turpin and his fellow highwaymen attempted to rob belonged to a period 500 years later than the thirteenth century. There are also some serious doubts that religious houses ever existed at Borley or Bures. The elopement legend does, however, make some attempt to explain the phantom coach and the ghostly nun phenomena which have been repeatedly reported from the Borley area.

Legend two focuses on the story of the murdered French Catholic nun, Marie Lairre, supposedly from a convent in Le Havre. The information about Marie seems to have come from automatic planchette writing obtained by Helen Glanville, sometimes sitting with her father and brother, and sometimes alone, at Streatham when the messages reached her. As outlined earlier, this hapless young nun was said to have been lured from her convent to marry one of the Waldegrave family, who subsequently murdered her in a previous building on the site of Borley Rectory. He either buried her body in a cellar or dropped it down a convenient, disused well. What were alleged to be her remains were eventually unearthed from the cellars under the burnt out ruins of

Borley Rectory in August 1943 and given Christian burial in Liston Churchyard by the Reverend A.C.Henning in 1945. Requiem masses were also said for her in Oxford and Arundel.

Legend number three replaces Marie Lairre with Arabella Waldegrave. The family left England in 1688 with James II and his retreating courtiers, because of the Protestant versus Catholic conflict. Tradition suggests that Arabella became a nun while she was in France, but subsequently renounced her vows and came back to England as an early precursor of Mata Hari, working as a spy for the Stuarts. She was apparently detected by counter-intelligence agents at Borley, who disposed of her there, and hid her body. According to this version of the ghostly nun legend, Arabella has haunted the place ever since.

Legend number four shifts to Simon of Sudbury, the Archbishop of Canterbury during the Peasants Revolt of 1381. Thoroughly disliked by the peasants involved in the rebellion, Simon was captured by them and beheaded on June 14th, to loud cries of approval. Sudbury is close to Borley and this involvement of the unfortunate Archbishop Simon with the hauntings is an alternative attempt to explain the headlessness of the male spectre said to have been seen along with the nun.

The fifth legend, which is one of the vaguest and least well substantiated, refers to a ghost which was said to be audible as well as visible. A young girl, presumably one of the many nineteenth century domestic staff in the huge Rectory, was said to have been seen clinging by her finger tips to the sill of an upper window. One assumption is that she had been standing on the outer sill to clean the window and somehow lost her balance. Screaming desperately for help, she fell through the glass of the verandah below and died of her injuries. A more sinister and salacious version of the legend suggests that she was trying to escape the attentions of one of the male servants — or even of the Rector himself — and had climbed out on to the sill to attract attention. Was she then deliberately pushed to her death to silence her?

The sixth case concerns Marianne Foyster, who believed she had seen the spirit of Harry Bull gliding around the vast old Rectory which he'd built. She reported several other paranormal phenomena as well. Some of those who knew and worked with Marianne while her husband was Rector of Borley apparently thought that she was possibly inclined to be rather an imaginative and excitable character, so perhaps some of her evidence should be examined with caution — which is not to say that it should be discarded. One curious coincidence — if it *is* pure coincidence — which the brilliant and thoroughly reliable Colin Wilson discovered in the course of his Borley research was that the Lionel Foyster had lived near Amherst in Canada, where the very striking Esther Cox poltergeist phenomena had occurred. Is it remotely possible that something paranormal had followed Foyster from Canada to Borley? Or had his previous knowledge and experience of Amherst somehow programmed and prepared him for the psychic experiences that awaited him in the strange Suffolk Rectory?

The seventh legend refers to an old gardener named Amos, who had been employed by the Bull family two centuries earlier. It was Harry Bull himself who reported that he had seen Amos's ghost near the Rectory. But unless a picture of the old gardener existed somewhere, it is difficult to understand how Harry could have identified a man who had died a century before he was born.

The last account relates to the mysterious "ghost of a man wearing a tall hat" which Ethel Bull reported seeing.

These eight areas would seem to cover and categorize most of the paranormal events that were reported from in and around Borley Rectory — or its ruined remains — during the period from 1863 to 1945, when the unsafe remnants were demolished. The old coach house, however, still survives, converted into an attractive private, modern dwelling, and currently known as "The Priory". The extensive Rectory gardens became the site of four post-war bungalows.

Harry Price, the psychic investigator who was most closely concerned with Borley, is almost as interesting as the house itself. A very entertaining writer and gifted story teller, Harry was often criticised for a lack of scientific rigour. There were those among his detractors who believed that he preferred creating a sensational effect to adhering strictly to some less dramatic truth. When Wyatt Earp was old and dying, a hopeful young journalist asked for the true story of the famous gunfight at the OK Corral, to which Earp replied: "Hell with the truth, kid, print the legend." Price's critics felt that he shared Earp's attitude.

In Price's own autobiographical *Search for Truth*, he described himself as the son of a rich paper maker from Shropshire. He also claimed to have travelled frequently between there and his suburban London home in prosperous Brockley, while attending a public school in the country. A scathing criticism of Price and his work, written by Trevor Hall, suggested that Price's father was only a modestly successful grocer in New Cross, who had seduced and then married Harry's mother while she was still a teenager. Young Harry, born in 1881, had attended the local Haberdasher's Boys' Secondary School, and the only connection with Shropshire that Hall could trace was that Harry's grandfather had been landlord of the Bull's Head at Rodington.

Price claimed to have been a Director of his father's non-existent paper-making company and to have spent his leisure time up until 1908 (when he married the wealthy Constance Knight) collecting coins and amusing himself as an amateur archaeologist. Hall's researches revealed something rather different.

Price had apparently earned his living by giving gramophone concerts, taking commercial photographs of local shop fronts for advertisements, selling a patent remedy for foot-rot in sheep, and performing as a stage conjuror — an area of skill that made some of his critics question his work in Borley in later years.

Attitudes to investigators like Price and their work seem to swing like pendulums. When his first book on Borley *The Most Haunted House in England* was published in 1940, it was favourably reviewed and received massive media attention, as did *The End of Borley Rectory* which appeared in 1946. His *Times* obituary in 1948 described him as having " . . . a singularly honest and clear mind on a subject that by its very nature lends itself to all manner of trickery and chicanery . . . "

But despite much effusive praise, and media attention, the termites were already busily at work on the all too vulnerable foundations of Price's fragile reputation.

Much was made of an account by *Daily Mail* reporter Charles Sutton who claimed that after he had been hit on the head by a pebble while accompanying Price on a tour of Borley Rectory he had found Price's pockets full of small stones and brick fragments.

Lord Charles Hope and Major the Hon. Henry Douglas-Home began to express serious reservations about the phenomena that had been witnessed in the Rectory when they had been there. They lodged official reports with the S.P.R. (Society for Psychical Research) and Douglas-Home accused Price of being less than honest over the matter of the Borley phenomena. One occasion to which Home referred involved a strange noise in the darkness which sounded for all the world like cellophane being crushed. Price was accompanying him at the time. Admitting that he had made a search of Price's suitcase later on, Home claimed that he had found a roll of cellophane in there.

Because of what Hope and Home told them, the S.P.R. appointed Eric Dingwall, Mrs Goldney and Trevor Hall to study the Borley phenomena and Price's role in the affair. The three investigators had access to Price's correspondence and other papers, and as he had died on March 29th, 1948, they were free from any fear of an action for libel when their scathingly critical Report entitled *The Haunting of Borley Rectory* was finally published in 1956.

In 1973 the pendulum swung back in Price's favour with the publication of *The Ghosts of Borley: Annals of the Haunted Rectory* by the highly reputable Peter Underwood, President of the Ghost Club, and his associate Dr Tabori.

However hard Price's work is hit by some critics, and however staunchly it is defended by others of equal status, the inescapable facts are that Borley Rectory and the area around it had an unenviable reputation long before Price became involved, and numerous other curious phenomena have been associated with the site since his death.

But Borley is anything but unique: ghosts and psychic phenomena similar to those reported there have been seen and heard in thousands of other places. A second-hand report, however, is still only a report, even when made by the most reputable witnesses in the best of good faith

Sir Edmund Hornby's story strikes a loud cautionary note which investigators of the paranormal should consider carefully. This account appeared in the *Nineteenth Century* magazine in 1884, which was nine years after the mysterious experience which he described so vividly. He had been a Judge of the Supreme Court of China and Japan at Shanghai.

"On the night of January 19th, 1875, the Judge records, he heard a tap at his bedroom door and a certain newspaper editor, with whom the judge was well acquainted, walked in. He ignored the Judge's request to leave the room and sat down on the foot of the bed. The time, Sir Edmond noted, was twenty past one. The purpose of the visit was to obtain the Judge's statement concerning the day's judgement for the morning paper. After refusing twice, the request was granted for fear that further argument would wake Mrs Hornby. Finally the Judge angrily told his visitor that it was the last time he would allow any reporter inside his house. The other replied: 'This is the last time I shall ever see you anywhere.' When he had gone, the judge looked at the clock: it was exactly half past one. Lady Hornby then awoke and the Judge told her what had happened.

"Next morning Judge Hornby repeated the story to his wife on dressing. When he went to court he was somewhat shocked to hear that his visitor had died during the night, at about one o'clock. In the dead man's notebook was the headline: 'The Chief Judge gave judgement this morning in this case to the following effect . . . ' and then followed some lines of indecipherable shorthand. The result of the inquest showed that he had died of some form of heart disease. The Coroner, at the Judge's previous request, ascertained that the dead man could not have left his house during the two hours before he died.

"When he got home the Judge asked his wife to repeat what he had said to her during the night, and he 'made a brief note of her replies and of the facts'.

The Judge records: 'As I said then, so I say now — I was not asleep, but wide awake. After a lapse of nine years my memory is quite clear on the subject. I have not the least doubt I saw the man — have not the least doubt that the conversation took place between us.' "

The *Nineteenth Century* arranged for some further research to be done. This purported to unearth some starkly direct contradictions. The newsman in the story was the Reverend Hugh Lang Nivens, Editor of the *Shanghai Courier*, and he had died at 9:00 AM not 1:00 AM. When the event supposedly took place, Judge Hornby wasn't married. The first Lady Hornby had been dead for two years and he did not marry again for a further three months. There was no inquest on Hugh Nivens.

When Hornby was told what the research had turned up, he said, "If I had not believed, as I still believe, that every word of it, the story, was accurate, and that my memory was to be relied on, I should not have ever told it as a personal experience." The question arises as to whether the Judge was right and the researchers for *Nineteenth Century* got it grotesquely wrong. Maybe another newsman had died at a slightly earlier or later period, when there was a Lady Hornby with the Judge. Or maybe he had just had a very vivid dream which had got confused with real life over the years. There is an important psychological adage that we tend not to recall an event but the first re-telling of that event. Numerous re-tellings can lead quite unconsciously to what are termed "retrospective falsifications". It's as if the mind likes to tidy things up as it sorts out and edits the data stored in the vast warehouse of memory.

The White and Grey Ladies of Dartington Hall are other examples of ghosts traditionally associated with death. A young postman saw one of the girls who worked at the hall waiting in a state of absolute terror by the end of the very long drive. He asked her what was wrong and she explained that she was terrified to walk up that long dark route alone. The good-natured postman went with her and saw her safely to the staff entrance. As he turned to go back down the drive he encountered the sinister wraith of the Grey Lady. She passed very close to him and went in and out of various hedges in a manner that no earthly being could have done. It also seemed to him that she was following a driveway that differed slightly from the one along which he was walking. The encounter shocked and horrified him out of all proportion, for there was nothing especially grotesque or frightening in the Grey Lady's appearance. Whether it was connected with this weird meeting or not, the previously healthy young postman died of meningitis not long afterwards.

The White Lady of Dartington was equally sinister, but seemed to confine her attentions to one old established family.

Ghosts of murderers and their victims form another wide category. A classic case in this genre concerns the village of Haddenham not far from Aylesbury. The ghost has been reported staggering along the road towards Haddenham clutching pathetically at a fatal wound in his chest. In 1828, a farmer had visited Thame market, but failed to return. Anxious because he was so late, his wife had gone to the farmhouse door to see if he was anywhere in sight. He materialised slowly in front of her with the handle of a heavy hammer protruding from his shattered chest. Terrified by what she had seen, the farmer's wife ran for help, and with a party of neighbours found her husband's body lying beside the road. The fatal wounds in his chest were identical to those she had seen in her vision of him. Not surprisingly, she herself came under suspicion, because she had raised the alarm, and had known about the cause of death before her husband's body was discovered.

Much later the truth came out. On his way home from market, the farmer had caught two sheep stealers, Tylor and Sewell, red-handed and had threatened to report them. In 1828 they would have been deported to Botany Bay, so they murdered him to silence him. On March 8th, 1830, they were publicly hanged outside Aylesbury Prison.

The ghost of Katherine Ferrers, one of the few highwaywomen who followed the same dangerous profession as Dick Turpin and Tom King, is frequently reported on the roads near Markyate in Hertfordshire, accompanied by the ghost of her huge black stallion. She was the daughter of George Ferrers who had married the widow of Humphrey Bouchier of Markyate Cell, an Elizabethan mansion incorporating parts of a much older building.

An arranged marriage with a sixteen-year-old husband, when she herself was only thirteen, did not turn out well for her, and historians suggest that it was her dull and unhappy home life which prompted young Katherine to take up her double life as a highway robber. After an audaciously successful career during which she killed several of her victims, she was herself fatally wounded by a shot from a coach guard.

She had a secret entrance to her hidden room at Markyate, where she normally changed back into ordinary clothes, and kept her highwaywoman's outfit, mask and pistols well hidden. She just about managed to stagger to this secret entrance before she died — still wearing her highwaywoman's outfit, complete with mask and pistols. The secret was out. Word spread like wildfire, although her room was bricked up and the family denied all knowledge of her nefarious adventures. A disastrous fire in 1841 completed the job of concealment.

No account of ghosts and hauntings would be complete without at least a passing reference to the Hairy Hands of Dartmoor: malign and inexplicable manifestations which threatened sinister evil to all who came within their orbit.

A statistically improbable number of coaches, carriages, and later on cars and motor cycles ran off the road at a spot between Postbridge and Two Bridges near the southern limits of Bellever Forest, in Dartmoor. Those who had been riding or driving the vehicles which were involved in these accidents, swore that they had seen a pair of hideous, disembodied, hairy hands which wrestled with them for control of the vehicle, causing it to run off the road.

The case reached something of a climax when a husband and wife were staying close to the place in their caravan overnight. The man was asleep and his wife was writing quietly at the caravan's folding table. She became aware of a strange, unearthly feeling and a sensation of abnormal cold. Turning round, she saw two large hairy hands at the window of their caravan, just above the place where her husband was sleeping. She made the sign of the cross and prayed fervently for a moment or two — and the terrifying hands disappeared.

There are a number of interesting theories which are put forward from time to time to explain phenomena such as those reported from Borley and thousands of other sites throughout the world. Not even the best of them seems totally adequate, and perhaps like the most effective medicinal cocktails of antibiotics, a mixture of hypotheses is needed in order to account for all the enigmatic phenomena lurking out there.

One interesting idea is that perhaps earth and stone, and the fabric of some ancient buildings, are capable of receiving and recording impressions of events. This may be enhanced when the events themselves are particularly emotional and dramatic — rather like increasing the input on a recorder, or amplifying the signal in some way. If a strip of magnetic tape can capture a picture and its accompanying sounds to be replayed repeatedly on a VCR, then maybe some of nature's "magnetic tapes" can capture and record events which sensitive and receptive people will continue to see and hear from time to time when the conditions are right. If this hypothesis is the correct one in a number of cases of paranormal events, then the so-called ghosts are no more paranormal than sitting down for a good evening's viewing with Schwarzenegger, Norris or Stallone on your video. It is just as natural to watch them re-performing their fights, chases and other adventures, recorded in distant studios and exotic locations long ago, as it is to watch "psychic" re-enactments of battles fought in the seventeenth century British Civil War.

It is, of course, equally possible that when we report having seen some paranormal manifestation, we are actually observing the disembodied spirit of someone who lived long ago, whose soul has returned to earth to fulfil an important purpose, or to pass on a message that was not completed during his or her earthly life.

There is also a neuro-psychological theory of perceptual malfunction which is well worth considering. Compare the human eye and brain to a computer controlled camera, just for the sake of the explanation. Occasionally, even the best equipment malfunctions, and instead of capturing the scene in front of its lens in the outside world, the computerised camera tries to record its own interior. Suppose that a parallel problem afflicts the human observer from time to time, and an *internal* thought, a dream, a visual idea, gets interpreted as an *external* one. If I am affectionately remembering a parent who has passed over, and that much loved and well remembered face and form appears sitting in a favourite chair, am I simply recording an internal view as if it was an external one?

If thoughts are more powerful than we usually give them credit for, is it possible that some so-called spectres and phantoms can be explained as *tulpas,* or thought forms, materialisations of ideas in our own minds, or in the collective minds of groups of people like the sitters at Victorian and Edwardian seances? If a group of like-minded believers are concentrating on contacting something paranormal, may they not sometimes conjure up their expectations? Does that go some way to explaining why the presence of a strong-minded cynic or sceptic can prevent the miracle from occurring? Has one hard, sharp, disbelieving mind got the ability to puncture the psychic balloon which the rest of the sitters are busily trying to inflate?

It may also be possible that some strange sightings are visitors from the past or the future, or from another probability track or unknown dimension? Could extra-terrestrial alien life forms appear in the guise of disembodied human spirits?

Of one thing we may be certain. It is not all imagination. Neither is it all psychosomatic — although some of it may be. The paranormal is not as Ebenezer Scrooge once thought "a fragment of undigested potato" — it needed something more mysterious than indigestion to conjure up Marley's ghost.

Reports of psychic phenomena remain one of the great central unsolved mysteries of the world. It is a field that is very well worth continual investigation.

THE STRANGE CASE OF THE BARBADOS COFFINS

What unknown power could have moved the massive lead coffins inside their sealed vault?

In a universe where commonsense cause and effect seem to govern most phenomena most of the time, the moving coffins of Barbados would appear to be an unexplained effect with no known cause.

The outline of the event is that in the Christchurch parish burial ground at Oistin Bay in Barbados — a bay which looks for all the world like a Caribbean holiday poster — the coffins inside one strangely troubled vault moved repeatedly but inexplicably between one interment and the next.

In Barbados at that time it was customary for the coffins of wealthy plantation owning families to be massively heavy, lead-lined constructions needing six or eight men to move them.

The Christchurch vault at the heart of the mystery was built of large coral stone blocks and closed with a ponderous slab of blue Devonshire marble. It was partly above and partly below ground level, and approached via a short flight of steps. The interior was four metres long and two metres wide, with a roof that arched when seen from inside but looked flat from outside.

The first person to be buried in the notorious vault was Mrs Thomasina Goddard. That happened during July 1807. A year later the pathetic little coffin of two year old Mary Anna Chase was interred. On July 6, 1812, Dorcas, her elder sister, followed her. There were dark whisperings that Dorcas had succumbed to an early nineteenth century medical problem that might have been diagnosed as anorexia in our own time. Some said that her father's brutality had led her deliberately to starve herself to death in a final desperate effort to escape from him.

Up until this time, all the burials in the notorious vault had been perfectly normal.

In August of 1812 everything changed. The Honourable Thomas Chase, reputedly the most thoroughly detested man in all Barbados, was being laid to rest in his infamous vault. The tiny coffin of little Mary Anna Chase had,

The Chase Vault at Oistin, Christchurch, Barbados, where the heavy lead-lined coffins moved around after the vault was carefully sealed by Lord Combermere.

(Photo © Simon Probert & Pamela Willson 1996, and reproduced with their permission.)

apparently, been thrown right across the vault and was now propped upside down in a far corner. Mrs Goddard's coffin had been rotated through 90 degrees so that it lay on its side with the back leaning against the wall. The first reaction of the white members of the burial party was to blame the coloured graveyard labourers. They denied it vigorously. Despite their understandable and fully justifiable resentment of their treatment at the hands of the plantation owners and managers, the coloured labourers were anxious to put as much distance as possible between themselves and this unquiet tomb. It is highly improbable that somehow they would have made their way secretly into the vault prior to Thomas Chase's burial and moved the previously interred coffins.

Every coffin was put back in its proper place and Thomas was laid reverently alongside the earlier occupants of the vault.

Time passed. On September 25, 1816, approximately four years later, eleven-month-old Samuel Brewster Ames was carried to the sinister vault. In the April before little Samuel's death, there had been a brief but bloody slave rebellion — they were not rare in early nineteenth century Barbados. It had been brutally quelled by the plantation owners with their usual ruthlessness.

The coffins in the notorious vault were once again in complete disarray. Once more the coloured workers were unjustly blamed for the desecration. This time the white plantation owners believed that the vault had been violated as an act of vengeance on behalf of those slaves who had been killed or maimed during the recent abortive uprising.

Upon reflection, however, this explanation failed to satisfy the investigators. It was recognized that the vault had only one entrance and the ponderous blue Devonshire marble slab was still securely in its place. It showed no signs of having been disturbed.

Then there was the question of the sheer weight and awkwardness of the coffins themselves. Mrs Goddard's casket was only a relatively light, wooden affair — flimsy compared to the others — and easy enough to move, but the unpopular Thomas Chase had been a big man, well over sixteen stone. His remains lay inside a solid wooden coffin encased in lead. It required nearly a dozen men to move it. When the vault was opened for little Samuel Brewster Ames on that fateful 25th of September in 1816, this massive lead-covered coffin was several feet from its original resting place and lying on its side.

Six weeks later, the vault was opened again. Samuel Brewster, father of little Samuel Brewster Ames, had actually been killed — clubbed to death by his slaves during the unsuccessful April rebellion — seven months previously. As a temporary measure during the emergency at that time, he had been buried elsewhere. Now he was being transferred to his final resting place in the family vault.

The marble slab was examined carefully. It seemed firmly in place. A crowd of curious onlookers followed Samuel's coffin. The slab was slowly moved aside. Sunlight revealed the interior of the vault : *once again the coffins had been radically disturbed.* They were randomly strewn about once more. Mrs Goddard's wooden casket had now disintegrated. The pieces subsequently had to be tied together and propped against one wall.

Photograph taken by gifted psychic Pamela Willson in 1996 showing what appears to be a paranormal presence hovering near the doorway of the Chase vault.

(Photo © Simon Probert & Pamela Willson 1996, and reproduced with their permission.)

Thomas Orderson, Rector of Christ Church, and three other men searched the vault thoroughly. Flooding was one possibility that occurred to them, and they tested for signs of dampness or recent moisture: but everywhere was perfectly dry inside the vault. Walls and floor were checked for any tell-tale cracks — nothing was detected.

There were some peripheral Voodoo traditions on Barbados at the time, but they were much less pronounced than on Haiti. The plantation workers were convinced that some form of supernatural curse was affecting the Chase vault, and they kept as far away from it as possible. Meanwhile plantation owners, managers, and visiting sailors all expressed a high level of interest and curiosity: the next interment was awaited with ill-concealed enthusiasm.

It happened on July 17th, 1819. Mrs Thomasina Clarke had recently died and the vault was to be re-opened for her. Understandably, there were a great many excited and curious onlookers, and the burial party included Lord Combermere himself, the then Governor of Barbados and a former cavalry commander in the Peninsular War: he had been one of Wellington's bravest and most reliable officers. Once again the coffins were in disarray — all except for the pathetic bundle of wood which had once contained Mrs Goddard. That was standing where they had left it propped against the wall three years previously. If anything would have moved easily because of some natural tremor, disturbance or flood, it would have been the precariously propped planks of that disintegrated Goddard coffin. But that was the only one which still stood —

Computer enhancement of the psychic photo taken by Pamela Willson clearly showing a human skull at the top of the strange figure in the doorway of the Chase vault.

(Photo © Simon Probert & Pamela Willson 1996, and reproduced with their permission.)

Authors and researchers Patricia and Lionel Fanthorpe at the Chase Vault in Oistin, Christchurch, Barbados.

unmoved as a dead Roman sentry at his post at Pompeii. Once more a thorough examination of the coffins and the vault was carried out. No clue to the disturbance was found. The coffins were laid back in their proper places: the three large leaden ones formed the foundation layer. Above them lay the children and the disintegrated pieces of Mrs Goddard's casket, tied together as before. On Combermere's orders, further precautions were taken. A thick layer of fine white sand was sprinkled over the floor to show footprints or drag marks. The heavy marble slab was cemented in place yet again, and Combermere and his party made distinctive marks in the wet cement using their seals.

Feelings of excitement and curiosity on the island were now running too high for Combermere to wait for the next interment. On April 18th, 1820, after he and a party of the island's leading citizens had been discussing the moving coffin enigma, they decided not to wait for another family death, but to re-open the vault and inspect its interior straight away. Neighbouring citizens were notified of the Governor's intentions; a party of very reluctant plantation labourers was assembled — and the grim work began. The blue Devonshire marble door proved to be a major problem. All the distinctive seals in the rock-hard cement were undisturbed and clearly visible, but after the cement was chipped free the door was still very difficult to move. The reason soon became all too clear: Thomas Chase's huge, lead coffin, weighing the better part of a

The entrance to the sinister Chase Vault where the heavy lead coffins moved repeatedly in the early 19th century, despite the seals on the door.

Interior of the macabre Chase Vault, looking from the rear of the vault towards the steps at the entrance.

ton, was wedged up against it at a steep angle. That in itself was totally inexplicable, but with the single exception of the fragments of Thomasina Goddard's wooden coffin, everything else was also in wild disarray. The sand, however, was undisturbed. There were no signs of dragging, of intruders' footprints, nor of flooding. Every part of the vault was as sound and solid as the day it had been built: there were no loose, movable stones, and no secret passages.

Combermere and his distinguished guests were completely baffled — and so were the onlookers. The tough old cavalry veteran, who feared nothing *physical*, decided that enough was enough. He gave orders for all the coffins to be reverently re-interred elsewhere: the Chase vault was to be left empty — and so it has remained until the present day.

A number of theories have been put forward over the years — the best of them are not entirely adequate: the worst are at least 180 degrees off target.

Wherever and whenever there is a really challenging and inexplicable phenomenon, there seem to be those who claim that it never really happened at all. The classic example is the eager denial by some atheists and agnostics of the very existence of the historical Christ — let alone his miracles and his resurrection. Their case is at best transparently flimsy, and such minute substance as it has is riddled with errors and fallacies: yet it seems to satisfy them. Small wonder, then, that some of those who appear to find the existence of unsolved mysteries uncomfortable and disconcerting should attempt to dispose of them by saying that they never happened. It is only the *legendary* ostrich — not the ornithological one — which buries its head in the sand to avoid unwelcome stimuli, but what a gift to orators, preachers and moralisers that mythical bird is! The fragile argument that the Barbados coffins never moved around in their vault, relies mainly upon the supposition that there was a sinister — but totally motiveless and unsubstantiated — Masonic Plot: Lord Combermere, the Rev. Thomas Orderson (who officiated at the interments), Nathan Lucas, Major Finch, Bowcher Clarke and other honest, respectable and reliable contemporary participants and witnesses were all said to have been Freemasons and to have concocted the whole story as a sort of Masonic fable about death and resurrection. That theory disintegrates more speedily than the unfortunate Mrs Goddard's wooden coffin.

What next? Of much more substance is the idea that giant, tropical, puff-ball fungi were responsible. An account of the Barbados coffins, written by Valentine Dyall, appeared in *Everybody's Weekly* on July 19th, 1952. Shortly afterwards Dyall received a letter from a Mr Gregory Ames, who then lived at 50 Bonser Road, Twickenham, Middlesex, UK. He enclosed a copy of a letter written by his great-grandfather on Christmas Day 1820. The writer, a close relative of the interred infant Samuel Brewster Ames, and almost certainly an eyewitness to the events in the Barbados vault, believed that huge fungi of a type known to grow in caves in Honduras were responsible for moving the coffins. He says that a very old plantation labourer told him that although the vault was originally built to hold the remains of the Honourable John Elliott, the mysterious sounds like muffled explosions which came from it led to John being interred elsewhere in 1724 — long before the Chase/Ames phenomena began. Were those unexplained "muffled explosions" really caused by the sudden collapse of enormous puff-ball fungi?

While giving a series of lectures on unexplained phenomena in East Anglia in the 1970s, we mentioned the Barbados coffins and the Ames letter. A farmer member of the group brought in a very large British puff-ball fungus which he had found in one of his barns. We duly sealed it inside a large plastic sack and the group kept watch on it week by week. At the end of the two term course, it still showed not the slightest sign of disintegrating into an undetectable nothingness. When Combermere and his team searched the vault and checked out the sand on the floor, they would have been certain to see and recognise the remains of any puff-ball fungi large enough to have moved coffins weighing up to a ton apiece. No-one at the time reported seeing such debris. The fungus idea is, nevertheless, just about tenable, but it's far from conclusive.

Seekers after a supernatural explanation have laid great emphasis on the behaviour of Mrs Goddard's wooden coffin. It alone did not move when the heavier, metal ones did. It was widely surmised at the time that the unhappy Mrs Goddard had taken her own life. If she had, there are precedents in the archives of supernatural case studies for strange disturbances and paranormal phenomena attending suicides. Yet, if Mrs Goddard's restless, earthbound spirit *was* somehow responsible for moving the Barbados coffins, that raises more questions than it lays to rest. Where do such unhappy spirits obtain their psychic — and physical — energy? In this case very significant amounts of energy? Why, when so many unfortunate people take their own lives, are cases like the Barbados coffins so extremely rare? To what extent — and this links across to poltergeist phenomena — can purely mental or spiritual energy possibly affect such large masses of matter? To "explain" the Barbados coffin phenomena in terms of Mrs Goddard's troubled spirit is like trying to explain the nature of water by saying that it has come out of a tap. To say that the power "came out of" Mrs Goddard's suicide, is not a full or satisfactory explanation of the true nature of that power.

Was it, after all, despite the vault being tightly sealed, the vengeance of those plantation workers who had been abominably treated by Thomas Chase? They had the motive, undeniably, but they were undeniably afraid of the "dark powers" which they believed the vault contained. It seems far more likely that they would have avoided the place than that they would have found a way to creep in and vandalise it without being detected. The vengeful labourers theory fails to explain the sealed door, the sound masonry (totally lacking in loose stones or secret passages) and the carefully sanded floor which showed no tell tale marks.

The rear of the mysterious Chase Vault showing the barrel arch ceiling, and the solid coral and limestone blocks of which it is constructed.

Flooding and minor earthquakes have both been suggested, but the great difficulty here is the localised nature of the disturbances. One vault does not flood leaving dozens of others perfectly dry. One set of coffins is not shaken violently out of position by an earth tremor that leaves all the adjacent vaults unaffected.

Some researchers have suggested that the coffins were moved by natural forces, as yet not understood by orthodox main-stream science. Ill-defined things like "negative gravity bubbles" have been proposed. Admittedly, they seem far more probable than the Masonic fable theories, but they're significantly less likely than Honduras-type puff-balls.

Inevitably, intrepid travellers on the boundaries of von Daniken Land, will suggest that extra-terrestrial aliens were responsible. To give that hypothesis the modicum of respect which it deserves, it is just about possible to imagine the alien observers carrying out a few simple experiments. Did they try out some sort of highly advanced, long range tractor beams? Perhaps they were able to move *metal* cases more easily than wooden ones — hence Mrs Goddard's coffin remaining in its place, while the leaden ones shifted significantly. As a corollary, might it be suggested that there were also psychological and sociological dimensions to those entirely hypothetical extra-terrestrial experiments? As well as trying out their tractor beams, were our postulated aliens studying the reactions of Combermere and the other investigators? Were they trying to find out how the human mind responded to a series of phenomena which it couldn't explain? Were they conducting some kind of cosmic IQ test on Combermere and his contemporaries? It's not high on the scale of probabilities, but it's not impossible given the great weight of pro-UFO evidence that has steadily accumulated over the centuries.

The overwhelming weight of evidence leads to the inescapable conclusion that the Barbados coffins were real, and on several occasions they moved significant distances inside a sealed vault. They do not seem to have been thrown around by vengeful intruders, by flood water, by giant fungi, by localised earthquakes, by extra-terrestrial aliens, or by nil-gravity-bubbles. Today, the tomb is empty — except for the intangible mystery which still clings to it.

Yet the Barbados vault is not quite unique. There are reports of *other* vaults where coffins were once alleged to have moved — and they are situated a long way from Barbados.

During July 1844 — nearly a quarter of a century after the strange events in the Chase family vault — odd things happened at Kuresaare, formerly called Ahrensburg, on what is now Saarema, but was then identified on maps as the island of Osel in Estonia. There were reports from visitors to the Ahrensburg cemetery that their horses were behaving strangely. They seemed nervous and unsettled when they were tethered after their riders had dismounted to attend the graves of family or friends. One report states that some horses went crazy with fear, and adds that at least one of the horses died in its frenzied efforts to get away from the hitching rail near the cemetery.

One of the Buxhoewden family was being interred on July 24th. The vault was duly opened. There were sudden cries of anger and amazement: most of the previously interred coffins had been stacked up untidily in the centre of the vault like logs on a bonfire. The coffins were reverently replaced, and the family made a formal complaint to Baron Guldenstubbé, President of the Consistory. His colleagues included the mayor, a local doctor, two craft guild representatives and an official secretary. Their formal verdict was that ghouls (either human or supernatural) had been responsible for the vandalism and desecration. Guldenstubbe acted swiftly — as determinedly and effectively as Lord Combermere had done on the other side of the world. New locks were added to the vault door, and guards were positioned in the cemetery. This had also been done — with great effect — in Bacton in Norfolk, UK, in 1828, when body-snatchers had attempted to steal corpses from the village churchyard during January of that year. The night guard had fired at the intruders, peppering them with heavy buckshot before they galloped away, never to trouble the Bacton dead again.

The carefully guarded Osel vault was inspected three days later. The soldiers reported no problems: all had been quiet while they had been on duty. All the locks were secure. But most of the coffins were again piled in a heap in the centre of the tomb, two or three others lay nearby on their sides. Guldenstubbé and the local Lutheran Bishop questioned everybody who might have had the slightest knowledge of the strange events. As in Barbados, a thorough search was made for a secret tunnel: but no trace of one was ever found. Guldenstubbé and the Bishop ordered two or three coffins to be opened: only naturally decomposing bodies were found inside. As in Barbados, a thorough check was made for flooding — it revealed nothing. Even the base of the vault was dug up and replaced. The chapel above was also carefully examined. Guldenstubbé made a third and final attempt: more new locks were provided; a ring of soldiers surrounded the vault; dry wood ash was sprinkled liberally across the floor as sand had been spread in Barbados.

Three more days passed and the vault was opened again: once more chaos reigned supreme. Coffins were scattered; some were up-ended; some had sprung open. The ashes on the floor showed no trace of footprints — nor of any other type of disturbance. Just as in the Barbados case, the coffins were re-interred elsewhere and the Buxhoewden vault was left empty. Another strange parallel with the Barbados case was that one of the young Buxhoewdens buried in the disturbed vault was rumoured to have shot himself.

Barbados and Osel were by no means the only sites where coffins were reported to have moved inexplicably. *Notes and Queries* for 1867 contained some correspondence from F.C.Paley, son of the Rector of Gretford near Stamford, UK. He reported that his father had told him of several heavy, lead lined coffins being disarranged in a vault in his parish. One was so heavy that six men could move it only with considerable difficulty. As in Barbados and Osel, some of these Gretford coffins were also found on their sides.

Yet another case was reported in *The European Magazine* dated September 1815, and commented on by Algernon E. Aspinall in his book *West Indian Tales of Old*. This time the vault concerned was at Stanton in Suffolk, UK. Once again, the coffins were lead lined, and standing on biers inside the vault. On several occasions when the vault was opened they were found to have been displaced. Once at least, a coffin was found resting on the fourth step of the flight that led down from inside the door to the floor of the vault. Subterranean flooding seems to have been the most popular explanation at the time — although witnesses noted that there was no sign of any such flooding when the Suffolk vault was opened.

The "moved-by-water" hypothesis, however, does have some unexpected support from an unusual and bizarre quarter: *The London Evening Post* of May 16th, 1751, carried a report that the *Johannes*, under Captain Wyrck Pietersen, retrieved a floating, wood encased, lead coffin containing the body of Francis Humphrey Merrydith. A month or so earlier, he'd been buried in the Goodwin Sands in accordance with his last request. Commander Rupert T. Gould, an authority on unsolved mysteries, and a very knowledgeable professional seaman, also supports the idea that such coffins can float. He made some reliable buoyancy calculations and reached the conclusion that a typical, lead lined, wood encased coffin weighed around 900 pounds, but had a displacement of over 1100 pounds. If the average corpse weighed less than 200 pounds, that would make such a coffin reasonably buoyant.

There is an account of the Baltic mystery in S.R.Vale Owen's book *Footfalls on the Boundary of Another World*. He was an American diplomat who obtained the information from Guldenstubbé's son and daughter in 1859. Reliable and well documented accounts of the Chase vault incident appear in the *Journal of the Barbados Museum and Historical Society, volumes XII and XIII,* which were published in 1945.

On more than one occasion and in more than one vault, heavy lead lined coffins have reportedly moved. If they were moved by some as yet unknown *natural* force, it could prove to be well worth pursuing. A close study of light brought in the miracle of the laser. An examination of silicon semi-conductors introduced the computer revolution. Fleming's observation of the behaviour of micro-organisms in the presence of certain moulds heralded the life-saving arrival of powerful antibiotics. A boy watching a kettle lid moving as the water boiled grew up to develop the steam engine . . . What might a perceptive and imaginative engineer discover from trying to replicate the Barbados vault phenomena on a scientific basis? If only Tesla had heard of the enigma and visited Barbados to investigate!

As we were putting the finishing touches to this manuscript, and making the final revisions, we received a very interesting phone call from Simon Probert and Pamela Willson of Penarth. Our lecture to the Annual Fortean "UnConvention" in London had been widely advertised and this year the subject was the Barbados coffin mystery. Simon and Pamela had seen a press report of it and invited us to call and see some photographs of the disturbed vault, which they had taken in September of 1996. As a well qualified and experienced professional funeral director, Simon is especially knowledgable about coffins. Pamela, a talented artist and expert picture restorer, is also a sensitive psychic and psychometrist. It was after lunch on that mid-September day that they visited the little church and graveyard at Oistin in Barbados. Having looked around the church first they went to inspect the infamous Chase vault. Surprisingly, as an iron grid is normally kept locked across it to prevent vandalism and damage, they found it was unbarred and open that afternoon. Simon took a photograph, which came out quite normally, and then Pamela descended to inspect the interior. She felt that the atmosphere was strangely *wrong*, and decided not to go in. Simon, however, did go in and Pamela took a photograph of him in the actual doorway where the blue Devonshire marble slab once rested, his hand raised in a cheery wave. When this picture was developed Simon seemed to have faded away into the darkness of the tomb's interior, while a curious, amorphous, wraith-like figure — not unlike a dead woman in a shroud — was standing on his left, to the right of the print. When this picture was subjected to computer enhancement, the shrouded woman could be seen quite clearly with a skull for a head. Another strange object behind her could have been a second skull, which appeared to Simon and Pamela as the four of us studied the picture together, to have a look of menace as though it was threatening the spectral woman. If the unfortunate Mrs Thomasina Goddard had in fact taken her own life because of Thomas Chase's cruelty, then the photographic evidence seemed to be suggesting that death had not ended her sufferings.

The very least that can be said about Simon and Pamela's photographs and the computer enhancement is that they are inexplicably strange, just as the coincidence of the vault being open that afternoon was strange, and my choice of lecture subject for the Fortean meeting was strange, and Simon and Pamela's seeing the note about that lecture in the *South Wales Echo* was strange — almost, perhaps, as if we were *destined* to meet and discuss the sinister Barbados coffin mystery.

THE MYSTERY OF THE
MARY CELESTE

Originally built in Nova Scotia as The Amazon,
the strange brigantine seemed to be jinxed.

The *Mary Celeste* was built by Joshua Davis (spelt Dewis in some accounts) — the first of twenty-seven identical vessels — on Spencer's Island, Nova Scotia in 1861, where she was originally named *Amazon*. Constructed from strong Nova Scotian beech, birch, spruce and maple, her cabins were finished with pine. She was a few inches short of 100 feet long, and just over quarter of that in width. Her depth was fractionally under twelve feet, and she was close on 200 tons displacement.

The corvel built (planks edge to edge, not overlapping like a clinker built ship) *Amazon* was technically described as a two-masted brigantine, although the records of the Atlantic Mutual Insurance Company listed her as "a half-brig". She was officially registered at Parrsboro on June 10th, 1861.

There are sailors with great knowledge and long experience who wonder whether certain ships carry a jinx, or curse. There were many of them who thought that about the *Amazon*: her first skipper, a Scotsman named Robert McLellan, died within forty-eight hours of taking command. On her maiden voyage she ripped a great gash down one side when she collided with a fishing weir off the Maine coast. Fire broke out and damaged her severely while the hull repairs were still being done: the Captain, John Nutting Parker, was dismissed.

She crossed the Atlantic uneventfully, but a collision in the Channel not far from Dover sank the brig with which *Amazon* had collided and led to yet another change of skipper. Under his command she ran aground just off Cow Bay, part of Cape Breton Island, Nova Scotia, in 1867, and was at first regarded as a total wreck. Incomplete records suggest that two men named Haines and McBean attempted to salvage her, but the deal went disastrously wrong, and bankrupted them.

Her next owner was John Beatty of New York, who sold her on again to James H. Winchester and his associates, Sylvester Goodwin and Daniel

Sampson. By this time various structural alterations had been made: she now had two decks; her length had increased to 103 feet, her depth to sixteen feet, and her breadth by just a few inches. Her displacement had increased dramatically to 282 tons. She was now American owned and registered; she flew the Stars and Stripes; and her name had been changed to *Mary Celeste*. Lloyds of London had once listed her as *Marie Celeste*, and there is a minor mystery about the name. One theory is that the odd mixture of French and English was simply due to a painter's error, even more oddly it has been put forward that the real name was intended to be *Mary Sellers*.

When Winchester and his associates discovered dry rot in the hull, they promptly rebuilt the bottom with a strong, copper lining. In their hands the *Mary Celeste* became as stout, as seaworthy and as reliable as any vessel of her size at that time.

For some two years she was under the command of Rufus Fowler, who had also acquired a share in her on 11th January 1870. On the 29th of October, 1872, he was replaced by Captain Benjamin Spooner Briggs, who also owned a few shares in the vessel.

Born at Wareham, Massachusetts, on April 24th, 1835, the second of Captain Nathan Briggs' five sons by his wife Sophia, Benjamin was thirty-seven years old, and the product of a New England puritan, sea-faring family background. His brothers also went to sea, and by the time he took over the ill-fated *Mary Celeste*, Benjamin had already commanded the schooner *Forest King*, the barque *Arthur*, and the brig *Sea Foam*.

Just before sailing into history, the *Mary Celeste* was anchored at Pier 44 in New York's East River. On Saturday, 2nd November, 1872, she was loaded with 1701 red oak casks of commercial alcohol, and everything in the hold was made secure. The shippers were a firm of New York merchants, Meissner Arckerman and Co. and the alcohol was destined for H.Mascerenhas and Co. of Genoa in Italy.

Although the Sandy Hook pilot ship took the *Mary Celeste* from Pier 44 to Staten Island's Lower Bay on November 5th, the Atlantic was so rough that Briggs decided to wait for two days before taking his ship out into open waters on November 7th.

Besides Briggs himself, the *Mary Celeste* carried his thirty-year-old wife, Sarah Elizabeth (daughter of the Rev Cobb, the Congregationalist Minister in Marion, Massachusetts) and their infant daughter, Sophia Matilda. Their son, seven-year-old Arthur Stanley, had been left at home in the care of his paternal grandparents. Poignantly, in her last letter, posted on Staten Island, Sarah Briggs said how much she was looking forward to getting a letter from her little son.

Twenty-eight year old Albert G. Richardson, the first mate, had been a soldier in the American Civil War, had married the niece of James H. Winchester (owner of the *Mary Celeste*), and was generally regarded as a brave and reliable seaman. He had sailed with Briggs before. The second mate was twenty-five-year-old Andrew Gilling, a New Yorker of Danish origins. He, like first mate Richardson, was highly regarded both for his character and seamanship. Edward William Head, aged twenty-three, served as cook and steward. He came from Brooklyn, and enjoyed the same good reputation as the three officers. The remaining crew members were German: Volkert Lorensen and his brother, Boy, were both in their twenties; Gottlieb Goodschall was twenty-three; and Arien Martens, around whom there was a slight air of mystery, was thirty-five. Although he was a qualified and experienced mate, he had signed on with Briggs as an ordinary seaman.

Before setting out on their last voyage, Briggs and his wife had dinner with Captain David Reed Morehouse, a Nova Scotian friend, and his wife. The two ladies were also friends. Morehouse was skipper of the *Dei Gratia*, carrying a cargo of petroleum to Gibraltar, and his ship was coincidentally moored not far from the *Mary Celeste*. Ironically, Morehouse was destined to be first on the scene after the tragedy. The four friends dined together for the last time at Astor House.

The *Mary Celeste* finally left the USA on November 7th. The *Dei Gratia* sailed on November 15th. For some ten days her voyage was completely routine and uneventful. Then, just after 1:00 PM on December 5th, John Johnson, who was helmsman at that time, sighted a ship about five miles off their port bow. Their position was 38 degrees 20" north by 17 degrees 15" west, and they were approximately 600 miles off the coast of Portugal. Johnson's keen, experienced eyes detected almost at once that there was something strangely wrong with the other vessel. She was yawing slightly, and her sails did not look right. He called John Wright, the *Dei Gratia's* second mate, and as soon as Wright had had a good look, they sent word to Captain Morehouse. He inspected the other ship for a few moments through his telescope and then decided that they needed assistance. By 3:00 PM, the *Dei Gratia* was only about 400 yards from the stricken ship. Having hailed her several times and received no answer, Morehouse sent a boat to investigate. Oliver Deveau, the first mate, went across with Johnson the helmsman and second mate John Wright. As they closed the distance, they saw that the other ship was the *Mary Celeste*, which had left New York eight days earlier than they had. Johnson stayed in the dinghy, while the first and second mate climbed aboard. Oliver Deveau, a big, muscular man, who was afraid of nothing, led that exploration. They searched the ship from end to end, but there was nobody aboard — alive or dead. They sounded the pumps to see how much water lay in the hold. One pump had already been withdrawn to let a sounding rod down, so Deveau and Wright used the other one. Recent storms had left a fair quantity of water between decks — but it was no great threat to the ship's buoyancy and stability. They found the main staysail lying across the forward housing, but the upper foresail, and the foresail itself, had apparently been torn away by the recent storms and lost overboard during the time the *Mary Celeste* had been deserted. The jib was set, as were the fore-topmast staysails, and the lower topsail. All the other sails were furled. The running rigging was in a chaotic mess. Much of it was fouled, some was dangling forlornly over the sides and the rest had been blown away and lost like the foresails. The vitally important main peak halyard, nearly 100 metres long — which was used to hoist the gaff sail's outer end — had snapped off short, and the greater part of it simply wasn't there. The binnacle had been knocked or blown over, smashing the compass, and the helm was spinning freely as wind and tide moved the rudder randomly.

Although the main hatch was in good condition and securely fastened down as it should have been, some ancillary hatches were open and their covers were lying on the deck. When Wright and Deveau checked the galley they found less than a foot of water in it, and almost all of the provisions were intact and usable. There was also a plentiful supply of fresh, clean drinking water aboard.

When they searched Captain Briggs' family cabin, they discovered the temporary, or slate, log, which showed that on Monday, 25th November, the *Mary Celeste* had been close to St Mary's Island in the Azores on a bearing of E.S.E. At 8:00 PM on the same day they had been within six miles of Eastern Point on a bearing of S.S.W. A child's garment, partly finished, lay in the sewing-machine which had not been put away.

The mate's cabin contained an unfinished calculation, which looked as though he had been called away very suddenly, and there was also a chart with a tracing of the *Mary Celeste's* track up until 24th November, when she had been 100 miles S.W. of San Miguel Island in the Azores.

In the crew's quarters, razors had been left out as though their owners had been about to shave when the disturbance occurred. Laundered underclothes still hung on a line to dry. Sea-chests, and treasured personal possessions like oilskins, pipes and tobacco pouches had also been left behind. An open bottle of medicine seemed to indicate that whoever had been taking it had deemed the emergency too acute to waste time putting the cork back in.

Two sections of rail had been removed to make space to launch the boat — a small yawl, which was normally kept above the main hatch cover. Wherever the passengers and crew had gone, some at least, appeared to have left in that yawl. They also seemed to have taken essential documents and equipment with them. The bill of lading had gone, so had the navigation book, the sextant and the chronometer. It was reasonable to assume from this that Briggs and his crew had abandoned ship for some reason that seemed vitally important to them at the time, and had taken with them the means of navigating their way into a main shipping lane to be rescued by another vessel, or to the nearest port the inadequate little yawl could reach.

Having discovered all they could, Deveau, Johnson and Wright returned to the *Dei Gratia* to report their findings to Captain Morehouse. After some discussion, it was agreed that Deveau with two men — Augustus Anderson and

Charles Lund — to help him would try to sail the *Mary Celeste* to Gibraltar to claim the salvage money. This was a risky undertaking for all concerned. Three men were a bare minimum skeleton crew for the *Mary Celeste*, while Morehouse would be left with barely enough men to handle the *Dei Gratia*. If the weather turned really bad, or if some other kind of emergency hit either vessel, they would be in desperate trouble. The safest thing seemed to be to sail in convoy.

This worked well until they reached the Straits of Gibraltar when a fierce storm separated them. The *Dei Gratia* arrived in Gibraltar on the evening of December 12th, and the *Mary Celeste* struggled in about twelve hours later.

The salvage claim should have been simple, straightforward and relatively generous. By great strength, courage, stamina and expert seamanship, the mighty Oliver Deveau had saved not only a valuable ship but its cargo as well. He and Morehouse and their men merited heroes' welcomes and substantial gratitude. What they got instead was the odious Frederick Solly Flood, whose arrogance and pomposity were inversely proportional to his IQ. Within two hours of their arrival, the *Mary Celeste* was placed under arrest by Thomas J. Vecchio of the Vice-Admiralty Court.

Fred Flood had the grandiloquent title of Attorney General for Gibraltar and Advocate General for the Queen in Her Office of Admiralty. He simply could not see that the *Mary Celeste* would have been abandoned unless there had been foul play. He obstinately refused to accept any explanations that did not involve murder and piracy, or, at the very least criminal collusion between Morehouse and Briggs.

Fred' s first broadside was fired at the *Mary Celeste's* crew, who were, of course, unable to be in Court to refute his wild accusations. He was convinced that they had broken into the cargo of crude industrial alcohol, got raging drunk and murdered Briggs, his family and first mate Richardson. When it was pointed out to him that raw industrial alcohol is not only very unpalatable, but so toxic as to produce severe internal pain long before it produced intoxication, he grudgingly abandoned that theory and looked around for another avenue of attack.

At Fred's request, marine surveyors examined the ship thoroughly. They reported her to be in excellent condition, with no sign of collision damage. However, they did comment on a curious groove which seemed to have been cut deliberately on either side of the bows. It did not damage or weaken the ship in any way: it was just inexplicable. Another marine carpentry expert, Captain Schufeldt, gave his opinion later that it was probably just the way that the curved timbers had naturally cracked and dried as a result of exposure to wind, sea and sun.

Fred's next line of attack was to suggest that some brown stains on the deck were blood. He also pointed out stains on the blade of an ornate Italian sword found in Briggs' cabin under his bed. Once more he put the circumstantial evidence together and saw only foul play. To everyone else's annoyance, Fred refused to disclose the results of the analysis: an almost certain indication that it was wine, paint or ship's stain and varnish — unless the cook-steward had spilt some brown soup while taking a tray to the Captain's cabin in rough weather!

It was the great good fortune of Morehouse, Deveau and their men that the actual members of the Admiralty Court were experienced and level-headed seamen, and totally unlike the obnoxious Fred Flood. The Court eventually found in favour of the *Dei Gratia's* Captain and crew, and awarded them £1700 salvage money: a considerable sum in those days, but only a fraction of the true value of their work.

What might have happened to the unfortunate people on board the *Mary Celeste* when tragedy overtook them in mid-Atlantic?

One theory concerns ergotine poisoning. It was not uncommon in Victorian times for ergot to infect the food supply, especially bread. The resulting toxin, ergotine, has grim effects on the victims. It produces agonising stomach pains, and hallucinations related to them. The victim may, for example, imagine that he is being attacked by a dangerous carnivore, an alien, a werebeast, a vampire, or a demon that is biting or clawing at his stomach. Sometimes the hallucinating patient sees his family, friends, doctors or nurses in these terrifying roles, and tries to defend himself against them accordingly. The ergot theory of the *Mary Celeste* explains the tragedy by saying that there was ergotine contamination aboard, and that the Captain and crew saw one another as monsters or demons as the agonising stomach pains and accompanying hallucinations took hold of them. Perhaps one or two uninfected survivors of the initial outbreak tried to escape in the yawl, only to find that they too were carrying the disastrous toxin with them. As recently as 1951 a bakery in southern France was infected and many of the victims hallucinated so badly that they leapt into rivers to escape the things which they saw pursuing them: many were injured, and some died.

Ergot fungus poisoning provides a useful and sensible explanation, but the problem with it is that Oliver Deveau and his crew lived on the provisions on the *Mary Celeste* — and they suffered no ill effects whatsoever. If ergot fungus had been present, it would certainly have affected them as well.

Sea monsters have always been mentioned alongside the *Mary Celeste*, and there can be little doubt that the oceans hold many secrets of which we as yet know little or nothing. There may well be gigantic and terrifying marine life forms capable of destroying Briggs, his family and crew. There are, however, problems with that explanation: why should the monster also have taken the chronometer, the sextant, the navigation book and the bill of lading?

A third theory concerns alien astronauts: did someone or something from another world abduct Briggs and his people for reasons of their own? Curiously enough, this was the theme of one of our early science fiction novels, *Fiends*, published by Badger Books of Hammersmith, London, as long ago as the 1950s. In this novel we suggested that the curious marks which really existed on either side of the bows were the places where the alien abductors in their UFO had extended a gigantic pincer-like appliance and gripped the *Mary Celeste* while the people were removed.

Along similar lines, theories have been put forward to explain the disappearances as the work of visitors from parallel worlds or other probability tracks, from other dimensions, or from the past or future: imaginative and remotely possible, of course, but not very probable.

One of the strangest theories ever advanced concerned the cargo of industrial alcohol and a horde of dangerously intoxicated rats. In outline, it suggested that carnivorous rats had broached the cargo, become dangerously aggressive and uninhibited as a result of drinking the crude alcohol and swarmed out of the hold to attack the passengers, Captain and crew. They had taken to the boat to escape, but the rats had swum after them and swamped the tiny yawl.

Even before brilliant horror writer Guy N. Smith had so much success with *Night of the Crabs*, a theory was put forward to explain the *Mary Celeste* tragedy in terms of an attack by an armada of flesh-eating crabs: unfortunately, like all the other theories, it doesn't account for all the facts of the case.

The vanishing island theory has several classical precedents, including ancient legends of whales so large that they were mistaken for islands and when they finally submerged inadvertently drowned the sailors who had gone 'ashore' to explore them. There is also, of course, the legend of the submergence of Atlantis to consider in these latitudes. Were the present day Azores once the mountain peaks of that mysterious lost continent?

One of the most ingenious and elaborate theories was in the form of a superficially plausible story told by various lovable old rogues who pretended that they had been stowaways aboard the *Mary Celeste* and subsequently not only the sole survivor, but the only person who knew what had *really* happened. With minor variations from one retelling to another the story went like this. There was friendly, sporting rivalry between Captain Briggs and first mate Richardson as to which of them was the better swimmer. The sub-plot of this imaginative drama was that baby Sophia Briggs loved to toddle up to the bowsprit and watch the water rushing past the bows. This naturally perturbed her parents, so Briggs ordered the ship's carpenter to build a little platform under the bowsprit with a good strong safety rail around it. The infant Sophia could then enjoy watching the water in perfect safety. This platform was duly constructed and let an inch or so into the ship's timbers for added strength and security. It was a relatively warm day for November in those southern Atlantic seas; there was only a slight breeze — ideal conditions for a swimming race. Briggs and Richardson decided on the spur of the moment to dive in off the bowsprit and race around the ship. The first man back at the bowsprit would be the winner. Word spread like wildfire. Sarah left the little dress half finished in her sewing machine. Richardson had already left his half completed navigational calculations. A crewman who was shaving put his razor down and walked up on deck to watch the race. Another crew member hastily swallowed his medicine and stood the bottle down uncorked so as not to miss anything. Briggs and Richardson were neck and neck all the way. It was a truly great race. In order to get a proper view of the finish, the eight spectators moved down on to the little platform. Just as the two powerful swimmers reached the finishing line together, the platform collapsed on top of them. Everyone except the unknown stowaway was floundering helplessly in the water. Risking punishment and imprisonment, he crept from his hiding place to see what all the desperate shouting and splashing was about — intending to throw a rope for them, or to try to launch the yawl to rescue them. Before he could do anything, a sudden squall hit the *Mary Celeste*. The wind drove her a hundred yards away from the strugglers in the water. The only two men who might have caught her again had been badly injured when the platform fell on them. The wind rose; the *Mary Celeste* glided unheedingly away from her drowning complement.

It was no easy matter for one man to get the yawl into the water, but the stowaway cut down some of the ship's rail and managed eventually. He rowed back to look for the others, but he found nothing except the little platform, still floating pathetically.

He rowed and drifted for days, finally landing on a deserted part of the Azores. Looked after by kindly locals, he gave a false name and said nothing about the *Mary Celeste* for several years in case of the legal consequences of his having stowed away.

It's a very *neat* story, and even its preposterous, but beautifully dove-tailed, details — such as the Captain and his first mate having a swimming race in November, and the carpenter building a playpen under the bowsprit — are almost credible because they fit together so well. But that's its problem: it fits *too* perfectly. Truth *is* probably stranger than fiction, but the strangeness of the stowaway's story is the strangeness of well crafted fiction, rather than the rougher strangeness of natural truth.

Some authorities have suggested that the passengers and crew of the *Mary Celeste* were adbucted by pirates or slave traders. Female slaves were still being traded illicitly along the North African coast in the 1870s. Was Sarah Briggs sold into what nineteenth century New England puritans would have euphemistically called " a fate worse than death" ? And did the others just walk the plank? But surely no pirate would have left the money, or the other valuables behind on the *Mary Celeste*? They'd have been far more likely to have taken the ship and cargo as well, changed her name board and flag, and sold her in a port where no questions were likely to be asked.

This slave trader theory, however, is supported by another strange version which purports to be an eye-witness account given by a seaman called Demetrius, who was one of the crew of the slaver concerned. He first told his story in 1913 — over forty years after the tragedy. In outline he claimed that when the *Mary Celeste* was near the Azores, she encountered another brig which flew a signal: "Short of provisions. Starving." The *Mary Celeste* signalled back: "Send a boat." A boat duly arrived with one man visible and a tarpaulin draped over what looked like empty cases to hold the requested provisions. As it drew alongside the *Mary Celeste* the tarpaulin went sideways and several armed men boarded Briggs's ship. He and his family and crew were ordered aboard the other brig. This was a slaver with fever aboard which had decimated the former captives and crew. The *Mary Celeste's* people also succumbed to it, and were flung overboard one by one as they died. The slaver itself was run down and sunk by a large steamer which did not stop, and Demetrius was the sole survivor of the collision. Not wishing to broadcast his criminal role in the tragedy, he had kept the facts to himself for forty years.

Other theories concern whirlwinds and waterspouts somehow sucking the hapless human beings away while leaving the ship itself relatively untouched. It's difficult to imagine a waterspout or whirlwind being so selective, and it's also pertinent to ask why everyone stood meekly on deck at the same time, passively waiting to be absorbed like inert biological dust into some huge, maritime vacuum cleaner. Loving and protective parents like Benjamin and Sarah would undoubtedly have got baby Sophia safely below decks — as far away from the thing as possible.

One of the darker theories which floated across the suspicious little mind of Fred Flood was that Briggs and Morehouse were in collusion to collect the salvage money: but Briggs' own shares in the *Mary Celeste* were more valuable than his percentage of any salvage money could have been — and, more to the point, he and Morehouse were both men of excellent character and unblemished reputation. They had far more to gain from pursuing their marine careers than from grabbing a few risky dollars of salvage money. As even Fred had to admit eventually, the collusion and conspiracy theory was far less watertight than the copper-bottomed *Mary Celeste*.

Another idea put forward by some researchers was that Briggs — admittedly a deeply religious man, although not a fanatical one — had succumbed to a bout of religious mania and thrown everyone else overboard as a sort of divine punishment for their real or imagined sins. In the first place it would have been completely out of character: Briggs was a very steady, quiet, sensible and reliable man. In the second place, it would have been difficult if not impossible to carry out. He was only of average size and strength — unlike the massively powerful Oliver Deveau of the *Dei Gratia* — and any two crewmen could easily have subdued and restrained him.

Mutiny has been put forward as another possibility. Was there some sort of plot being hatched by the four German sailors? Martens was a well qualified and experienced mate who could have taken command and navigated the *Mary Celeste* without difficulty. But it wasn't the ship that vanished — it was the people. Mutineers characteristically make off with the ship, abandoning their rightful Captain and those loyal to him — as was the case with Bligh of the *Bounty* (1754 - 1817).

The most logical and rational explanation would seem to be the one connected with the nature of the cargo itself. As the ship moved towards warmer waters, the casks might well begin to sweat and leak a little. Potentially explosive fumes would accumulate in the hold. There would be disquieting noises, like old timbers settling into slightly different positions in a centrally heated house when the system is switched off or on. Winchester himself testified that although Briggs was an excellent and experienced Master, he had never carried a cargo of industrial alcohol before. If there had been a lot of visible vapour, or small explosions from the hold, Briggs might well have decided that the whole 1701 casks were in imminent danger of going up — taking the *Mary Celeste* with them. His decision would have been influenced by the presence of the wife and baby daughter that he loved more than his own life. He would have launched the yawl, packed everyone into it, and secured it to the *Mary Celeste* with the longest line which was quickly available — the missing halyard. The cargo did not explode, but the halyard broke. Desperately, Briggs and his crew row in pursuit of the *Mary Celeste*, but wind and current are against them. Their yawl overturns in heavy seas. The *Mary Celeste* sails on alone into legend.

After the lengthy and totally unnecessary difficulties with the unpleasant Fred Flood in Gibraltar, the *Mary Celeste* was sent back to James Winchester, and her new skipper, Captain George W. Blatchford safely delivered her cargo to Genoa. Glad to be clear of the problem — and probably half-convinced that there really was a jinx on the *Mary Celeste* — Winchester then sold her at a loss, and concentrated on making a fair profit from his other vessels. During the following thirteen years the unhappy ship had seventeen different owners, and her maritime history was a miserable trail of disasters. She lost men, sails and cargoes. She ran aground and caught fire.

The end came in 1884 when she was purchased very cheaply by a Boston consortium, who were supposed to have loaded her with bread, beef, ale, codfish and expensive furniture. All of these goods were very heavily insured. Her unscrupulous Captain, Gilman C. Parker, ran her on to a coral reef off the coast of Haiti, but the underwriters were highly suspicious and sent an investigator. Unfortunately for Parker and the other conspirators, there was plenty of the *Mary Celeste* left to investigate. What was supposed to be very expensive cutlery turned out to be cheap dog collars. Casks labelled ale were full of water: nothing was what it seemed, and nothing was half as valuable as it had been declared to be.

Captain Parker and the first mate both died before they could be charged. The majority of the traders involved in the attempted fraud went bankrupt, and one of them committed suicide. It was almost as if the ill-fated *Mary Celeste* had brought her destroyers down with her.

Certainly loneliness and tragedy seemed to extend to the families whose people had vanished from the *Mary Celeste*. Benjamin Briggs' mother had already lost her eldest son Nathan, who had died of yellow fever in the Gulf of Mexico. Maria, her only daughter, had drowned in a shipwreck, and Benjamin's brother Oliver went down in the Bay of Biscay. Albert Richardson's heart-broken widow, Frances, never remarried and died at the age of ninety-one in Brooklyn in 1937. The grieving parents of the Lorensen brothers did not learn of the tragedy until 1873.

As a footnote or corollary to the story of the *Mary Celeste*, it is interesting to recall what happened — and what may yet be happening — to a much more recent mystery ship, the *Baychimo*. She left Vancouver, on July 6th, 1931, with a crew of thirty-six, under the command of Captain John Cornwall. She went through the Bearing Straits and on into the notorious North West Passage. Thousands of dollars worth of furs were purchased all along the Victoria Island coast, but on her return journey the *Baychimo* was caught in the pack ice. According to the records of the Hudson Bay Company's Digital Collection, history was made when Captain Cornwall and his men were rescued by air. The previously ice-locked *Baychimo*, however, had mysteriously slipped away from her icy shackles and vanished. The following spring, she was observed 300 miles to the east near Herschel Island. Leslie Melvin, a trapper, found and boarded the *Baychimo* and reported that she had seemed to be in first class order, and totally seaworthy. A party of Eskimos found her in 1933, but she disappeared again in the ice. Elizabeth Hutchinson, a Scotts Botanist, reported seeing her again in 1934. Over the years, sightings have continued from trappers, whalers, prospectors and explorers: one the most recent being in March 1962, when local fishermen saw her moving north in the Beaufort Sea.

If Fred Flood doubted that the *Marie Celeste* could have gone on for ten or eleven days without a crew, he would have found it impossible to accept the amazing — and continuing — saga of the *Baychimo*.

WHO WAS KASPAR HAUSER?
His origin unknown . . .
His untimely death a mystery . . .

Kaspar Hauser arrived suddenly in Nuremberg — and metaphorically from nowhere.

One of the most picturesque cities in Bavaria, Nuremberg has a long and fascinating history and there were other mysteries in the vicinity long before Kaspar arrived.

In the seventh century a holy hermit named Sebaldus, also known as Sigibald, was preaching in the area, converting the people to Christianity from their former faith in the old nature gods like Wodan, god of heaven, and Donar, god of the weather. Many of the early Christian missionaries like Sebaldus were killed by the tough, local Teutons, who were not the easiest of people to convince. But those rare charismatics like Sebaldus who survived the various hazards and ordeals of the time — with the help of God plus their own raw strength and courage — were hailed as very special indeed and venerated accordingly. Sigibald went on to become a patron saint of the local farmers and fishermen, and many miracle stories have grown up around him over the intervening centuries. Just before the old holy man left this earth, he gave orders that his body was to be placed in an ox cart and buried wherever the oxen stopped of their own accord. The Saint Sebaldus Church was erected at that point, and pilgrims soon began flocking to Sigibald's sacred grave.

Apart from the spiritual benefits which it brought to the pilgrims, the holy man's shrine brought trade and prosperity to the town: pilgrims need food and shelter. In response to demand an inn soon sprang up beside the Church, justifying the wisdom of the old German proverb: *"Wo der Herr eine Kirche hinbaut, setzt der Teufel ein Gasthaus daneben."* (Where the Lord builds a Church, the devil sets up an inn close by.)

Kaspar reached Nuremberg just at the time when a similar attraction was definitely needed. Apart from the good influence of Sebaldus, there had been an era under the strict, but supportively paternal, rule of the Hohenzollens, when Nuremberg had been important and prosperous. That era was over by 1828, the year that Kaspar arrived, and the Bavarian industrial revolution — which would bring a different kind of fame and prosperity to Nuremberg — still lay a few decades in the future. In that sense at least, the timing of whoever, or whatever, had brought Kaspar to Nuremberg was fortuitous.

On May 28th, 1828, the city was almost deserted: it was Whit Monday — a public holiday, the *Ausflug*. Georg Weichmann, a shoemaker, was practically the only citizen in Unschlitt Square at the time of Kaspar's arrival.

Strolling into the square, Georg noticed a youth of about sixteen, leaning weakly against a building and moaning softly to himself, as if ill or greatly distressed. The kindly Weichmann walked over to the young man and offered assistance. Was he ill? Did he need a doctor? Was he hungry or thirsty, perhaps? The only answers the friendly shoemaker received were unintelligible mumbling sounds, but the boy had an envelope in his hands and Weichmann read the address on it. The letter was intended for "The Captain of the Fourth Squadron of the Sixth Cavalry Regiment, Nuremberg."

Weichmann was sturdy as well as good-natured and, according to one account, he supported the staggering youth all the way to Captain Wessenig's house. He was out, but his servants said he was expected back shortly, and invited Georg and the stranger to wait. Hospitably, they produced the customary refreshments for their visitors. Georg and Wessenig's servants watched with amazement as the newcomer wolfed down bread and water as if there was never likely to be any more on earth, but he shied away from cold meat and beer — apparently revolted by the smell of them. When cooking odours drifted in from the kitchen, he almost fainted. He was also very nervous of the big grandfather clock, treating it like some monstrous beast that was capable of attacking him. Curiosity prompted him to try to pick a candle flame as though it were a flower. He cried out in pain and surprise when the flame burnt his finger. Every time Weichmann or members of Wessenig's staff asked him a question he responded with "*Weiss nicht*" meaning "Don't know".

Captain Wessenig then arrived, listened attentively to what his servants and Weichmann had to tell him, looked quizzically at Kaspar and opened the mysterious envelope. There were two letters inside. The first, in an illiterate, disguised hand ran as follows, and purported to be from the boy's mother:

> "This little one has been baptised. He is called Kaspar, but you must give him his second name. Please take care of him. His father was once a soldier in the cavalry. Take him to the 6th Cavalry Regiment at Nuremberg when he is 17. That was his father's old Regiment. Please, I beg you, look after him until he is 17. His birthday was April 30th, 1812. I cannot care for him myself because I a very poor girl, and his father is dead."

The second letter, ostensibly from the mysterious guardian to whom the impoverished young mother had sent the infant Kaspar, said:

> *"Honourable Captain,*
> *I am sending to you a young man who wishes to serve his King by*
> *joining the Army. A poor young woman brought him to me on*
> *October 7th, 1812, and I myself am only a poor workman with a*
> *family of my own to raise. His mother begged me to take care of*
> *him, so I have tried to treat him as a son. I have never let him*
> *outside my house, so nobody knows where he was brought up. He*
> *does not know the name nor location of our home. No matter how*
> *you question him, Honourable Captain, he will not be able to*
> *show you where my home is. I brought him at night so that he*
> *will not be able to retrace his steps. Because I have nothing, I have*
> *not been able to give him any money at all. If you do not wish to*
> *keep him, you can hang him or strike him dead."*

Both letters appeared to have been written by the same person, whose clumsy attempt to disguise the style and degree of literacy was an abject failure.

All that Kaspar was able to add were the words "Horse, horse," and "Want to be a soldier like father."

Wessenig concluded that the young stranger was either " . . . a primitive savage or an imbecile . . ." and sent him to the Police Station, where he was given a pencil and paper. He managed to write the words "Kaspar Hauser" but simply answered "Don't know" to all questions.

Sergeant Wüst stripped and searched him, and wrote an official report:

> *"He is a sturdy, broad-shouldered boy of 16 or 17, with a*
> *healthy complexion, light brown hair and blue eyes. His hands*
> *and feet seem to be disproportionately small. Although at first he*
> *appeared to be crippled, closer inspection revealed that his feet*
> *were badly blistered as though he were unused to walking. His hat*
> *and shirt are too large for him. His boots are too small. His*
> *shapeless jacket and trousers are too large, and the jacket appears*
> *to have been cut down from an old frock coat."*

The sergeant and other officers compared Kaspar's childish, irregular scrawl with the writing on the letters. There was no possibility at all that Kaspar himself could have written either of them. Not quite sure what to do with the lad, the Nuremberg Police decided that the best course of action was to keep him in a cell for a few days to give higher authority a chance to come to a decision.

Herr Hiltel was the experienced old warder who kept Kaspar under observation during these early days. His reported observations of the young man make very interesting reading:

"He can sit for hours without moving his limbs at all. He does not pace the floor nor does he attempt to sleep. He sits quite still and rigid without appearing to be uncomfortable. He prefers it to be dark rather than light, and he can move in the dark as well as a cat can."

Apart from repeating "Want to be a soldier like father," Kaspar's only replies to Police questions were the monotonous reiteration of "Don't know".

Kaspar, however, suddenly caught the public imagination, and the citizens of Nuremberg began to take a keen interest in him. This was due in part to the theories of Jean-Jacques Rousseau (1712-78), the writer responsible for putting forward 'the child of nature' myth. According to Rousseau, it was civilisation and society that 'corrupted' people. If then, as was now beginning to seem likely in Kaspar's case, the Mystery Boy of Unschlitt Square had grown up largely insulated from these 'corrupting' influences, he might turn out to be one of Rousseau's almost perfect 'children of nature'.

Crowds of sight-seers visited him daily. They gave him pieces of paper on which he wrote "Kaspar Hauser" but nothing much else. Many of his reactions were characteristically infantile, as though he were somehow compensating for having missed out on his normal childhood development. He was fascinated by a ticking watch. He built coins into little stacks. He was engrossed by the pictures of Kings, Queens and Jacks on ordinary playing cards. He did not at first seem to recognize any difference between the genders, but referred to both male and female visitors as *junge*, the word for 'boy'. He did not seem to have any awareness of the passage of time, and knew nothing of day and night, nor of hours, minutes and seconds. At first he showed no preference for privacy with toilet functions, but would excrete and urinate in public as unaffectedly as he would eat or drink.

The greatest success, and for Kaspar the major stimulant of these early days in Nuremberg, was a wooden horse. He adored it. He festooned it with ribbons. He played with it constantly like a happy toddler. He 'fed' it each time he ate.

His learning curve was a steep one. By July he was able to talk fluently enough to give Bürgermeister Binder and the town council an account of his past life. They issued an official version of what Kaspar told them and called it "Bulletin Number One".

"He knows neither who he is nor where he came from. It was only here in Nuremberg that he first entered the world. Before coming here he always lived in a hole and sat on straw on the ground. During that time he heard nothing, and saw no bright lights. He would wake and sleep and wake again. When he woke he would find a pitcher of water and a piece of bread beside him. Sometimes the water tasted unpleasant. Then he would sleep. When he woke again he would be wearing a clean shirt. The face of the man who came to him was always hidden. He had ribbons and two wooden horses to play with. He does not remember ever being ill or

sad in his hole. The man brought a wooden table into the hole and put it over Kaspar's feet. There were pieces of white paper on this table and the man made marks on them with a black pencil. When he had gone Kaspar copied the marks the man had made. Finally the man taught Kaspar to stand and then to walk. At last he carried him out of his hole. Kaspar is unsure of what happened after that until he found himself here in Nuremberg carrying the letter."

The Nurembergers adopted Kaspar and placed him in the care of Professor George Friedrich Daumer, who enjoyed something of a reputation as a philosopher and educationalist. Daumer — like many of his contemporaries — was a committed passenger on the Rousseau bandwagon. He regarded Kaspar as a prime example of a feral child and studied him accordingly, keeping meticulous records as he did so.

Daumer discovered that Kaspar's natural senses were unusually well developed. The young man had exceptionally acute hearing and could see in the dark. Conversely, he had difficulty at first in adjusting to normal light. His sense of smell was abnormally keen, almost as good as a hound's. He could track an animal by its scent, and he could recognize human beings in the dark in the same way. He was also able to distinguish different trees merely by the scent of their leaves.

If his natural, animal senses were strong, his knowledge of basic physics and of simple cause and effect in the ordinary world were almost totally absent. He was unsure of the difference between living things and non-living matter. He would look behind mirrors to try to locate the person he had seen reflected in them. He thought that a rubber ball was alive and was bouncing because it wanted to jump.

According to Daumer's reports, Kaspar was highly intelligent, and learnt fast. Certainly some of Kaspar's surviving drawings show that he was capable of finely detailed and accurate art work.

Daumer and Kaspar decided to collaborate on his autobiography, which was duly completed in August of 1829. It proved to be something of a disappointment and anticlimax. Perhaps the rumours and speculation surrounding Kaspar had led readers to expect something far more sensational, or at least some significant *new* disclosures as the boy's vocabulary and powers of expression and comprehension increased. The book was much longer than Kaspar's original statements had been, but it contained nothing fresh.

On October 7th, Kaspar was found unconscious in Daumer's cellar with a head wound. On regaining consciousness, he was unable to give much information to the Police other than that he had been attacked by a 'a man with a black face'. This undoubtedly referred to a mask, and tied in with Kaspar's account of the masked man who had brought him his bread, water and changes of clothes while he was confined in his straw-lined hole. The Nuremberg authorities took the attack seriously and moved Kaspar to a safer location with two policemen as bodyguards.

A curious incident which Hauser found hard to explain involved what he said was the 'accidental' discharge of a pistol. Hearing a shot from Kaspar's room, the two guards rushed in to investigate. They found that he was unharmed but very shaken and upset. He told them that he had been looking out of the window, had leant over too far and consequently clutched wildly at the wall as he feared he was going to fall out. In his frantic attempts to get a grip on something to prevent the fall he had inadvertently snatched down the pistol from its support and it had gone off.

However, the question of the continued expense of keeping Kaspar's guards on duty protecting him caused considerable dissension among the Nuremberg tax-payers. Did Kaspar justify what it was costing the city to maintain, guard and educate him? There was a vociferous minority who felt that it did not. Far from the exciting and romantic theories of his origin spread by his supporters, these detractors suggested that he was either a foreign vagrant, or the discarded offspring of an over-large peasant family. There were also critics who thought that the whole thing was an elaborate hoax, perpetrated by Kaspar himself, to obtain the attention and free board and lodgings that he wanted.

Despite the arguments, Kaspar stayed at the home of his latest guardian, von Feuerbach, until the old man had a stroke and died in May, 1833 — one of several people who had been in close contact with Kaspar and died unexpectedly. The circumstances of von Feuerbach's death were not, perhaps, sufficiently strange on their own to invite Police investigation, but taken with a string of others they were significant enough to deserve comment. It was known that — immediately before his death — von Feuerbach was in the process of compiling a detailed legal report on Kaspar, a report that might have contained a number of findings which some people might have wished to suppress.

The rather eccentric English aristocrat, Lord Stanhope, came on the scene next, took a keen interest in Kaspar and said that he'd like to adopt him. The Nuremberg Council seemed not to want to lose their star attraction entirely, but they never the less negotiated a deal which allowed Stanhope to have temporary care and custody of the young man, provided that his Lordship contributed to the City's coffers to offset part of Kaspar's upkeep.

Stanhope took Kaspar on tour, showing him off to various minor royalty and his other friends among the European aristocracy. The tour was not an unqualified success. Rumours constantly linked Kaspar with the Royal House of Bavaria, and with the Grand Duchess Stephanie de Beauharnais of Baden. The deeply offended Royal Bavarians threatened a law suit. Predictably, the unusual Kaspar and the eccentric Stanhope quarrelled periodically, and, later in 1833, by arrangement between Stanhope and the Nurembergers, Kaspar was transferred to Ansbach, twenty-five miles away, where he was placed in the care of Dr Meyer. Just in case there were any further attacks on Kaspar, Stanhope arranged for him to be protected by Captain Hickel, a soldier who was working with the Ansbach Police.

Whereas Daumer had been an enthusiastic Hauser supporter who had praised and encouraged him, and commented positively on the young man's intelligence, Meyer and Kaspar did not work harmoniously, and the doctor estimated that Hauser's mental age was no higher than eight or nine.

Things came to a violent and dramatic climax on Saturday, December 14, 1833. Kaspar staggered home from the public park known as the *Hofgarten* clutching a wound in his chest and shouting: "Knife . . . Man stabbed . . . Gave purse . . . Look quickly . . . Go Hofgarten!" Mrs Meyer helped her husband to put Kaspar to bed and then sent for a doctor. When he arrived he confirmed that Kaspar had been stabbed, but did not think that the wound was unduly serious. Captain Hickel, meanwhile had raced to the Hofgarten in pursuit of Kaspar's attacker. He failed to find him, but he did find the mysterious purse which Kaspar had shouted about. There was a note inside, but it was written in that odd back-to-front style which Victorian children used to enjoy playing with, and which has to be held up to a mirror in order to read it. It said:

> "*Hauser can tell you who I am, what I look like and where I come from. To save him the trouble, I shall give you that information myself. I come from . . . on the borders of Bavaria, on the River . . . My name is M.L.O. . . .*"

Anxiety was growing steadily about Kaspar's failure to improve. The wound was, in fact, slowly proving fatal, and he died on December 17. The subsequent post mortem revealed that the knife had pierced the diaphragm and entered the lower part of his heart. All three medical examiners were certain that the assailant had been left-handed. Two were not sure whether the wound could have been self-inflicted: the third was adamant that it could not have been. Hauser's own last words were: "I didn't do it myself."

Before he died Kaspar had told a strange story about the attack, and told it repeatedly to the cluster of priests, medical men, local government officials, civic dignitaries, military and police officers gathered in his sick room.

In essence, Kaspar claimed that a man had arranged to meet him in the Hofgarten and had promised to reveal the secret of his true identity. When he arrived in the park, a tall man with dark whiskers, who was wearing a black cloak came over and asked: "Are you Kaspar Hauser?"

When the young man said that he was, the sinister stranger had handed him a silk purse and then stabbed him. The purse had fallen in the snow, the attacker had disappeared, and Kaspar himself had struggled painfully back to Dr Meyer's home.

Captain Hickel was doubtful because he had found only one set of prints in the snow — Kaspar's own — at the spot where the purse had been dropped. He and Dr Meyer urged Hauser to confess and clear his conscience. This he stubbornly refused to do. He reminded those present of the previous attack that had been made on him in the cellar in Nuremberg.

He was buried in Ansbach Cemetery where his grave marker still stands. It reads: *"Here lies the Enigma of our Time — His Birth Unknown, his Death a Mystery."*

What is the *truth* about Kaspar Hauser?

The wildest and most imaginative theories suggest that he was teleported from some distant place, that he came from another planet, a parallel universe, another dimension, or even that he was a time traveller. It was Anselm von Feuerbach who provided much of the fuel for the interplanetary traveller theories by writing of Kaspar: *". . . one might feel oneself driven to believing that he is a citizen of another planet brought by some miracle to our own."* If we regard all these ideas as too improbable to be the answer, what remains?

One possibility is simply that the letters accompanying him on his arrival in Nuremberg were the simple truth after all. His mother was too poor to rear him. She passed him over to a kindly, but almost equally impoverished, neighbour, who did his best as long as he could, and was grateful to deposit the teenager in Nuremberg as a potential recruit for the Cavalry Squadron.

Detailed versions of the history are at variance over one or two important points. One researcher records that Weichmann, the helpful shoemaker, accompanied the lad to Captain Wessenig's house. Another version of the story suggests that Georg simply led Kaspar as far as the New Gate guardroom and gave him instructions as to how to reach Wessenig's house from there. If that is correct, it conflicts with the version which suggests that Kaspar was incoherent, and lacking a large enough vocabulary to say more than "Don't know".

Was Hauser simply a crafty young confidence trickster who enjoyed the limelight, and was happy enough to settle for good publicity and free board and lodgings? Was he, as Meyer said, of very low mental ability? If Meyer rather than Daumer was closer to the truth about Kaspar's intelligence level, how could someone who was so intellectually challenged have accomplished all that Kaspar achieved? His pictures and the notes accompanying them do not seem to be the work of a slow learner.

If, as seems seriously possible, Hauser *was* the abducted heir of a royal, or aristocratic family, hidden away for dynastic or political reasons, then who was responsible and what did they have to gain by the boy's lengthy incarceration in the allegedly dark, straw-lined hole?

At the time there was a strong candidate: Caroline Geyer, the beautiful, young, morganatic wife of the elderly Duke Karl Frederick of Baden. When the widowed Duke had married her, there had been several offspring by his earlier marriage in line to inherit his Duchy. It was rumoured that they had almost all died with quite unnatural rapidity, some in rather questionable circumstances, soon after their father's morganatic marriage. The theory involving Caroline with Kaspar Hauser had suggested that he had been the last and youngest of the legitimate heirs who would have taken precedence over her children. Rather than have a child killed, Caroline had arranged to have him incarcerated until her eldest son was safely on the Ducal Throne. Kaspar was duly released with the intention that he would simply slip away into obscurity. Caroline and her minions had not reckoned on the international publicity which accompanied the Mystery Boy of Nuremberg. Fearful in case the truth somehow came out, she changed her original plan, and decided that her safest course now lay in silencing him permanently — hence the abortive attack in Daumer's cellar in Nuremberg, and the successful later attempt by one of her assassins in the Hofgarten in Ansbach.

If there had been a ruthless and sinister, high level conspiracy to silence Kaspar, it is possible that it extended further afield. Von Feuerbach died suddenly. Bürgomeister Binder also died.

Although the Mystery Boy of Unschlitt Square holds a unique position in history, there was a less well known case which is interesting because it illustrates the double impostor theory. For Kaspar to have become such a celebrity, it may be argued that someone else — perhaps several other people — had to be party to the fraud. But fraud, in the sense of deliberate deception or hoaxing, may not be quite the right concept. There are illusions and self-deceptions which when shared can reinforce one another, until in the minds of the participants the boundaries between fact and fiction, between data and speculation, have become hopelessly blurred. This certainly seems to have happened in the partially parallel case of the Princess Caraboo.

On the night of April 3, 1817, a girl turned up at a cottage near Bristol, apparently speaking an unknown language. She was taken before Magistrate Samuel Worrell, who took her to stay at his home, where she attracted the attention of linguists from far and wide, none of whom could make any sense of her unknown speech and writing.

Manuel Eyenesso, however, listened attentively, and then said that she was speaking Malayan. He went on to interpret and relay her account. She was, he announced, the Princess Caraboo of Java, who had been kidnapped by pirates. She had managed to escape from them and make her way to England. This news was received with great excitement: as the arrival of the real-life Pocahontas, daughter of Chief Powhattan, had been in 1616.

To the embarrassment of Manuel and the Princess, however, a Mrs Willcocks arrived from the Devonshire village of Witheridge, and proclaimed that the mysterious girl was her daughter, Mary. Thus confronted, Mary was alleged to have confessed to the hoax, and was promptly sent off to obscurity in America.

Had she and Manuel deliberately worked some clever trick together, or had one impostor simply come across the other by accident? Did one or both of them suffer from what psychologists refer to as the *Munchausen Syndrome*, a mental abnormality distinguishable by the sufferer's compulsion to tell improbable and wildly exaggerated stories about his or her experiences? The historical Baron Munchausen, after whom the syndrome is named, lived from 1720 - 1797 and served in the Russian Army against the Turks. Rudolph Erich Raspe wrote the fictional version of the Munchausen narratives which were published in 1785, and included such tales as the deer which the Baron shot with a cherry stone, and which was later found with a cherry tree growing from its head.

The Princess Caraboo affair, like the Kaspar Hauser mystery, is a very convoluted one, containing much contradictory evidence and the inevitable counter accusations of fraud and deception.

A second version suggests that it was Mrs Worrell, unhappy about her husband's interest in the attractive young Malayan girl, who went to Devonshire in search of Mrs Willcocks — or someone who could be bribed to *say* that she was Mrs Willcocks. Mrs Worrell was then alleged to have paid this impostor to say that Caraboo was only her daughter, Mary, who was mentally ill and made up gibberish languages while pretending to be a Malayan Princess. This account adds that Mrs Worrell also paid for the girl to go to America, where far from vanishing into obscurity she continued to demonstrate her uncanny unknown speech and writing. Was Mary Willcocks' ability in that area something akin to the phenomenon known as *glossolalia*, defined by Drever's *Dictionary of Psychology* as "*a fabricated language or speech in an unknown tongue, occurring in religious ecstasy, in hypnosis, in mediumistic trances, and in certain pathological mental states*"? This, of course, assumes that Princess Caraboo *was* only Mary Willcocks from Devonshire and not a genuine Javanese Princess who had been kidnapped by pirates.

This multiple imposture theory may well have its counterparts in the Kaspar Hauser problem — which still remains stubbornly unsolved. Was he the genius Daumer believed in, or the slow learner of Meyer's reports? Was he an abandoned, impoverished peasant boy, the lost heir to the Throne of Bavaria, or the victim of a time-slip? Was he brutally murdered in the Hofgarten by an unknown assassin, or did he die of a stupidly self-inflicted wound intended to restore flagging public interest?

GUARDIANS OF THE GRAIL

*The ancient wooden cup of Nanteos — believed by
many to be the Holy Grail — still exists . . .
carefully guarded in its secret British hiding place.*

T he great problem in researching the many and varied Grail traditions is
that they overlap and apparently contradict one another at so many
points. Yet running through them all are certain highly significant
shared threads, which, when followed carefully — like the life-saving strand in
the Labyrinth of Minos — lead out of an otherwise bewildering and seemingly
inescapable historical and literary maze.

Like some great fortified palace which has survived over the centuries, the
Grail tradition has been altered and modified, revised and rebuilt, expanded and
extended, until it is almost impossible to locate its original foundations. Yet
those ancient foundations exist; they are still traceable — and it is vitally
important to any true understanding of the Grail mystery to see just how deeply
they penetrate the rock on which the contemporary Grail structure stands.

Probably the best known of the legends is associated with Glastonbury, in
Somerset, UK. In outline, this tells how St Joseph of Arimathea (who was
possibly Jesus's uncle) brought the Grail to England some time between 40 and
65 AD. Joseph was alleged to have been acting on the instructions of St Philip,
and the Grail that he brought was said to be the one which Jesus himself had
used at the Last Supper. In this version of the story, Pilate had allowed Joseph to
have the Grail, and he had used it to collect some of Christ's blood at the
crucifixion. All through Joseph's long missionary journeyings, covering many
years, this Sacred Blood had remained fresh and uncorrupted.

Coming safely through many dangerous adventures, Joseph and his faithful
band of disciples reached the coast of Somerset in south-western Britain during
the middle years of the first century and landed there. They travelled eastwards
towards Glastonbury Tor, where they rested on what has been called Wearyall
Hill ever since. The legend goes on to say that when St Joseph paused for prayer
at the foot of the Tor, he thrust his staff into the ground where it immediately
took root and grew buds. Joseph and his followers took this as a special sign

from Heaven that they had reached their journey's end. This was the place where they knew they were to build the first British Church and establish their permanent headquarters.

A variation of the Joseph legend says that he and his followers found that the first tiny church had already been built for them when they arrived, exhausted, in Glastonbury. This variation says that the small wattle and daub structure was built by the risen Christ himself — still to that extent a carpenter. It was known as *Vetusta Ecclesia*, meaning the Ancient Church.

In trying to trace the origins of the Grail legends, and the secret hiding place of the Grail itself, it is worth noting that St Joseph allegedly buried the Grail at the foot of the Tor in what is now known as Chalice Well. Joseph is also credited with bringing to England the Spear, or Lance, of Longinus the Centurion, the weapon which pierced Christ's side at the end of the crucifixion. In much the same way as the Cup is credited with enormous magical powers, so is the Lance, but it is important to note in this connection that a mysterious and immensely powerful Lance, Cup and Sword feature in numerous ancient pagan legends, their power being at its zenith when they are united. These older pagan versions are completely separate from the much later Christian traditions involving Jesus and Joseph of Arimathea. They almost certainly pre-date the Christian era by many centuries.

Round about 1180, Chretien de Troyes wrote *Conte du Graal*, or the Story of the Graal. He completed only 9234 lines of it — or, at least, that is all that has survived. Scholars are not certain whether his great work was unfinished, or whether part of it was lost over the intervening years. Is it possible that the missing ending is carefully hidden somewhere, like the Grail itself? And if it is, what coded clues to the location of the Grail might Chretien's lost ending contain?

It was often considered advisable by writers of his period to give their work additional weight and authenticity by adding references to older works on which their own accounts were allegedly based. This popular literary device did not invariably mean that such older works did not exist. Nor did it guarantee that *some* medieval authors had not, in fact, consulted genuine ancient sources. Chretien, for example, claimed that he had consulted an ancient book passed to him by Philip, Count of Flanders, and this may well be true.

There can be little doubt that the medieval troubadours of Chretien's time acquired great reservoirs of information — some of it undoubtedly ancient and esoteric — as they made their way from one castle to another in Europe and the Middle East, especially during the Crusades.

Eleanor of Aquitaine (1122 - 1204) provides a vital link between Chretien and this knowledgeable troubadour culture. She was the grand-daughter of Guilhem IX of Aquitaine, the first troubadour whose work still survives. When she was fifteen, Louis VII of France married her for the sake of her inheritance, and they had two daughters before her implacable enemy, Bernard of Clairvaux,

A selection of letters and documents relating to the famous Nanteos Cup, part of an ancient olive wood drinking vessel, believed by many to be the Holy Grail.

persuaded Louis to divorce her. The pious, ascetic, puritanical and fanatically celibate Bernard undoubtedly feared that Eleanor's gigantic energy and strength of character (which exceeded his) combined with her liberal, southern worldliness (which was total anathema to him) would be a bad influence on Louis and his Parisian court.

The spirited and attractive young Eleanor immediately married Henry Plantagenet of Anjou, destined to become Henry II of England and father of Richard the Lionheart. After Henry's death, Eleanor became a very effective Regent while her famous son was away fighting in the Crusades.

But it was through one of her daughters by Louis VII, Marie de Champagne, that the troubadour culture reached Chretien. Marie became Countess of Champagne when she married Count Henry in 1164. She established a flourishing centre of troubadour culture at Troyes, modelled on Eleanor's own cultural centre at Poitiers. It was while working and writing in Marie's court that Chretien had close contact with many of the leading troubadours: men such as Jaufre Rudel, Bernart de Ventadorn and Raimbaut d'Aurenga. It is also highly significant that their troubadour culture was well established in the south-western parts of France known as the Midi — the area where the mysterious village of Rennes-le-Château is situated, where there were several Templar strongholds, and where the strange, heretical sect known as the Cathars or Albigensians once flourished.

When their almost impregnable fortress of Montségur fell in 1244, four Cathar mountaineers escaped with a great treasure, noted down in the Latin records as *pecuniam infinitam*: literally "unlimited money". Might that priceless Cathar treasure have been the Lance or the Grail — or *both*? And what became of it after it left Montségur? After a period of safe storage in Rennes-le-Château did it finally cross the North Atlantic with Sinclair and his refugee Templars to find a safe new hiding place in the strange labyrinth below Oak Island, Nova Scotia?

The hero of Chretien's version of the Grail story is Perceval, who seems to be based on the very much older history of the great Welsh hero Peredur, sometimes rendered Pryderi, from the *Mabinogion*. These stories from ancient Welsh history appear in *The White Book of Rhydderch* and *The Red Book of Hergest*. Both of these volumes date only from the fourteenth century, but the material in them seems to be much older, its *original* sources pre-dating the Christian era by many centuries. The mysterious and heroic Perceval reappears as Parzival in Wolfram von Eschenbach's book of that name, which was put together round about 1205.

Von Eschenbach was a Bavarian knight, who claimed that his version of the story was accurate and that Chretien was wrong. Wolfram records that he got his information from Kyot de Provence, and that Kyot discovered it from Flegetanis, who is described as "a heathen scholar renowned for his high learning". Kyot was otherwise known as Guiot the Troubadour, and he was one of many who attended the great Festival of Mayence in 1184, when the sons of the Holy Roman Emperor, Frederick Barbarossa, were knighted by their father. Almost every poet and troubadour in medieval Christendom would have been there: Wolfram would certainly have attended, so it seems reasonable to argue that it was at Mayence that he and Guiot probably exchanged vital information about Parzival and his quest for the Grail. It is also significant to note that both Guiot and Wolfram were enthusiastic supporters of the Templars, who seem at one time to have been the guardians of the Grail, as well as protectors of the pilgrim road to Jerusalem.

In the Parzival story itself, the Grail is kept at Munsalvaesche (the Mount of Salvation) which may be intended as a coded reference to Montségur (the Mount of Security). According to one tradition, the Grail Castle is supposed to be in the Pyrenees, and Rennes-le-Château is in the foothills of the Pyrenees. Parzival's hermit uncle tells him about the powers which the Grail possesses. It can heal. It can postpone or prevent death. It can rejuvenate the dying phoenix. It can provide limitless food and drink like the legendary cornucopia. It is not a cup but a mysterious stone called *lapsit exillis*. What if *lapsit exillis* is a corruption of *lapsit ex caelis*, meaning "the stone that fell from the sky"? Or perhaps it's a corruption of *lapis elixir* , the Philosopher's Stone sought by the alchemists, transforming base metals to gold and holding the secret of eternal life?

Parzival, originally from Waleis (Wales?) reaches the Grail Castle and meets Anfortas, the wounded Fisher-King, but fails to make the correct response when the Grail is brought in by a beautiful and mysterious woman called Repanse de Schoye. Her name itself is highly significant: *réponse de choix* — the chosen response — or *réponse de la joie* — the joyful response. The visitor to the Grail Castle seems to be required to make the right response: to ask the appropriate and acceptable questions. But what *are* those questions, and what *is* the right response? Is Wolfram suggesting that there is some sort of key, or password that unlocks the secret powers of the Grail?

Again, according to Wolfram, the Grail may not be a cup but a magical stone or crystal — which connects with the strange medieval legends of Prester John. At a time when the Crusaders were faring badly against the Saracens, there were persistent stories of a great Christian King who was referred to as Prester John. His huge and fabulously wealthy country lay far to the east of Palestine, and his invincible armies were said to be on their way to destroy the Saracens from behind and link up with the Crusaders. Among the many stories told of this great Christian ruler was that he bore a sceptre made from pure *emerald*.

One of the most enigmatic, semi-historical, semi-legendary characters of ancient Egypt was Thoth, scribe of the gods, whose powerful spells were engraved on *emerald* tablets. He was also known as Hermes Trismegistus (Hermes the thrice blessed) whose powers resided in certain esoteric and arcane *emeralds*. It is possible that this same paranormally powerful benign being was also known in antiquity as Melchizedek, the Priest-King of Salem, to whom even the great patriarch Abraham paid tribute, and who was said to have been "without father or mother, having neither beginning of life nor end of days". Was this ageless Priest-King of Salem later to be known as Prester John, the Priest-King who carried an *emerald* sceptre? And was that powerful emerald sceptre the *lapsit exillis* of Grail Castle? Is the Grail legend saying in code that whatever the priceless object eventually turns out to be, it is really *lapsit ex caelis* — the stone that came from the skies — and did Melchizedek come to Earth with it?

Historically, Prester John never arrived to assist the forces of Christendom in their long struggle against the Saracens — but someone else did. Huge forces from the far east won devastating victories over the armies of Islam, but these were *not* the Christian armies of Prester John coming to reinforce the weary soldiers of western Christendom. They were, in fact, the terrifying and invincible Mongol hordes of Genghis Khan, who ravaged Europe in 1221. Eventually the peace which his vast Mongol Empire enforced enabled Europeans such as the fearless Venetian adventurer, Marco Polo, to visit Peking in 1275. Polo claimed to have found the lost Kingdom of Prester John and its then ruler King George, who was undoubtedly a Christian. But what Polo found was the little Kingdom of Tenduk — not the vast, wealthy and militarily awesome empire of the Prester John legend. In fairness to Polo's evidence,

The Nanteos Cup — perhaps the Holy Grail — in its glass bowl inside its wooden case, preserved by the Guardian at a secret safe house somewhere in western Britain.

however, it must be accepted that he was a scholarly and careful writer, who wrote of his travels with meticulous honesty and accuracy.

One of the modern Grail legends which can be passed over swiftly is the sensational suggestion that the Grail was actually a *person*, not an object, and that this mysterious woman carried the Holy Blood genetically. Various contemporary Rennes-le-Château researchers have suggested that the supposed "secret" of that mysterious French village was that Jesus was married to Mary Magdalen. She subsequently came to live in the south-west of France with their children, and they in turn became part of the arcane dynasty of Merovingian Kings. It is remotely possible that Jesus was married to Mary. It is even more remotely possible that after his death, resurrection and ascension, she took the children to safety in France, where they did merge with the Merovingians — but the "Grail-is-a-person-or-lineage" theory fails to fit the facts. All the stories, myths and legends show the Grail as an *object* of some description (a cup or stone) which has immense and mysterious powers. The Grail is a source of incomprehensible and overwhelming might: if the Grail was personified, that person would also have been shown to have massive strength and force. No such super-being features in the Grail legends, unless we count Hermes (alias the mighty Melchizedek?). In fact, the reverse is true: most of those such as Parzival and Anfortas who were involved with the Grail had all too many human weaknesses and handicaps.

One of the most remarkable — and persistent — Grail traditions concerns the Nanteos Cup. When Henry VIII turned his avaricious eyes on the land and wealth of the monasteries during the sixteenth century, brave old Abbot Whiting of Glastonbury became one of several victims of what was tantamount to judicial murder. Shortly before his death, Whiting sent seven of his bravest young monks to Strata Florida not far from Aberystwyth in Wales. They carried with them a strange *wooden* cup — believed by many to be the Holy Grail.

By a strange piece of synchronicity, we had the privilege of being the friends of a grand old priest, Canon Noel Boston, who was Vicar of Dereham in Norfolk, UK, in the 1950s and '60s. It was Noel who officiated at our wedding in 1957. He shared our interest in researching the paranormal, and one day, in the course of an otherwise mundane chat, he said: "Incidentally, I've seen the Holy Grail. I know where it is. It's in the keeping of an old, noble family, and it has amazing healing powers. It's not metal, it's wood — but it has two silver bands around it to hold it together because it's so old." Then the subject of the conversation changed — but we never forgot what Noel had said about the Grail.

In the course of our work on the *Fortean TV* programme in 1997 on Channel 4 and S4C in the UK, the research team turned up some amazing material about the mysterious Nanteos Cup. It too was said to be wooden — just like the one of which Canon Noel Boston had told us forty years earlier. The guardian, a lady, lived alone in a small British village within 100 miles of Cardiff. Her anonymity and secret location were the only protection which she and the Cup had. Our research colleague arranged through a trusted neighbour of hers that we could visit her to ask whether she would allow us to tell the story of the Nanteos Cup as part of our TV show. She is a very kindly, but shy and nervous lady, and we were pleasantly surprised when she agreed to see us. After a brief chat, she took the Nanteos Cup reverently from its hiding place and showed it to us. Made of ancient olive wood, darkened by the centuries, the Cup is about five inches in diameter, and only the lower portion of it still remains. There were no signs of the silver bands which Noel had described to us so many years before. Neither of us is particularly psychic, but we both felt that there was an atmosphere of great antiquity and holiness surrounding that simple, wooden Nanteos Cup.

The guardian told us as much as she knew of its history. Abbot Whiting's men had brought it to Strata Florida, hoping that Henry VIII's scavengers would not visit such a small and remote Welsh religious house. They were wrong. Before long the King's men were asking difficult and dangerous questions in the area. Not knowing what else to do, the monks turned for help to some local landowners, the ancient and noble Powell family of nearby Nanteos. The rugged and independent Powells — afraid of nothing, not even Henry VIII — took pity on the monks and their precious old wooden Cup, and gave them refuge in Nanteos when Strata Florida became unsafe. Time passed.

The last of the monks died. By default, the Powells then became the official guardians of what was destined to become known as the Nanteos Cup. This arrangement continued for almost four centuries until the direct line of Powells died out in the 1950s. The precious wooden Cup and its guardianship then passed to a niece. When she died, the guardianship passed to one of her daughters: that lady is the present custodian. She it was who provided all the background information for us in 1997, appeared in silhouette on our TV show, gave us holy water from the Cup, and allowed us to photograph it.

During the time that it was in the Powells' keeping, no genuine, reverent request for its healing aid was ever turned down — and no charge was ever made for its use. That still remains a condition of its guardianship today.

There are many valuable old records in the hands of the present guardian, which show when the Nanteos Cup was borrowed by sick or injured people and when it was returned. The words "healed" or "cured" are written alongside the lending entry. She also has many more recent records — often in the form of letters of thanks from those who have experienced miraculous cures.

We were hesitant to enquire about the silver band discrepancy but the guardian herself solved the problem for us quite spontaneously, without our having to ask.

" A few years ago," she said, " the Cup was getting so frail that it was thought necessary to put a silver band round it to protect it — but that seemed to reduce its healing powers, so it was taken off again." The implication was that our friend Noel had seen it during the period when the silver band, or bands, were in place.

The guardian told us of many cures that had taken place within her time or her mother's time: one of the most spectacular and immediate being the healing which the Cup provided for Father Wharton. This good priest suffered very badly from arthritis, which affected both his knees, making it all but impossible for him to kneel. He was a singularly devout and reverent man, and it was a constant source of distress and disappointment to him that his infirmity prevented him from kneeling to pray as he would have dearly wished to do.

He visited the guardian and asked for water from the Cup. Within minutes of taking it, he felt the arthritis easing in his knees. Within the hour he was able to kneel and rise to his feet again as easily as if he had never had the illness: and Father Wharton is just one of thousands who have benefited from the healing power associated with the Nanteos Cup over the years.

How much of such healing is due to powerful psycho-somatic forces within the mind and body of the believer? Medical research seems to accept that mind over matter is no mere illusion. Quite what the link is and exactly how it operates are mysteries which still remain unsolved, but the essential point is that the psycho-somatic link really works: the mind can undoubtedly aid the body's healing processes quite substantially and dramatically. The insuperable *will to live*, the all out mental drive towards health and full recovery, can often be the most critical survival factors when illness or injury strikes.

Jesus himself taught on many occasions which are recorded in the Gospels that the *faith* of the sick person was a crucial ingredient in the healing process. The classic example was the woman with the haemorrhage who knew that if she could only touch the hem of his garment as he passed by her through the dense crowd, she would be healed.

Yet the faith of the person longing to be healed is not entirely self-sufficient: there must also be real, objective, *healing power* in the person, or object, towards which that faith is directed. Ultimately it seems to be the *person* with whom the healing object is closely associated: the robe heals the woman's haemorrhage because it is Christ's robe. The Nanteos Cup heals because it is the ancient and holy cup which *may* have been the one which Christ used at the Last Supper. At the very least it is an old and holy object which the monks of Glastonbury and Strata Florida have sanctified by many years of their prayers.

Another hypothesis worth noting in connection with the true origins of the Nanteos Cup is that Jesus was a carpenter before he began his preaching and teaching mission. A carpenter planning such an enterprise would make the necessary provisions well in advance — like a good soldier making provision for a lengthy campaign. Jesus might well have made a simple, wooden cup as part of his provision for the journey. If a first century carpenter decided to make a cup, he would almost certainly have made that cup of wood.

When we ourselves examined the Cup closely, with the guardian's permission, we could see that its base bore the marks of having been turned on a lathe. Were lathes used by carpenters in first century Palestine? If they were not, then whatever else it was, the Nanteos Cup could not have been the one which Jesus used at the Last Supper. Research into the history of the carpenter's lathe, suggested that it was almost as old as the potter's wheel — and that had certainly been in use at the time of the prophet Jeremiah — centuries before Jesus was the village carpenter at Nazareth. The Nanteos Cup *might* then have not only been the one which Jesus used at the Last Supper — it might have been one which he made himself in his workshop at Nazareth specially to carry with him on his mission. To think that Christ might actually have *made* it, as well as to think that he might have *used* it, makes the Nanteos Cup uniquely precious. It is not possible to prove conclusively — beyond the least shadow of doubt — that the Nanteos Cup is definitely and absolutely the Holy Grail, but it is possible to prove that it has as good a chance as any of its rival claimants to be the true Christian Grail.

Whatever else it is, and however strong and benign its healing and blessing powers may be, it is certainly *not* the mysterious stone or emerald which Wolfram indicated in his version of the tale. Neither is it the sinister old Celtic cauldron which allegedly restored life to the dead, nor the mysterious pagan Cup of Power which was associated with the Magical Lance and Sword. The Grail Quest is complicated and confused because the legends have become intertwined and welded together. They need to be separated again if any real progress is to be made.

Assuming that there is a solid core of historical truth in the Joseph of Arimathea story, then the Christian Grail, the Cup which Jesus made at Nazareth and used at the Last Supper, may well be the ancient Healing Cup of Nanteos, still safely in the hands of its reliable and devoted guardian at her secret location in western Britain.

What are the possible *locations* of the other strange, powerful, magical objects — the ancient, pre-Christian objects — which were sometimes called the Grail? The existence of more than one such artifact and its associated traditions helps to account for the confusing number of sites where thaumaturgical treasures were once believed to have been concealed. The Arthurian Quest stories — interwoven with the idea of the Christian Holy Grail, and the legend of St Joseph of Arimathea — can be abstracted and simplified until they come down to *a prolonged and determined search for something powerful and valuable during a violent and dangerously unstable era of history.* What has most value at such times? Not wealth, but *superior weaponry!* Did the shadowy Romano-British war leader sometimes known as Arthur send his men looking for some mysterious, quasi-magical super weapons, popularly known as the Grail, the Lance and the Sword?

Was it rather a Celtic Arthur the Bear, head of his ancient and mysterious clan, who sent dauntless Welsh, Irish or Scottish warriors in pursuit of the strange artifacts that could turn the tide of war in their favour? Was it Bran, owner of the Cauldron of Life and Death, whom they sought? Was Bran — as the scholarly Roger Loomis suggests — one and the same person as the wounded Fisher-King, Anfortas, of the later Grail traditions? After all, Bran was a *sea-god* in the ancient legends, and the Fisher-King was necessarily associated with the sea.

Bardsey Island, known in Welsh as *Ynys Afallach,* was always a place of holiness and healing in the oldest Welsh traditions: some even suggest that it was to Bardsey that the wounded Arthur was brought — not to die, but to recover and to travel to his other provinces in Armorica in France. But dare it be asked whether a confusion arose in the legends between the French Armorica and the *Americas* that lay far to the west? Did the healed and rejuvenated Arthur carry the magical and mysterious Grail (whatever it *really* was) across the Atlantic to some unknown hiding place on the east coast of Canada? To Newfoundland, or even to Oak Island, Nova Scotia? The probability is very low — but it is not impossible.

The remains of an ancient fortress, or perhaps an early monastery, on the coast at Tintagel in Cornwall have been associated with King Arthur's Camelot and the Grail Quest for many centuries. Just a short distance along the coast is Rocky Valley, where a curious circular maze design of great antiquity has been carved into the rock. Very close again is the amazing waterfall at Nectan's Glen, where the saint's remains lie buried under the bed of the river from which the holy man once drank. Tintagel Castle, a hidden cave within Rocky Valley, or a secret hiding place in the river bed at Nectan's Glen are all *possible* locations for the mysterious treasure for which the legendary Arthurian Knights once searched.

Cadbury Castle — a rival site for Camelot — is yet another possibility. Returning to Glastonbury, we are confronted by its impressive Tor — and the very strong likelihood that some ancient sacred and mysterious thing was buried there long before the Joseph of Arimathea legend Christianised the story. Is the *Christian* Grail tradition centred on Glastonbury because a much *older* Grail tradition was focused on Glastonbury centuries before Joseph ever reached Britain?

Otta Swire in *Skye: The Island and its Legends* makes out an interesting case for the *Stone* of Destiny — and Wolfram describes the Grail as a *stone* — to have found its way to the Isle of Skye. A.E.Waite in *The Hidden Church of the Holy Graal* records how Joseph of Arimathea died in Scotland. Barry Dunford's thought provoking research in *The Holy Land of Scotland* provides and sorts a substantial amount of useful evidence which leads again and again to mysterious Fortinghall in Scotland — yet another possible treasure site.

The ancient Monastery of Slane in Ireland was founded by Bishop Erc, who lived during a period when there was considerable conflict between the early Christian missionaries and the Druids. Following the theory that the Christianised Grail legends were a symbolic overcoming of the older western religions by the new faith from Palestine, Erc's victory over the Druids may be seen to represent the triumphant Christianisation of an older, pagan Grail tradition strongly associated with the Hill of Slane. Could it be that that older Druidic teaching indicated that Slane was a possible hiding place for the original, pre-Christian Grail? Certainly, Slane was a place of refuge for the infant Dagobert II in 653. He was recalled from there in 674 to claim his French Kingdom and to play his brief, tragic, enigmatic part in the Rennes-le-Château mystery. As we have seen, Rennes — like Oak Island, Nova Scotia — is a strong contender for the role of Grail hiding place.

Yet another theory that is well worth serious consideration is the work of Dr Graham Phillips, author of *The Search for the Grail*. In essence he suggests that in 327, when the Empress Helena, sent search parties to Palestine looking for holy relics, they found the Grail for her. A hundred years later when barbarians were threatening to pillage Rome, the Grail was sent to England for safety. It reached the old Romano-British city of Viroconium, near present day Shrewsbury, and when the Legions eventually had to withdraw, it came under the protection of a Welsh speaking King or Warlord known as The Bear. Was this the famous Arthur again? Dr Phillips believes that it was. With the Norman invasion in the eleventh century, what had once been The Bear's property passed to a Norman leader called Payn Peveril, and a contemporary monk chronicler reported that the Grail had passed into Peveril's hands. Dr Phillips believes that it remained in the family until the middle of the nineteenth century. At that time the last of the Peverils, Frances Vernon, married Thomas Wright. Tragically, their son died, and they decided to hide the Grail for distant posterity.

Wright, however, cleverly re-wrote a seventeenth century poem, written by an early Peveril. He added two lines of enigmatic Roman numerals to the concluding couplet of the poem which referred to " . . . the shepherd's songs . . . " On the assumption that the shepherd referred to was King David, the Old Testament Psalmist, Wright carefully selected verses from the Psalms that would lead to the spot where he had concealed the Peveril Cup in a cave at Hawkstone Park in Shropshire.

When Wright died, Frances re-married and had children by her second husband. In 1920, Walter Langham, her grandson by this second marriage, went in search of the Cup which Wright had concealed: and found it by following the Psalm clues attached to the poem he had altered.

It was Langham's great-grand-daughter, Victoria Palmer, who finally met Dr Phillips, and the ancient onyx cup came to light. Their story contains several remarkable parallels to our own quest for the Nanteos Cup: at this distance in time it is impossible to say categorically which — if either — is the real Christian Grail.

There are also worthwhile claims from Spanish sanctuaries . . .

It would take the strength and stamina of the legendary Lancelot or Galahad to track them all down.

OGOPOGO AND OTHER LAKE MONSTERS

Just like Loch Ness, the Canadian lakes may well be inhabited by huge unknown creatures.

Although Loch Ness is probably the first name that springs to mind when lake monsters are mentioned, the Canadian lakes probably provide a more fruitful area of research than even the Scottish and Scandinavian ones. Scores of reliable witnesses have reported sightings of strange creatures in the deep and mysterious inland waters of Canada — and those reports have been frequent and recent.

The indigenous Canadians included numerous accounts of lake monsters in their own history long before the arrival of any Europeans. Frequent references are made in particular to *Ogopogo*, which is reported from Lake Okanagan, an eighty mile long stretch of water deep inside British Columbia on the Pacific coast. The popular name has more in common with a music hall song from the twenties than with the genuine Okanagan legends about the monster's origin. Apparently a man known as Old Kanhek was murdered in the vicinity and the lake was named as a memorial to him. The gods punished the murderer by transforming him into a giant water-serpent, and doomed him to remain in that form at the scene of his crime forever. In the legend, the monster lives in underwater caves just off Squally Point near Rattlesnake Island, and local people appease it by throwing small animals into the water as food. This is reminiscent of a piece of Finno-Ugric mythology in which a water monster resembling an enormous frog — and known as a *Vodyanoi* — frequented mill pools. The millers tended to throw unwary travellers into the water to feed their local *Vodyanoi* and thus protect themselves and their families.

Again, according to the old Okanagan legends, the water-serpent has been seen at both ends of the lake as well as in and around his favourite haunts between Rattlesnake Island and Mission Valley.

Folklore and legends of strange aquatic creatures are widespread throughout Canada and North America. Almost 100 lakes and rivers have their own local stories of being inhabited by monsters. The Micmac people of Nova Scotia have traditions of a thing they call the great water-snake, as do the Algonquin whose territory lies to the west of the Micmac zone. The Micmac also have mysterious traditions of semi-aquatic, semi-human entities. In one of the old Micmac stories, the hero Wsitiplaju marries a beautiful and mysterious sea-woman who is the sister of the killer whale. She can remain with him in her human form only as long as he keeps her inland. If she visits the shore again, she will resume her original form and return to her killer whale family in the sea, taking their children with her. After many years together, they are caught in a great storm and lose their way, inevitably returning to the shore, where the spell is broken and he loses her to her sea people once more.

The upper New York State Iriquois tell of a great water beast known as *Onijore*, and the Potawatomi of Indiana have legends of a monster that inhabits Lake Manitou on the Wabash. The Potawatomi lodged strenuous objections to the proposed construction of a mill on a site there in the mid-nineteenth century on the grounds that it would seriously interfere with the water-beast.

Farther west again the Shawnee have a remarkable story of a duel between one of their great hero-magicians from the remote past and a semi-aquatic monster. A young girl is involved and plays a vital role in enabling the hero to destroy the monster. The story bears an uncanny resemblance to St George saving the princess from the dragon, to Perseus the son of Zeus saving Andromeda, to Cadmus of Thebes killing a monster with the assistance of the goddess Athena, and to the help given to Jason by the enchantress Medea when he overcame the monster guarding the Golden Fleece. It even resembles the curious tale about the wealthy and bored Catherine de Medici obtaining a "water monster" from somewhere to entertain her guests at a water festival.

Aturki is the local name of the water monster known to the Kalapuya people of Oregon's Willamette River, but there is possibly some confusion over the name of "Champ" the famous monster of Lake Champlain which was supposedly discovered there by the great French explorer Samuel de Champlain in 1609. The redoubtable French navigator and fearless adventurer does indeed recall his encounter with a formidable aquatic monster, but that was much farther to the northeast in the vicinity of the St Lawrence Estuary.

If most sightings were genuine, or at worst bona fide mistakes by honest and honourable observers, there was a case from Perry near Silver Lake in New York State which turned out to be a blatant hoax. There was a great sensation there in 1855 when reports of a monster in the lake circulated wildly. These sightings continued for two years and more, and naturally attracted many tourists. Then a fire broke out in a local hotel, and when the brigade arrived to extinguish the blaze they discovered the "lake monster" in the attic. The hotel proprietor had constructed it to run on compressed air, in the hope that its appearances on Silver Lake would attract tourists and improve his trade: it did both. After an initial reaction of anger and disappointment, the citizens of Perry now hold an annual festival to commemorate the enterprising hotelier's ingenuity.

Serious and carefully detailed reports of the *Basilosaurus, zeuglodon* or *ogopogo* tend to agree that the creature is anything up to seventy feet long. The body is approximately two feet thick, and the head is described by many witnesses as like that of a horse, a cow, or a sheep: with horse being the most frequent comparison.

One witness who actually collided with something large and heavy while she was swimming in Lake Okanagan as a teenager made a full report to J.Richard Greenwell from the International Society of Cryptozoology. Preferring to conceal her identity simply as "Mrs B.Clark" she told Greenwell that it was around 8 AM on a warm July morning in 1974 that she was swimming across the lake to a raft which also acted as a diving platform, and which was situated about 500 yards from the beach. She had almost reached it when she felt something bumping against her legs. Whatever it was was enormous, very massive and heavy. Understandably surprised and frightened by the unexpected underwater collision, she pulled herself up on to the raft as quickly as she could. The *ogopogo* was less than twenty feet away and the water was clear. She described the creature as having a hump or coil — like the ones usually attributed to the large creature which is still persistently reported from Loch Ness in Scotland. The hump, or coil, which "Mrs Clark" described was about nine or ten feet long and rose nearly five feet out of the water. It was moving forward through the water as she watched it. She said that it was travelling north and moving away from her. The tail that she saw was about ten feet behind the hump, and she described it as resembling the tail of a whale: that is, it was horizontal and apparently almost divided into two halves. She estimated it at somewhere around six feet wide. As part of the strange creature's swimming technique, the tail rose as the hump or coil went down into the water, and "Mrs Clark" thought that at one point it broke surface by a few inches — perhaps as much as a foot. She had the creature in view for four or five minutes, but found it very hard to categorise. In some ways it reminded her more of a whale than a fish, but she also felt that it was far too slender to be a whale. The colour was a very dark grey, and it gave her the impression that it had no neck as such: the head just joined the body like the head of a fish.

Expert cryptozoologists, however, accept that such a variety of proto-whale did once exist, although the fossil records suggest that it has been extinct for at least twenty million years. It is normally classified as *Basilosaurus,* otherwise known as a *zeuglodon.*

When European settlers reached Okanagan in the mid-nineteenth century, they learnt from the indigenous Canadians in the area that a huge, snake-like monster which they called *Naitaka* resided in the lake. This was the one which had, in legend, formerly been a murderous human being.

In the 1870s it was observed from both sides of the lake simultaneously, and the witnesses concerned then described it as looking very much like a floating log that suddenly came to life and started to swim independently against wind and current.

Something that does not correspond at all with the known zoological format or expected feeding habits of a *Basilosaurus* or *zeuglodon* attacked a trader who was crossing Okanagan in the 1850s. He maintained that some huge aquatic beast equipped with either hands or tentacles, pulled him down into the water, but he managed somehow to break free and escape. The horses, however, were less fortunate and all of them drowned. A similar thing happened to John MacDougal a few years afterwards. He, too, struggled wildly and managed to escape, but lost his horses in the battle with the *naitaka*.

There is nothing to prevent *two* totally different species of aquatic monster from inhabiting Okanagan: the less numerous carnivorous predators with a taste for horses perhaps living on the supposed herbivores, although it would be far more likely that the less aggressive species would be fish eaters rather than lake-weed eaters.

The possible existence of two or more varieties of aquatic monster — one perhaps preying on the other — is supported by an account from July 2nd, 1949, when a group of witnesses in a boat close to the shore of Okanagan reported seeing a specimen of *Basilosaurus* which was partly submerged. The witnesses were about thirty yards away when they saw it. They described its forked, horizontal tail — exactly the same pattern as "Mrs Clark" saw in 1974 — and its undulating movements. They reported that the creature's head was under water, and deduced that it was feeding while they were observing it.

Oliver Goldsmith's famous work *A History of the Earth and Animated Nature (1842 Edition)* contains this comment on the whale's enemies:

> There is still another and more powerful enemy called by the fishermen of New England the killer. This is itself a cetaceous animal, armed with strong and powerful teeth. A number of these are said to surround the whale, in the same manner as dogs get round a bull. Some attack it with their teeth behind; others attempt it before; until, at last, the great animal is torn down . . . They are said to be of such great strength, that one of them alone was known to stop a dead whale that several boats were towing along, and drag it from among them to the bottom.

The Miller and Marten families saw what might have been a sub-species of *zeuglodon* in July of 1959, but clearly described its head as being snake-like, rather than bovine or equine. It was swimming behind their motor cruiser as they were returning from a trip on the lake. Mr Marten, who was at the helm at the time, turned the boat towards the creature so that they could all get a closer and more detailed view of it. This movement of the boat which it had been following seemed to discourage the *zeuglodon* from making any closer contact, and as they watched from about sixty yards away, it slowly submerged and vanished from sight. R.H.Miller, who was also on board, was editor of the *Vernon Advertiser*, and having witnessed the creature for himself had no hesitation in giving it maximum publicity.

A 1968 sighting involved a group of young water-skiers with a power boat capable of thirty-five knots. Sheri Campbell saw about six metres of the mid-section of a *zeuglodon* basking on the surface not far from her with neither its head nor tail visible. Not surprisingly, her concentration faltered and she dropped her ski-rope. By the time the boat came back to rescue her, the *ogopogo* had started moving. Sheri said that she could clearly see blue-green-grey scales that shone in the sun like a rainbow trout. The water-skiers got within a couple of metres of the thing before it submerged and made off at high speed: they tried to catch up with their power boat, but *ogopogo's* speed was greater than their thirty-five knots, and they soon lost sight of him.

Another sighting was reported by the captain of a Canadian Fisheries Patrol, who said it was rather like a floating telegraph pole with a sheep's head at one end.

Two visitors from Montreal named Watson and Kray saw what they described as something with a thirty-foot long sinuous body with five undulating humps each of which was around two metres long. These humps were about a metre apart. They described the tail as forked, but saw only one half of it above water.

A visitor from Vancouver saw *ogopogo* swimming within 100 metres of her. She said he was a truly wonderful sight with a head like a horse or cow, and glistening coils that looked like two huge wheels going through the water. She also commented on ragged edges along the spine, resembling the teeth of some great saw. As she watched it rose and submerged at least three times before submerging again and making off out of sight below the water. Her testimony was particularly interesting, as she had known nothing of the legends or the history of any previous sightings before visiting Okanagan.

Another amazing report came from Lake Utopia in New Brunswick in 1867. Men working in a lumber camp and at a mill beside the lake described how they had seen a huge animal splashing about in the water. Their account appeared in *Canadian Illustrated News* a few years later in 1872. The creature they described had a barrel-sized head and a pair of ferociously snapping jaws. It was said to appear most frequently just after the winter ice had thawed. This linked in with some European research into lake monsters in which Norwegian sightings also increased notably when cold water flowed down from mountain lakes. Sightings were also most frequent when there were timber mills beside the rivers concerned. Could it be that the "patches of churning water" which almost invariably accompany reports of sightings of aquatic monsters are in some way due to vast amounts of industrial waste (accumulations of discarded sawdust, perhaps?) which decay and give off large quantities of fumes? Do those fumes in turn energise the sawdust waste sufficiently to send portions of it agitatedly to the surface to be mistaken for *ogopogo* or a close cousin of his? One or two distant and uncertain sightings, maybe, but it wasn't a clump of gaseously propelled sawdust that frightened Sheri Campbell and then escaped from the water-skiers' power boat at a speed in excess of thirty-five knots.

Walgen Lake, once called Alkali Lake, situated in the heart of the Nebraskan grasslands, is totally different geologically and geographically from the northern lakes where most sightings have occurred. And the Walgen monster was brown rather than a dark greenish-bluish-grey. A Nebraskan farmer who reported seeing this creature said that he watched it spouting water as much as six metres into the air. A group of five witnesses together also recorded an encounter with the Walgen monster. They estimated its length at six or seven metres.

Turning from these lake creatures to the stranger and larger denizens of the sea, the most impressive witnesses are undoubtedly Captain Peter M'Quhae and his officers and crew of the *Daedalus*. During the afternoon of Sunday, 6th August, 1848, the 19-gun frigate, *Daedalus,* was on her way home to England from the East Indies. She was in 2000 fathoms of water, over 1000 miles south-east of St Helena and about 350 miles off Africa, when nervous young Midshipman Sartoris reported to his Officer of the Watch, Lieutenant Edgar Drummond, that he had seen something he could not identify off to starboard. At the moment when the midshipman reported his strange discovery, Drummond was talking to Navigation Officer Bill Barrett and Captain M'Quhae himself. All three came to the rail to investigate. All three were intelligent, observant, and experienced officers in the British Royal Navy — an organisation renowned for its efficiency and rigid discipline, especially in their century. In addition to Sartoris and the three senior officers of the *Daedalus,* the creature was observed by the helmsman, the bosun's mate and the quartermaster.

M'Quhae described the thing they saw as resembling an enormous snake, or serpent, at least sixty feet long, and with its head and shoulders a good four feet clear of the water. The witnesses were unable to see any method of propulsion, but the sea-serpent was keeping up a steady thirteen or fourteen knots, and maintaining an absolutely straight south-westerly course — even after passing astern of the *Daedalus's* and going through the frigate's wake.

Whatever it was, M'Quhae and his men had it in sight for twenty minutes, and they carefully observed its dark brown overall colouring with a patch of yellowish white around the throat. They also saw something along its back which they described as similar to a horse's mane.

Lieutenant Drummond fully endorsed M'Quhae's report and added a few minor details. He said that the head was approximately ten feet long, pointed and flattened at the top. The upper jaw projected substantially over the lower one. It gave him the overall impression of a large snake or eel, and he was unable to discern anything resembling scales.

There was incandescent controversy among zoologists and the admiralty hierarchy, but M'Quhae and his complement had well deserved reputations as solid and reliable men, and their report was duly accepted.

M'Quhae's own sturdy response to his critics is well worth noting:— *"... I deny the existence of excitement, or the possibility of optical illusion. I adhere to the statements, as to the form, colour, and dimensions, contained in my official report to the admiralty..."*

If M'Quhae had needed corroboration, he would have nodded approvingly at the evidence provided some thirty years later in 1879 by Major H.W.J.Senior. Standing on the deck of the *Baltimore* as she cruised through the Gulf of Aden, Senior saw a sea-serpent very similar to the one M'Quhae had seen. His shouting for other passengers and crewmen to come and look, brought Mrs Greenfield and Dr Hall, the ship's surgeon, swiftly to the rail beside him. More passengers and crew, including the officers joined them after Dr Hall's cry of amazement. What they saw was a creature whose head and neck were just under a metre in diameter. It reared up over twenty feet out of the water, opening its huge jaws as it did so. A moment later, the jaws closed again as it prepared to dive. It moved at great speed below the surface and reappeared very rapidly almost 100 yards ahead of the *Baltimore*. Major Senior said that the head reminded him of something like a cross between a dragon and a bulldog. He noted particularly that, as it progressed, the creature raised its head repeatedly and let it fall again with a great splash so that water rose on each side of its neck — for all the world like a small pair of wings.

Brian Newton writing in *Monsters and Men* includes a graphic account of a German submarine, registered as U28, which sank the British steamer *Iberian* with a torpedo in 1915. As the *Iberian* went down she exploded under water with enormous force. The U-boat Commander, Georg Gunther Freiherr von Forstner, and his crew watched in amazement as a huge sea-creature was thrown up into the air by the explosion. The German witnesses said that it was at least sixty feet long, and looked like a huge crocodile, but with four webbed feet and a pointed tail.

Aristotle (384 - 322 BC) wrote in *Historia Animalium*: "In Libya the serpents are very large. Sailors going along the coast have told of seeing the bones of many cattle which, it seemed to them, had been eaten by the serpents. And as they sailed on the serpents came to attack, throwing themselves on one trireme and capsizing it."

Livy (59 BC - AD 17) wrote of an enormous sea-monster which demoralised even the fearless Roman Legionaries during the Punic Wars, and was finally destroyed by their heavy catapults and ballista, which were normally reserved for knocking down fortifications around towns and cities.

Pliny (23 - 79 AD) who wrote a *Natural History* mentions a Greek squadron exploring on the orders of Alexander of Macedon which was attacked by thirty foot sea-serpents in the Persian Gulf.

Huge, fast and powerful as these sea-serpent-like creatures would appear to be, they pale into relative insignificance compared to *something* which an Australian diver going for a depth record in what was then the latest gear reported from the South Pacific in 1953. The diver was followed by a fifteen foot shark, which seemed more curious than aggressive as it spiralled down just above him. The diver reached a ledge and paused there. Below his ledge lay a huge trench which seemed to go down forever into unknown darkness.   He had no intention of attempting to go any lower, but just stood on his ledge observing things. The shark was about ten yards away and twenty feet above him.

Suddenly the water grew colder. *Something* was coming up from the depths of the great black hole below the diver's ledge. He described it as a flat brown *thing* the size of a football pitch, dark brown in colour and pulsating slowly. It floated up past his ledge as he stood absolutely motionless. The shark was immobile too: either from the intense cold which the *thing* had brought with it from the chasm, or from sheer terror — if a shark's brain is capable of experiencing that kind of emotion. The terrified diver watched as the huge living sheet from the depths touched the shark, which twitched helplessly and sank down with the monster. The diver continued to watch as it vanished into the darkness. The temperature gradually returned to normal and he returned thankfully to the safety of the surface.

So what might sea-monsters be? Is there one all-embracing theory, or are we looking, perhaps, for several specific hypotheses tailored to fit the different sightings? The first and most probable explanation is that we are observing either survivors from earlier epochs or mutant descendants of those survivors which have evolved along different evolutionary paths. The world is still big enough, and its lakes and oceans deep enough, to contain regiments of gigantic and mysterious creatures which no human eyes have yet seen. Terra incognita has not entirely vanished, and we know less about the depths of the oceans than about the surface of Mars.

Wilder speculations may concern themselves with the possibility that not only are sea-monsters alien to us as land people, but alien to the planet as well. Things that size would require a larger ship than was used for the human Moon landings, of course, but size need not be a final barrier to interstellar travel. So many ancient peoples worshipped strange water-gods that the speculative classical historian is sometimes left wondering whether weird semi-aquatic beings came from *elsewhere*, and have perhaps left their steeds, their pets or their descendants in the hidden places of the deepest oceans.

As Bishop Erik Pontoppidan of Bergen wrote in his *Natural History of Norway* in 1755:

> "Were it possible that the sea could be drained of its
> waters, and emptied by some extraordinary accident, what

incredible numbers, what infinite varieties of uncommon and amazing Sea-monsters would exhibit themselves to our view, which are now entirely unknown! Such a sight would at once determine the truth of many hypotheses concerning Sea-animals whose existence is disputed, and looked upon as chimerical."

THE MYSTERY OF THE DEVONSHIRE FOOTPRINTS

Who or what left a mysterious 100 mile trail in the snow across the wide estuary of the River Exe in 1855 ?

On the night of February 7th, 1855, Devonshire experienced an abnormally heavy fall of snow. On the morning of February 8, a Topsham baker named Henry Pilk came out of his bakery door and admired the smooth white blanket of snow. Then he spotted a line of odd-looking footprints running from his yard's six foot wooden fence to the door of the bakery and back again.

For a moment or two, Henry thought the trail had been made by a stray donkey or pony: then he realised that the strange little donkey-shaped prints were one behind the other in a straight line. No donkey the baker had ever seen walked like that. Come to that no animal he had ever seen walked like that. Only some bipeds — such as human beings — made single tracks of foot prints, and even then they were not in a single line unless the human being concerned was trying to walk a tightrope.

Henry had too much work waiting in his bakery to spend more than a couple of minutes worrying about marks in the snow, no matter how weird they looked. He didn't bother to inspect the other side of his fence: he just got on with his baking.

Albert Brailford, the Topsham schoolmaster, arrived an hour later at the head of a small posse of excited villages. They had followed the trail to Henry's yard. It was, as far as they had been able to tell up to now, all over the village. They had seen it on the road, in gardens, along paths, in yards and fields. It went up to the walls of houses and reappeared on the far side. It went up to fences as much as twelve feet hight and then carried on as if they weren't there.

The group of searchers grew as it travelled. Housewives and young children, apprentices and tradesmen, shopkeepers and their customers . . . almost everyone joined in the hunt. The farther they followed the weird trail, the more disconcerting it became. Nothing physical proved much of an obstacle for it.

The tracks did not seem to vary at all, nor did they show tell-tale signs as though the animal had stopped to feed, or look around. Nowhere did the mysterious track-maker seem to have doubled back. The line of prints never circled round nor crossed over itself: and Topsham was by no means the only village where the phenomenon was seen that morning.

Although Topsham marked the northern limit of the area where the prints could be followed, they had also appeared as far south as Totnes, 100 miles down the coast. Every village between had been visited and so had many of the lonely farms and isolated cottages. From Dawlish to Torquay, from Powderham to Newton, from Teignmouth to Luscombe . . . and from a score of other villages, reports of the strange footprints came in continually. Farm workers found them crossing fields and surmounting haystacks. Priests noticed them around their churches, graveyards and rectories. Wealthy landowners and squires tracked them along their wide lawns, garden paths and carriage sweeps. Foresters found them among the trees and bushes in their woods and coppices. Fishermen noticed them on bleak beaches and cobble-stoned quaysides. The mysterious trail ran almost everywhere.

The prints had to have been made during the fateful, snow-shrouded night of February 7th, yet no one in any of the locations had heard or seen anything which could have been responsible for the inexplicable track.

Dr Benson of Mamhead thought he was hot on the trail of whoever, or whatever, was responsible. He followed the trail across open ground to a

The wide Estuary of the River Exe which was crossed in some unknown way by the strange trail of weird footprints in 1855.

haystack almost twenty feet high. The stack was covered with snow, and that snow was not marked in any way. Yet when Dr Benson moved around to the far side of the stack he saw at once that the frightening trail continued just as if whatever had made it had either stepped over the stack or somehow dematerialised and glided through it. Either possibility was disconcerting.

If a twenty foot stack could not impede the track-maker, neither could the two mile wide estuary of the River Exe. The great estuary lay between Powderham and Lympstone, but the uncanny track vanished on the western bank and re-appeared on the eastern side of the estuary — as if the track-maker had flown over the river, swum it, or walked calmly across its bed. At Teignmouth, the strange marks again crossed a wide estuary as if it wasn't there, simply vanishing on one side of the water and reappearing on the other.

Two veteran huntsmen, both expert trackers with years of experience, followed the marks for hundreds of yards through thick undergrowth. Nothing on the bushes showed the slightest indication that any creature with fur or feathers had been that way. Inexplicably, the tracks suddenly vanished — just as they had done on the banks of the two estuaries. The huntsmen looked for them in all directions, but there was no trace of them on the ground.

Then they spotted them again, travelling in the same direction as when they had vanished, but the tracks were now on a cottage roof several hundred yards ahead of where the hunters had last seen them on the snowy ground. Beyond the cottage, the weird tracks descended again and ran on in a straight line to Mamhead, where they continued boldly along the village street.

It was not necessary to have had hunting and tracking experience in order to distinguish the so-called "devil's footprints" from all natural marks left by birds, beasts or human beings. The unknown track consisted of a remarkable single line of small, horse-shoe shaped impressions, each approximately ten centimetres long by six wide, and the prints were almost invariable twenty centimetres apart. Their spacing, like their size, was unusually regular, more like the trail left by a mechanical device than by a living thing which would have been expected to vary its stride to suit the ground it was crossing, and its own energy level.

As the day wore on and the tracks began to thaw a little, some of the melting snow collapsed, giving the impression of cloven hoofs — and that really accelerated the superstitious rumours. There were many who were now prepared to believe that Satan, or one of his minions — with their traditionally cloven hoofs — had made the tracks.

The next question was *why?* Not a few local clergyman took advantage of the situation to suggest that their congregation should mend their ways: drink less, gamble less, swear less and attend church more frequently. The innocent curiosity and interested excitement of the morning and early afternoon were giving way to fear by evening. As dusk drew in, only the hardiest and boldest of the Devonshire men continued their search. By now they were as

Co-author Patricia Fanthorpe at the ford in Clyst St George where the strange trail of footprints was seen.

miscellaneously armed as the grim crowds pursuing still grimmer monsters in the old Hammer horror films. Blacksmiths carried hammers; woodsmen had their axes; ostlers and grooms carried pitchforks. Farm workers took their scythes or sickles. Landowners and gamekeepers had their guns with them, double charged and loaded with heavy shot. The mood was tense. No-one knew what effect an axe or gun would have on a quarry who could fly over twenty foot obstacles and wide river estuaries. But these were Devonshire men, like Hawkins and Drake, and they were more than prepared to fight. These were western men of the same stock as those who had once marched fearlessly on London to rescue Bishop Trelawney from the querulous King James. Devil, demon or monster — whatever it was that had made the track these sturdy and resolute men would tackle it somehow.

Daniel Plumer lived in Woodbury where he was known as "Daft Danny". He wore a curious costume of feathers and was hiding in the woods near his home when a group of monster hunters from Topsham found him. Unable to give a coherent explanation, the terrified Daniel gibbered wildly. These inhuman sounds reinforced the Topsham men's belief that they had indeed captured the sinister track-maker. Heavy cudgels were raised. Hammers clicked back on shot guns. In the nick of time, a local J.P., Squire Bartholomew, arrived. For Daniel's own safety, the Squire put him in protective custody until the hue and cry died down.

Greatly exaggerated versions of the sightings of Danny and his odd costume began to spread. So did other weird rumours each one stranger than its predecessor: some said that the footprints glowed like hot coals; they faded as you scrutinised them but then reappeared as you looked away again. Some villagers thought they'd seen a great horned figure hovering above Powderham Castle. Others with hyper-keen hearing claimed to have heard faint echoes of demonic laughter from beside the track.

Theories ranged from hoaxers to the supernatural, but none fitted all of the facts. It would have needed upwards of twenty hoaxers to make all the tracks over so great a distance in the course of a single night. That would have needed co-ordination and planning of a crisp, military nature. The more people who are involved, and the more elaborate the plot, the less chance there is of keeping it secret — as Guy Fawkes found out to his cost. No hoaxer ever went public and claimed to have made the trail; no Devonshire Sherlock Holmes or Miss Marple ever identified the hoaxer.

What about the tracks of some bird or animal? Britain in the mid-nineteenth century was home to a small army of amateur and professional botanists, zoologists and ornithologists. They kept the letter columns of the local and national press bristling with assertive, argumentative correspondence. The tracks were caused by a kangaroo which had escaped from a circus or menagerie. They were made by migrating frogs, toads, rats, mice, sea birds driven inland by the bad weather, deer, badgers . . . almost every mobile living thing the writers could imagine was suggested as an explanation at one time or another. Nothing they thought of came within a mile of providing an adequate explanation: there was often almost a negative correlation between the vehemence of the theoriser and the credibility of his, or her, theory.

The old story about the church cleaner who found the Vicar's sermon notes is illuminating in this context. As well as the précis of his address in blue-black ink in the centre, the priest had written notes on how to deliver it in red in the margin. "Raise the right arm. Look round the church. Lean forward and point to someone. Stroke chin thoughtfully." Then printed in block capitals and underlined: *"Argument very weak at this point, shout loudly."*

If it was not the track of some known bird or animal, and if it was not the work of hoaxers, what could it have been? If we choose to theorise inside a mysterious, metaphysical universe which is allowed for the sake of the argument to contain angels, demons, poltergeists, djinns, devas, vampires, ghouls, were-creatures, zombies and assorted returning spirits of the dead, then a long track of unusual, horse-shoe shaped prints ought not to be too difficult to explain.

But this leaves us in a realm of pure speculation — as unbounded and amorphous as a piece of fantasy fiction. In Alice's Wonderland, the Devonshire footprints would look reassuringly mundane — but solutions that apply in Wonderland, don't answer questions posed on Earth.

A sinister, wind-riding, spirit creature, the Wendigo, is said to occupy the remoter parts of Canada and the north-western states of the U.S.A. The Wendigo of legend leaves a track of circular prints and forces its victims along at

The trail of inexplicable Devonshire footprints passed along these peaceful country lanes 150 years ago. Who or what could have left the strange track?

the same terrifying pace until their own feet are burned down by friction to agonised miniature replicas of its own huge ones. Whatever supernatural being made the tightly spaced "devil's footprints" — if indeed it was a paranormal being — was nothing like the Wendigo of the Canadian legend. In so widely speculative an area, there are no clues. Werebeasts would tend to lope on all fours like their animal counterparts. Dracula wore boots or shoes. No-one has yet given a detailed and definitive description of a ghoul — either real or imaginary. There are no persistent myths or legends of any paranormal beings — benign or hostile — which leave regular tracks of horseshoe shaped prints.

So if the answer cannot be traced to the misty realms of the supernatural, do the wilder boundaries of physics provide any clues? Do theories of teleportation, telekinesis, extra dimensions or extra-terrestrials hold out any hope?

A wheel with horseshoe shaped printmakers attached around its perimeter and controlled by a being (human or otherwise) with strong telekinetic powers could have been whirled around the strange track made during the night of February 7, 1855, in the limited time available. The question of *motive* then arises. *Why* would an intelligent man, woman or extra-terrestrial have *wanted* to do something so apparently pointless?

Yet another theory concerns the possibility that the tracks were in some way *phenomenalist* in origin. Phenomenalism is a philosophy, an attitude to life, which has something to commend it. In essence, we can accept that certain objects in the universe around us probably deserve the rank of " real, hard facts". These are things like your hand, the keyboard you're typing on, the chair you're sitting on, and the floor on which that chair rests. At the furthest end of the scale are absurd dreams, pink chocolate and cream river fantasies, and jokes which you know to be made up and unreal: situations like those in Larson's brilliantly funny Far Side cartoons, where a dog is dynamiting his owners' house, or a tyrannosaur is complaining bitterly at the breakfast table because its partner won't — or can't — pass the marmalade. Somewhere in between these two polarities — the indisputably real and the incontrovertibly unreal — there lies a grey area which contains all those inexplicable things which *sometimes* appear to belong on one side of the " thin crust known as reality" and *sometimes* on the other.

A phenomenalist ventures into this mysterious universe of ours wiling to accept everything that comes in through his, or her, own sensory inputs, or is reported by fellow beings as one of their experiences. But acceptance in this phenomenalist sense does not entail absolute *belief* in any of these first or second-hand reports of the appearances of what we think of as the "external" universe. Phenomenalists do not set out to explain — except with tentative and temporary theories. Neither do they unreservedly accept other people's explanations. So between the concrete end and the rainbow's end, phenomenalists see the universe as having a vast, grey, indeterminate area of things which might or might not be "real". In this mental *terra incognita* they cheerfully impound a vast range of paranormal reports: stigmata, levitation, lake monsters, Nostradamus, Mother Shipton, telepathy, telekinesis, teleportation, ghosts, poltergeists, werebeasts, fairies, the appearance of Kaspar Hauser and the vanishing of Benjamin Bathurst. A phenomenalist would undoubtedly declare that the Devonshire footprints were part of this huge collection of inexplicable, paranormal things which have a quasi-reality. That declaration is of *some* help: phenomenalism does not deny the footprints — neither does it say that honest and reliable eye-witnesses were fools or liars. It is intellectually preferable to place the footprints in the phenomenalist category than to assert dogmatically that they were definitely made by hoaxers, by little green aliens riding monocycles, or by something like a west country UK version of the Canadian Wendigo. Phenomenalists would say that from the evidence available it would seem likely that something as yet unknown performed a strange feat in Devonshire during the night of February 7th, 1855 — and they would leave it at that. The phenomenalist door remains permanently open. Like the bat-wing doors of the old Hollywood Wild West saloons — always ready to admit another customer — the Phenomenalism Saloon is always open to accept another new theory, or to let a discredited one slink quietly away. The disadvantage of the phenomenalist explanation is that it isn't the sort of explanation most of us hope for. Mysteries, like detective stories, are fascinating and entertaining — but we *do* want Poirot, Holmes, Columbo or Inspector

Morse to solve it for us at the end. Detective Superintendent Phenomenalism, however, only tells us that we can please ourselves as to whether we think the prints were an elaborate hoax, the track of an unknown terrestrial animal, an alien visitor, someone or something from another dimension . . . or anything that *we ourselves* can think of. He will most happily and intelligently discuss the case with us, will point out that certain probabilities are stronger than others — but that is the limit of his help. If he said more, or brought in his own definitive verdict, he would cease to be a true phenomenalist.

The Devonshire trail of February, 1855, was by no means unique. Equally mysterious tracks have appeared in other places and at other times. In 1840, Sir James Clark Ross, a dauntless Victorian explorer, visited Kerguelen Island close to Antarctica. It was a bleak and desolate place inhabited, as far as he could tell, solely by gulls and seals — yet across the Kerguelen snow Ross saw a strange track of horse-shoe shaped prints " . . . like those of an ass or donkey" extending in a single line. Similar prints were seen in Scotland in the same year. These were observed in the mountainous area where Glenorchy, Glenlyon and Glenochay are joined. Other Scottish prints like the Topsham set appeared around Inverness at the same time as the Devonshire trail was reported. Very similar prints were also reported in Galicia, from Piashowa-gora, a name which means "the sand-hill". This happened repeatedly during the years following the Devonshire episode. The Galician trail was said to appear quite regularly in the winter, and was regarded by the local residents as something paranormal.

Author Eric Frank Russell, whose science fiction and unsolved mysteries are still well worth reading half a century on, saw similar tracks for himself in 1945 while he was serving with the Allied Forces during the Ardennes Campaign. The nearby villagers couldn't explain them in terms of any local wild life. Unfortunately, there was no film available for non-essential use because of the war, so Eric was unable to make what would have been a unique and vital photographic record. His integrity and reliability as a witness, however, are beyond question. If Eric Frank Russell said that he saw them, that's good enough for us. A century and a half after they puzzled the good people of Devonshire, the enigmatic footprints continue to baffle investigators today.

WHO WERE THE GREEN CHILDREN OF WOOLPIT?

Reliable twelfth century records tell how two green children suddenly appeared in a Suffolk harvest field.

K ing Stephen of England (born 1094, crowned 1135, died 1154) did not enjoy a particularly prosperous or peaceful reign — and the most memorable event in it was an extremely unlikely one: two green children, a boy and a girl, reportedly arrived mysteriously in a Suffolk harvest field.

Stephen was the son of Adela, daughter of William the Conqueror. He had a brother, Henry, who was Bishop of Winchester at an opportune moment as far as Stephen was concerned. With a generous portion of that collusion and political plotting for which the medieval church was unfortunately renowned, Bishop Henry connived to get Stephen crowned.

The chronic problem throughout the whole of Stephen's reign was Matilda, daughter of Henry I, who reigned from 1100 - 1135. By any standards of justice and fair play, she should have been Queen. Stephen had, in fact, promised her his allegiance and full support until his brother Henry had prompted him to go for the throne himself.

While Stephen and Matilda were fighting for the crown like the Lion and the Unicorn in the famous old nursery rhyme, there was no strong, central power to keep the barons in check. With every local baron able to behave more or less like an absolute and autonomous monarch in his own little kingdom, life for the majority of ordinary people was hazardous and uncertain.

Social and psychological historians occasionally comment that at times of uncertainty and weak central government, there is a tendency for strange and inexplicable phenomena to be reported. It is almost as though cultural and political instability encouraged a crop of weird Fortean phenomena as welcome diversions and distractions from the general threats of war and exploitation that most individual citizens can do nothing about. Were the Green Children of Woolpit

The mysterious old "wolfpits" — now flooded — from the village of Woolpit where the strange green children emerged from their lost tunnel.

perhaps a response to social anxiety rather than tangible, objective phenomena? A contemporary parallel might be the suggestion that social anxiety about nuclear war, global warming, the approach of the Millennium, and holes in the ozone layer, may account for a substantial number of UFO and abduction reports. A document dating from the English Civil War period (1642-1648) was discovered in the Colman Library in Norwich, Norfolk, UK. It gave a clear and detailed account of what the observers described as church steeples taking off into the air, accompanied by a sound like a whole regiment of drummers beating in perfect unison. Would a seventeenth century listener say that about a rocket engine?

The document begins:

> *"Upon the one and twentieth day of May in the afternoone in this year 1646, there were very strange sights seen, and unwonted sounds heard in the ayre in several places as followeth . . . "*

It goes on to tell how " . . . *diverse and severall persons of credit from Norfolk, Suffolk and Cambridgeshire . . . "*

vouched for the truth of the phenomena. In the district between Thetford and Newmarket, for example:

> *". . . a pillar of cloud did ascend from the earth, with the bright hilt of a sword towards the bottom, which pillar did ascend*

> *in a pyramidall form, and fashioned itself into the form of a spire or broach steeple."*

Soldiers at the village of Comberton near Cambridge:

> *". . . did behold the form of a spire steeple in the sky, with divers swords set around it."*

It was also reported that at Brandon:

> *". . . the inhabitants came out of their houses to behold so strange a spectacle as a spire steeple ascending up from the earth.*
> *". . . there descended also out of the sky the form of a pike or lance, with a very sharp head or point, to encounter with it. Also at a distance there appeared another speare or lance, with a very acute point, which was ready to interpose but did not engage itself.*
> *". . . about Newmarket, there were seen by divers, honest, sober and civill persons, and men of good credit, three men in the Ayre, striving, struggling and tugging together, one of them having a drawn sword in his hand.*
> *". . . in Marshland, within three miles of King's Linne, a captain and a lieutenant, with divers other persons of credit, did hear a sound as of a whole regiment of drums beating a call with perfect notes and stops, much admired by all who heard it. And the like military sound was heard in Suffolk on the same day."*

Assuming for the sake of argument that the evidence preserved in the document is basically reliable, does it give us a broad idea of what a seventeenth century witness would say if he or she saw and heard a rocket propelled spacecraft landing, taking off again, and performing some sort of manoeuvres involving the crew in space suits making a rendezvous with a second vessel and carrying out repairs or adjustments?

In the case of the Green Children of Woolpit, the chronicler is Ralph, who was Abbot of the Cistercian monastery at Coggeshall. He lived and worked close enough to Stephen's unpropitious reign to have known eye-witnesses to the Woolpit episode.

The name Woolpit is interesting in itself, and has given rise to several possible interpretations. It may simply refer to an early owner named Ulf; it may mean that Wolf-pits were dug there to trap the wild wolves that once ran through the East Anglian forests; or it may refer to the prosperous mediaeval wool trade in that area.

There is some evidence in a volume called *Suffolk in the XVII Century: a Breviary of Suffolk* that the present village of Woolpit was once the old Roman

**The Woolpit village sign, commemorating the strange children who
appeared there from nowhere many centuries ago.**

town of Sitomagus. The Romans were great brickmakers, and Woolpit has
extensive ancient brick-kilns.

There was a strong religious connection with Woolpit long before Ralph's
time. In 1006 the village belonged to Ulfketel, Earl of the East Angles, but he
gave it to the Abbey of St Edmunds, where it remained until Henry VIII 's
dissolution of the monasteries led to Woolpit Manor being leased to the Darcy
family in 1542.

During the reign of Stephen, the local supremo appears to have been Sir
Richard de Calne from Wikes, or Wyken Hall — twelfth century spellings are
notoriously variable — and Ralph the Chronicler may have known one of his
descendants, although traditionally he obtained the story from Sir Richard
himself.

Another chronicler was William of Newburgh, or Newbridge, Priory. His
account is preserved in Manuscript Number 3875 in the Harleian Collection in
the British Museum. Freely translated from the Latin it says:

> *"Concerning the Green Children . . . It does not seem right
> or proper to leave out a miracle unknown for centuries which is
> said to have happened in Anglia during Stephen's reign. For a
> long time I hesitated about recording it although many people
> knew and spoke of it. There is no rational explanation for it,
> and it seemed foolish to me to present such an obtuse matter to*

people as though it deserved belief. At last, however, I was compelled to accept it because of the overwhelming weight of evidence. I was amazed by events which I cannot understand or fathom out, no matter how hard I concentrate my mind upon them. There is an East Anglian village a few miles from the Monastery of the Blessed Martyr King Edmund. Close to this village there are some ancient excavations, which in English are referred to as "Wlfpitts" which means wolf pits. From these the village takes its name. At harvest time, while the harvesters were busy in the fields collecting their crops, two children appeared — one boy and one girl — with completely green bodies. They were also wearing clothing of a strange colour made from unusual material. As these bewildered children wandered through the fields, the harvesters caught them and took them to the village. Many people gathered to see the strange sight. It was a long time before they would eat anything, although it was clear that they were almost fainting from hunger. Food was offered to them in plenty, but they would touch none of it. It was discovered by accident, while beans were being gathered in from the fields, that the children tried to eat the pith from inside the stalks. They cried with great sadness because they could not find any. However, one of the harvesters took pith from a pod and gave it to them. They ate this eagerly. For some months they ate nothing except this, but gradually they got used to bread, and their colour slowly changed until it was like ours. They also learned to speak our language, and were baptised. The boy, who appeared to be the younger of the two, died soon afterwards, but the girl who now looked indistinguishable from our women married a man from King's Lynn. When they had mastered our speech, they were questioned about who they were and where they had come from. They said that they came from The Land of St Martin, a place where that Saint was greatly venerated. They had no idea where their own land was, nor did they know how they had come to be in the field where they were found by the villagers. They recalled that they had been tending their father's animals in the fields of their own country, when they had heard a great noise like the bells ringing from our Monastery of St Edmund. While they were puzzling over this sound, they found themselves in the Woolpit fields with harvesters all around them. When they were asked about the faith of the people of St Martin's Land they said that they were Christians and that there were churches there. When questioned about the movements of the sun, they replied that it did not rise in their country as it does in ours.

They said that the light is much weaker than ours: about the same as early morning or just after sunset. They also said that they could observe another country across a wide river. These things and many besides were spoken of by the children when people asked them about their country. Readers can say what they will as they think about these very strange things. I do not regret writing down these astounding events: the story is too strange and complicated for human intelligence to unravel."

Piecing together the records and traditions, the two children with green skin and, possibly, green clothing of some unusual material, turned up in the harvest fields. They themselves seemed to have thought that they had come through a tunnel or passageway of some kind. Their description of their home in St Martin's Land makes it seem a very normal and terrestrial place, but there are odd discrepancies. If there was little or no light there, how did the necessary photosynthesis in the grass take place to enable their father's animals to graze it? What was "the bright country" which they claimed to be able to see in the distance? If it was the simple, Suffolk harvest fields of Woolpit, what "great river" lay between? Again, if it was merely a terrestrial tunnel that separated their father's mysterious land from Woolpit, why could neither the children nor their new friends in the village find the entrance again?

Woolpit village centre: the unknown green children were led through these same streets almost 1000 years ago. Were the villagers the first terrestrial human beings the children had seen?

Mysterious tunnels and subterranean passages figure prominently in myths and legends. In Grantchester near Cambridge there is a tunnel entrance which begins in the cellars of the old Manor House and was said to have been excavated from there all the way to King's College Chapel. The theory was that in times of plague or epidemic the King's College men could have escaped along it to the cleaner, healthier air of Grantchester. An investigation a few years ago, however, revealed that what was left of the tunnel seemed to go towards Grantchester Church rather than towards Cambridge itself. A field near King's was marked on an eighteenth century map as "Fiddler's Close" and there was a legend that at some previous time an adventurous fiddler had set out to explore the King's College end of the tunnel. Playing as he went, he had gone ever farther and deeper, while his anxious friends and supporters — following above ground as best they could — had heard his music growing fainter, until it finally tailed away into silence. The dauntless fiddler never reappeared.

A similar legend is attached to Binham Priory in Norfolk, where another long subterranean passage was said to connect Binham with Walsingham. Ghost stories dating back for several centuries told of a grim spectral monk who walked above ground along the line of the secret tunnel as though he was looking for something he could never find.

Apparently, part of the tunnel collapsed at the Binham end during the early nineteenth century, and while a crowd of bystanders peered down into the passageway, Jimmy Griggs the Fiddler arrived followed by his faithful dog, Trap. Playing his fiddle just as the dauntless fiddler had done in the King's College legend, Jimmy and Trap ventured off along the tunnel, with their friends and supporters following the music. Once again the sounds grew ever fainter and more distant until they faded entirely. Days later, a terrified, shivering Trap re-appeared with his tail between his legs — but fearless Jimmy Griggs was never seen again.

Several ingenious theories have been advanced over the years. There was alleged to have been a similar episode in Spain where two green children appeared in Banjos in Catalonia. In this account some agricultural workers found two strange children crying at the entrance to a cave. They spoke a language that the villagers could not understand. Experts from Barcelona could not understand it either. The children were wearing clothes of an unusual fabric, and their skins were green. Just like the Woolpit children they went hungry for days, finally eating beans. The boy soon died, but the girl survived and learnt enough Spanish to tell her friends in Banjos about her homeland. Her description of it was exactly like the St Martin's Land of the Woolpit story: twilight, a wide river, and a bright country in the distance. There was also a reference to a loud noise that had immediately preceded their arrival in Banjos. The villagers failed to find the entrance to the mysterious 'tunnel' which had transported the green boy and girl to Banjos. Just as in Woolpit, the girl lost her green colour, but died after five years instead of marrying a local man as the

Woolpit girl had done. The Spanish green children were said to have had almond eyes, but otherwise they resemble the Suffolk children very closely — rather too closely, perhaps. The Mayor of Banjos who took the lead in befriending them was said to have been a certain Ricardo de Calno — which sounds uncannily like a Spanish version of Sir Richard de Calne in Suffolk. In fact, the whole Spanish tale seems to have been only an imported version of the Woolpit story, and to have no foundation in fact. The Catalonian village of Banjos does not even seem to exist — unless a very strong magnifying glass has to be applied to the map of Catalonia.

So who might the Green Children of Woolpit have been, and where did they come from?

Some researchers think that the story may have been a badly re-hashed version of the Babes in the Wood legend. It's a sensible idea and worth investigating, but the dates present an insuperable problem.

The story of the Babes was first published by Thomas Millington of Norwich in 1595, but there is reason to suspect that it was written by the Thomas May who took over Griston Old Hall — the Wicked Uncle's House — in 1597. There is a strong tradition among old local inhabitants that carvings of the story were in evidence in the house as late as 1805. The popular story tells the tale of a boy and a girl whose parents died and who were then placed in the care of their uncle. The latter stood to inherit if anything happened to the children. He ordered two murderers to take them into Wayland Wood and kill them; the assassins quarrelled because one felt pity for the children. They were left to wander in the wood until — overcome by exhaustion — they curled up under an oak tree where they died and were covered with leaves by the sympathetic robins. Uncle fell under a curse: his sons were lost at sea, all his enterprises failed and he died bankrupt.

The version in the old ballad is a fanciful variation of a historical episode at Griston which took place towards the close of the sixteenth century — the heyday of Shakespeare and Elizabeth I. Young Thomas de Grey lost his father, Thomas senior, in 1562 when the boy was only seven years old. He was a ward of Queen Elizabeth and as was customary he had been "sold in marriage" to Elizabeth Drury. This arrangement could account for the brother and sister tradition in the old ballad — but the children concerned were actually affianced instead, according to sixteenth century custom.

Young Thomas's uncle Robert stood to inherit the estate if the boy died, and the will provides some evidence of a quarrel between father and uncle. Robert was an adamant recusant Catholic and the local country people who were strongly Protestant disliked him accordingly. Young Thomas went off to visit his step-mother (his late father's second wife Temperance Carewe who had remarried Sir Christopher Heyden of Baconsthorpe) and died either there or on the way home — perhaps even in Wayland Wood as the original ballad says.

The locals raised a cry of foul play, but Robert went ahead boldly. He claimed the dead boy's estate and then over-reached himself by trying to claim the dower lands from the child bride. She and her family refused to be dispossessed and a great court case involving two bishops was fought. Robert was ordered to return a significant portion of the land.

After the furore had died down he was persecuted and repeatedly imprisoned and fined. His sons attempted to reclaim the family fortune for him by going off on a privateering expedition. They took as their example the good fortune of Thomas Cavendish of Trimley St Mary in neighbouring Suffolk, who had rebuilt his shattered fortune in 1586 by taking up privateering and successfully capturing a Spanish treasure ship. The de Grey boys were not so lucky: both of them were drowned at sea. Wicked uncle Robert died owing £1780 in fines — about £100 000 today. The Green Children of Woolpit made their surprising entrance to the Suffolk harvest fields about three centuries before Robert de Grey arranged for the murder of his orphaned nephew. However, the idea that the Babes and the Green Children might have been one and the same involves a poison theory rather than the more widely known death from exposure hypothesis. If Robert had attempted to use cyanide or something similar on the Babes, the argument goes, the toxicity might have accounted for their green colouring. It doesn't, of course, account for their description of the twilit St Martin's Land and their story about looking after their father's farm animals. Neither does it contribute any solution to the problem of their diet.

So if confusion with the Babes in the Wood can be discounted, where *did* the Green Children come from?

In what appears to be the historically valid version of the event, although the boy died shortly after being rescued by the Woolpit villagers, his sister grew up, lost her green colouring entirely, became a happy, healthy young woman and married a man from King's Lynn. Sir Richard, who employed her for the few years until her marriage — and it is necessary to remember that in Shakespeare's Elizabethan world Romeo and Juliet were married in their early teens — said that she was inclined to be "somewhat loose and wanton in her ways". Sexual behaviour tends to vary from culture to culture, and Sir Richard's remark may be one of the most significant in the whole record. Were the Green Children from somewhere — call it St Martin's Land, or whatever we choose — in which a different code of sexual ethics was the norm? In the records of the Kaspar Hauser case, the Mystery Boy of Nuremberg would perform his excretory functions in public without the slightest idea that it was not acceptable in the culture of early nineteenth century Nuremberg. Is it sensible to ask whether the Green Girl was sexually uninhibited because she had been reared in a more open and permissive culture than that of twelfth century Suffolk?

It is extremely unlikely that the Green Children travelled through time, across whatever barrier exists between parallel worlds and probability tracks — if, indeed, such tracks do exist, from another dimension or from another planet. Yet how else can the so-called "tunnel" connecting Woolpit with a twilit land bounded by a great river be explained?

Folklorists and students of myth and tradition will suggest that there are several features in the account which point in legendary or supernatural directions. 'Martins' were imps or little demons: so was the strange, dimly lit St Martin's Land meant to symbolise the outer boundaries of hell? Perhaps it was purgatory? In C.S. Lewis's *The Great Divorce* he describes purgatory as a huge, sprawling, twilit city in the grey, drab, industrial midlands of the 1930s depression.

Beans were also the traditional food of the dead, and green was the colour of fairies, gnomes, elves, leprechauns and 'the little people' in general. Can the Green Children be explained in supernatural terms? Again, it seems highly improbable.

Explanations have been put forward that they were escapees from one of the notorious early copper mines that employed enforced child labour. Snow White's Seven Dwarfs were thought by some researchers to have been child miners whose growth had been stunted by long, arduous toil and exposure to huge amounts of copper. Could those conditions have induced a green pigmentation as well?

The mystery is as deep now as it was during Stephen's reign. Researchers remain as puzzled as the Woolpit harvesters of almost nine centuries ago.

WHO ENGRAVED THE YARMOUTH STONE?

Does the mysterious Yarmouth Stone refer to a trans-Atlantic Viking voyage?

It was our great friend George Young of Queensland in Halifax County, Nova Scotia, who first put us on the trail of the mysterious Canadian Yarmouth Stone. This 400 pound boulder was discovered in a salt marsh by a Yarmouth doctor, Richard Fletcher, in 1812. He was an army surgeon who had retired and gone to live in Yarmouth in 1809, subsequently dying there in 1819. He actually located the stone close to the shore on a point of land that then ran out between the outlet of the Chegoggin Flats and the western side of Yarmouth harbour. There are only fourteen characters in its short inscription and these have been puzzled over by the experts for close on two hundred years.

The stone has now been carefully preserved and advantageously displayed in the fascinating Yarmouth County Museum, at 22 Collins Street. Its Director and Curator, Eric J. Ruff, the Historian, is a mine of valuable information about the mysterious old stone and its possible origins. This is what he told us during a recent interview which he allowed us to record and which we found very helpful and informative.

"The Yarmouth Runic Stone is very interesting in the history of Yarmouth. Most people think that it was left by the Vikings — that's the general theory — but there are lots of other theories. Basically it was found towards the end of Yarmouth harbour in 1812 by a Doctor Fletcher. Some people, notably the descendants of Dr Fletcher, always felt that he did the carving, because he was apparently a practical joker: and his family always felt that he did it. Lots of others have felt that the Vikings left the stone, and it's been translated a couple of times by various people from the Runes. One translation was made by Henry Phillips Junior round about 1875, and he felt that the Runes read either 'Hako spoke to his men' or 'Hako's son spoke to his men.'"

(Phillips subsequently published a paper on it in 1884 according to a note made by Harry Piers, a former Curator of the Provincial Museum, and suggested that this Hako was a member of the Karlsefne Expedition of 1007.)

Co-author Patricia Fanthorpe with Eric J.Ruff (Museum Curator) and the Yarmouth Runic Stone, discovered by Dr Richard Fletcher in Nova Scotia in 1812.

Eric Ruff also told us that in 1934 Olaf Strandwold had translated the Runes on the stone.

This Strandwold translation is particularly interesting linguistically. Olaf Strandwold, was the County Superintendent of Schools in Benton County, Washington, and an eminent Norwegian scholar, who believed that the characters were certainly Runic. He interpreted them as: "Leif to Eric raises {this monument} . " The idea of "this monument" in the sentence is an understood object. It is not actually contained in the letters of the Runic inscription itself. The sense of such an understood grammatical construction can also be found in requests for assistance such as "Please help me up {from this ditch} " where the idea of "from this ditch" is understood because the people to whom the remark is addressed can see the ditch and the predicament of the speaker — both of which make the understood words superfluous! In exactly the same way, the physical presence of the substantial Yarmouth Stone renders the addition of "this monument" superfluous. As Confucius might wisely have written in one of his aphorisms: *"He who carves deep letters on hard stone will choose fewer words than he who writes on paper with smooth ink and small brush. "*

In 1934 when Olaf Strandwold did his work, Georges St Perrin was in charge of the stone and the Yarmouth Library that then housed it. Georges' description of it to Olaf in 1934 says clearly: " . . . shows very few signs of erosion. The cuts show, except in a few isolated spots, a distinct V-shaped

Co-author Lionel Fanthorpe with Eric J.Ruff (Museum Curator) and the
Yarmouth Runic Stone, discovered by Dr Richard Fletcher in Nova Scotia
in 1812.

section . . . the stone is of very hard texture . . . the cuts are so well tooled that a
highly tempered instrument must have been used by the inscriber . . . "

What Strandwold did so effectively was to search carefully through
established Runic alphabets and locate known equivalents from authenticated
sources which matched the Runes carved on to the Yarmouth stone. He then
laid these out in parallel with a third line below which gave the Latin alphabet's
equivalent of the Rune above. Strandwold took several closely cross referenced
pages to establish and verify each of the fourteen Runes on the stone and finally
came up with the Latin version:

LAEIFR ERIKU RISR

Allowing for the minor discrepancies between ancient Runic and Ogham
characters carved at slightly different angles, there is also a remarkable similarity
between the Glozel Alphabet from central France, and the inscription on the
Yarmouth stone, as the following diagram illustrates.

Yarmouth Stone	⌄ ⌐ ∟ ⋈ ⊢ ⋉ ⋀ ⌊ ⟨ ⋁ ⟩ ⊢ ⋔ ∘
	or
Glozel Alphabet	⌄ ⌐ ∟ ⋈ ⊢ ⋉ ⋀ ⌊ ⟨ ⋁ ⟩ ⊢ ⋔ ·
	Ӂ
Morlet's Numbering	4 16 15 31 24 65 41 32 15 16 14 24 43 1
	or
	44

In order to keep the views of the various Runic experts fairly balanced, it needs to be said that in 1966, some thirty years after Strandwold's work was published, Dr Liestol of the Norsk Polarinstitutt in Oslo expressed his doubts about whether the inscriptions were Runic at all.

A totally different scholarly approach to the problem was made by Julius Frasch Harmon in his paper entitled *Concerning the Carvings on the Braxton and Yarmouth Stones* which appeared in *West Virginia History* Volume XXXVI in January 1976. Harmon suggested that the inscriptions were entirely *numerical* and referred to the statistics of an expedition which had set out on the orders of King Erik XIV of Sweden.

Eric Ruff then went on to explain several other very interesting ideas. "There's an early Basque theory which says that the stone reads: 'The Basque people have subdued this land,' and that would have come from 350 BC. The Mycenaean theory, which would be earlier than that, translates the stone as "Exalted throne: the pure lions of the Royal Household sent into the sunset to protect, to seize, and to make a hole in the mighty waters at the summit have been sacrificed — the whole corporate body." I think that's marvellous — how you can get that out of just a few Runes: I don't put much faith in that one, as you can tell. Other theories include the Japanese theory, fourteenth century Scandinavian, and tree roots. So you can take your pick. I like it when our visitors come in and say, 'Is it real?' and I say, 'Yes, it's a real stone.' We do have a bit of a problem with the stone. One of the Presidents of the Historical Society in the thirties thought that the carvings were getting faint so he re-chiselled the stone, so we've lost anything that we could have got from the original, although we do have photographs of the original. Anyway that's the way it goes. Naturally, it belongs to the Yarmouth Public Library, and it's on loan from them since the Museum was opened in the 1950s.

"My own favourite theory is the Basque Theory because I've taken a Basque-French dictionary and looked up the Runes in a Basque book of Runes, and I understand how they can equate those to the Basque words. It makes sense to me: certainly you can see "*Basque*"; you can see "*people*"; you can see "*land*". There was another stone found in Yarmouth about 1895. It had Runes like our Rune-stone and then it had three more letters below them — that translates in Basque as 'The Basque people have subdued this land and dwell here.' There's some speculation about that stone because it happened to be found in the grounds of a hotel which had just opened in 1895, and that stone has since been lost.

"Our stone was found in 1812 and that was before people even thought about the Vikings. It could be Viking. I certainly don't doubt that Vikings were here. I'm sure they could have been here. They were certainly in Newfoundland."

This point is strongly supported by Birgitta Wallace. She was working with a German film crew in 1995, and had shown them the Viking site at L'Anse Aux

Meadows in Newfoundland, which she supported as being undeniably authentic, before bringing them down to Nova Scotia to film the Yarmouth stone.

Eric went on to explain how the stone had crossed the Atlantic before World War I.

"The stone was taken over to England at one time to be approved or translated. It was taken prior to the First World War, and when it was ready to be returned, War had broken out, and it was decided not to risk bringing it across with the U-boats. Apparently it sat crated on the London Docks during the First World War.

"Chips have been taken from the back of the stone to determine where the stone came from. It would have been good to think that it came from Scandinavia somewhere, but it just turned out to be local stone."

Laura Bradley, the very helpful and informative professional Archivist at the Yarmouth County Museum, also recorded an interview for us: "I've seen several researchers who were here specially to look at the stone. Early researchers and translators were not actually able to see the stone, so they were working with photographs and rubbings, so they were not able to determine what was a natural mark on the stone and what was man made. One theory which keeps coming back is that the marks on the stone were naturally made — and it's hard to determine because the integrity of the original carvings has been interfered with by the re-carving and it's difficult to view it in the same way. However, two geologists within the last six years have looked at the stone and they've told me that they do not believe that these marks were made naturally. And yet our local expert, well really the North American expert in this field, Birgitta Wallace who works with Parks Canada, says that these markings are definitely not Norse Runes but that they're naturally made. So we have qualified experts taking opposite views.

" The jury is still out for me. I know the stone was found in 1812, and the man who found it was an army surgeon. The possibility of his actually making these markings seems remote to me. And then I'm speaking with geologists and they feel that it's not naturally made, or not a natural occurrence, and then speaking with this Norse expert who says it's absolutely not Runes, I really feel I would like to give an informed opinion, but unfortunately at this point I'm not able to do that. This is one of Yarmouth's greatest mysteries, and I really for the life of me, having looked at the documents with all of these experts . . . I don't know how those markings found their way on to that stone. It is quite a mystery for me."

What, in outline, is the substantiated Viking history with which the controversial old Yarmouth stone may at last prove to be involved? Eric the Red, otherwise known as Eric Thorvaldsson, flourished in the closing years of the tenth century AD, as the founder of the earliest Scandinavian settlement in Greenland. His son, Leif Ericsson, was the first fully accredited European discoverer of North America. Eric the Red headed west in the spring of 981 with

The Yarmouth Runic Stone, discovered by Dr Richard Fletcher in Nova Scotia in 1812.

about thirty of his family, friends and neighbours and a quantity of live stock. Their clinker built Viking ship was less than 100 feet long, and conditions at sea on such a voyage must have been far from easy. Prevented from landing on the east coast by a wall of drifting ice, they made their way round the south point and then steered up the west coast of what is now Julianehaab. Having found the land to their liking, they named it Greenland, and later spoke of it so highly that their enthusiastic contemporaries made up an expedition of some twenty-five boatloads of potential colonists and live-stock. Only fourteen of these boats containing between 300 and 400 colonists in all, actually established themselves there in what was later known as the Eastern Colony.

In 999 Eric's middle son Leif, variously known as Leif Ericsson, and Leif the Lucky, sailed from Greenland to Norway via the Hebrides instead of going on the more usual Icelandic route. On his way back the following year, he made the return voyage without calling at any intermediate land, and was hoping to strike the southern end of Greenland. Having missed it in bad weather, he encountered the North American mainland instead: probably Labrador, perhaps Newfoundland, perhaps even as far south as Nova Scotia. Realising that wherever this was it was not his father's home in Greenland, he turned north up the coast and reached home safely before autumn. The tantalising question remains unanswered: did Leif Ericsson land anywhere near Yarmouth and inscribe the controversial stone while he was there?

The Yarmouth Stone is not by any means the only inexplicable ancient carving to be found in Nova Scotia. In 1983 Edward Hare was using heavy earth-moving equipment on his land at Mount Hanley when he hauled up a very unusual cuboid boulder. Almost a metre long, half that in width and depth, the stone came out in two halves. The broken halves matched perfectly, and as Edward fitted them together he noticed some very curious, deliberately chiselled markings which matched up when the two halves were rejoined. Our expert friend, George Young, was called in to examine the stone and his extensive knowledge of ancient languages — Ogham in particular — led him to suspect that the inscribed stone Edward Hare had found was genuinely ancient and that its inscription was historically significant.

Ogham may well have been developed by the early Celts as long ago as 1000 BC and carried with them as they travelled westwards. This raises the question of just how far west the early Celtic traders and sea warriors were able to voyage.

Following the trail blazed by that renowned pioneer of ancient languages, Professor Barry Fell, George Young expertly deciphered the Mount Hanley Stone as a work that had been carved by inscribers whose own language was Gaelic, and that it was most probably a memorial stone: not so very different in style or purpose from our present day gravestones. The letters MUI which he found were, in his opinion, most probably an early version of the name Muir, or Murrey, and the MAC or MC in front of it would have indicated "son of" — the early equivalent of today's McMuir or McMurrey. The LU characters, he thought, represented the name Lew or Lewis, while the DAI MAB HU lettering would have been Dai son of Hugh, which would be rendered as Dai Hewson, or Dai McHugh today. George Young's further discoveries on the Mount Hanley Stone inscription produced other early Gaelic-sounding names including Loi, mother of Mu, and a reference to the pre-Christian Celtic sun-god Bel, not totally unconnected with the Middle Eastern god Baal and his consort, Ashtoreth.

George's work on the Mount Hanley Stone raises three important questions. How old is the inscription? Where did the people who inscribed it come from originally? And what happened to them?

He offers some exciting possibilities as answers. He noted that the earliest Ogham found in Iberia and North America had no vowels. Its characteristic style was found mixed with other scripts in languages from the same era — especially Punic which came from Lebanon and Syria in the beginning, then made its way to Carthage, where it subsequently became blended with certain Greek dialects. It travelled from there to Cadiz in Spain.

Later Ogham from Ireland and Scotland did contain vowels and probably dates from the 500 year period between 100 AD and 600 AD.

With the arrival of Christianity in Ireland, Ogham marks and marker stones were frequently destroyed or obliterated as they were regarded as either Satanic, or, at best, pagan, in origin.

George favours the idea that the Mount Hanley Stone was inscribed by people from Ireland, or from a large Irish colony which had established itself in the New Hampshire/Vermont area. He would date the main colony's existence between 300 AD and 600 AD, and suggests that a small settlement of colonists lived on Mount Hanley at or around that time.

George comments that Herodotus, Plutarch and other early chroniclers refer to colonies of Carthaginians and other 'Greek men' in what must have been North America and Canada as early as 250 BC. He also mentions the Nordic Sagas' references to a country they called 'Greater Ireland' on the western side of the Atlantic. Was this territory Newfoundland or Nova Scotia? George examines the possibility that this so-called 'Greater Ireland' could have been the result of Brendan's colonizing voyages in the fourth century AD.

George also makes some telling points about the Roman departure from Britain in the fifth century, and the fierce Scoti tribes from Ireland who raided Caledonia by sea at that time. Did they or some of their contemporaries head west across the Atlantic instead and found the Mount Hanley colony?

The settlement there seems to have been a permanent one: traces of their stone drainage system have been unearthed, and stone drains are not a feature of a transient, nomadic camp. As to where they went, or what became of them, George thinks that conquest by, or assimilation into, one of the indigenous tribes is the most likely explanation.

He believes, with good reason, that the Mount Hanley Stone, could eventually prove to be one of the most significant historical discoveries ever made in Canada.

So the riddle of the inscribed Canadian stones remains. Some may be hoaxes. Others may be the work of natural erosion, which can at times look confusingly similar to the remains of a weathered inscription. Some may be Celtic, Norse, Basque or even Phoenician. They may be written in an indigenous Canadian or American language, in Runic, in Ogham, in Glozelian, or some completely unknown script representing the lost language of an older and stranger race from far away.

VAMPIRES AND GOATSUCKERS

Did a fearless girl and her brothers in Croglin Low Hall fight and destroy a hideous vampire?

Vampires in legend go back a long way. Some versions of the myth of Lilith, or Lilis, supposedly Adam's first wife, suggest that she was a special type of vampire who was particularly dangerous to children. The Latin word *strix* was sometimes applied to a vampire, although it is more appropriately used for a screech-owl, which also links it with the Lilith myth. Graeco-Roman literature contains a sprinkling of vampire stories, but there are earlier traces of them in the East. The word *vampir* is found in the Magyar language, and the Lithuanian word *wempti*, meaning "to drink" is also associated with it. A Russian document dating back to 1027 uses the phrase *upir lichy*, meaning "wicked vampire".

Some old traditions maintain that vampires are the offspring of a witch and a werwolf; others suggest that witches, wizards and black magicians become vampires after death, or that suicides run the risk of changing into vampires.

It is possible that the vampire legend originated in the Far East and travelled to Europe along the silk and spice routes. From the Mediterranean, the vampire tradition reached the Carpathians and became popular among the Slavs. Another route may well have been the one thought to have been followed by the original Romany Gypsy tribes who migrated from northern India, and were thought to have arrived in Bohemia and Transylvania during the thirteenth and fourteenth centuries — and Transylvania has been synonymous with the vampire legend ever since Bram Stoker introduced Dracula to the world.

The original form of the name was Vlad Dracul, and he was also known as Vlad the Impaler. Vlad was born in Sighisoara, or Schassburg, round about 1413. His father "Vlad the Devil" or "Vlad the Dragon" was a member of the Dragon Order, who were pledged to make ceaseless war against the Turks. This is reminiscent of the Carthaginian Hannibal's sworn hatred of the Romans, since as an impressionable boy he was made to take a solemn oath against them by his father, Hamilcar Barca.

Young Dracula was allegedly captured by his Turkish opponents when he was only thirteen, and seems to have acquired his notorious taste for torturing and impaling his enemies during that captivity. For several decades from 1456 onwards, he was the stern terror of Wallachia, where, even allowing for exaggeration and the propaganda put around by his enemies, he launched thousands of victims into eternity via the spikes below his castle walls. This accounts for his alternative title of *Tsepesh* or *Tepes*, meaning 'impaler'.

Dracula was said to have been killed by one of his own men by mistake: he had disguised himself as a Turk to watch the outcome of a battle from behind enemy lines. He lacked all vestiges of mercy and morality, but like Macbeth, he wasn't short of crude physical courage. Seeing that the field was all but won, he raced to the top of a hill to watch the last few Turkish soldiers being slaughtered — fatally forgetting his own disguise. He was mistaken for a Turk and killed.

His tomb was opened in 1931. It contained a crumbling skeleton, a serpent necklace, a cloak of red silk with a ring sewn into it and a golden crown. These unique Dracula souvenirs were eventually stolen from the Bucharest Museum, and have never been recovered.

Turning from the historical Vlad to the folklore of vampires in general, they were feared not only because they were deadly and secretive killers, able to assume the form of a bat and fly up to the intended victim's bedroom, but because they carried with them the deadly infection of vampirism: once drained by a vampire, the victim was doomed to join the vampire's ranks. Traditionally,

Croglin Low Hall, scene of the alleged vampire attack on Amelia Cranswell and her brothers in the 17th Century.

Croglin Low Hall: the window (now bricked up) to the right of the door as you leave the Hall is traditionally the one through which the vampire gained entrance to attack Amelia.

vampires show no reflections, cast no shadows, and are unable to cope with bright light. Sunlight is fatal.

It was believed that vampires were unable to enter a house unless they had been invited — but once the householder had made that fatal error, they were able to come and go at will.

The traditional vampire's longevity was so great that it almost amounted to immortality, and this was combined with massive physical strength and relative invulnerability. The rules of the game, however, were not loaded entirely in the vampire's favour. It disintegrated almost instantly in the presence of strong sunlight. A good sharp stake through the heart was also terminal: iron and wood being equally satisfactory. Beheading, severing the limbs and burning the pieces of the dismembered torso were also considered effective. Some vampires are said to be unable to cross water, refinements of this tradition say that the water has to be *flowing* in order to stop them. They are helpless between sunrise and sunset and must then rest in their coffins on some of the soil in which they were originally buried. Holy water sears them like concentrated acid. Being touched with a cross, preferably a silver one wielded by an ordained priest who sincerely holds the faith, burns vampires as devastatingly as a red hot branding iron. Like werebeasts, they can be shot with silver bullets or cut with a silver knife. They are deterred by garlic, but not totally halted by it.

Vampire folklore exists almost universally. In Ashanti legends, for example, they are called *Asasabonsam* and live in trees deep in the forest. This African vampire tradition gives them iron teeth and feet like hooks, which dangle from trees to trap the unwary.

The southern States of the U.S.A. — especially Louisiana — have legends of a vampire-like monster called *Fifollet* or *Feu-follet.*

In Australia there are stories of *Yara-ma-wha-who*, a small red humanoid, not much over a metre tall. The mouth is exceptionally large and the hands are covered in suckers. When it captured someone by dropping down from its perch in a fig tree, it would drain the victim's blood until the unfortunate man or woman was helpless. *Yara-ma-wha-who* would return later, swallow the victim whole, take a long drink of water (an interesting practical detail from a terrain where water was particularly scarce) and then sleep. When it awoke, the undigested portion of the victim would be regurgitated — *still alive.* This swallowing and regurgitating process was repeated until the victim had shrunk to the size of a *Yara-ma-wha-who* and slowly turned into one. Although many factors here differ from the European vampire legends, the *Yara-ma-wha-who* shares the traditional power to infect and transform the victim.

A particularly interesting Bulgarian vampire was known as an *Ustrel*, and was believed to be the spirit of an unbaptised child. Slowly working its way out of the grave, an *Ustrel* would emerge on the ninth day after death to attack sheep and cattle in order to drain their blood.

Co-author Lionel Fanthorpe on the road to Croglin Low Hall in Cumbria, where the alleged vampire attacked Amelia Cranswell three hundred years ago.

This links in with the sinister *chupacabras*, or "goatsucker", reported recently from Mexico, Puerto Rico and parts of Central and South America. Numerous reliable and reputable witnesses have described the *chupacabras* they saw as resembling an enormous porcupine, but with disproportionately powerful hind legs like a wallaby or kangaroo, and strange-looking appendages — almost like thin horns — all the way down its spine. It attacks by day as well as by night, and seems to live on a diet of goats, chickens and household pets. Despite every effort by the authorities, no specimen of *el chupacabras* has yet been killed or captured. Some researchers have suggested that it may be a genetic engineering experiment which has gone horribly wrong and broken out of a laboratory: was someone attempting to create a monster that would be ideal to launch against enemy troops? If such a creature could be bred, and programmed to attack selectively, it could be much less dangerous to the user, and much more useful militarily than indiscriminate germ or chemical warfare. It would also be tactically preferable to unleashing any type of nuclear radiation to blow around indiscriminately for years after the conflict — contaminating friends and foes alike with grim impartiality.

Other theories suggest that it has alien origins: some reports describe it as resembling a hybrid between one of the "grey" ufonauts and an unspecified terrestrial animal.

So far, no human beings have been attacked by *el chupacabras*, but a young girl in Cumbria, UK, was not so lucky.

Some popular accounts of the Croglin Grange, or Croglin Low Hall, vampire which attacked her date from the 1870s. Augustus Hare presents most of the facts in *The Story of My Life*, and he says he obtained his account from a Captain Fisher who once lived at Croglin Grange.

The whole Croglin story is shrouded in mystery and misunderstanding. To begin with there's a bloodcurdling, mid-nineteenth century 'penny-dreadful' called *Varney the Vampire, or the Feast of Blood*. Written by James Malcolm Rymer (1804 – 1882) it certainly contain a few minor parallels to the Croglin story, and some researchers have regarded *Varney* as evidence to invalidate the entire Croglin account.

Rymer was a successful and prolific writer: his 220 chapters, first published in 1847 were re-published as 'penny parts' in 1853. They then amounted to nearly 900 pages.

To seek to discredit a factual, historical episode on the grounds that someone has written a piece of fiction which is vaguely similar, and that the real life history, therefore, is not history at all but just additional fiction based on the first piece, is not a substantive argument. *Fictional* stories of espionage, of detection, of warfare and romance cannot invalidate the historical truth of Rahab and the Israeli spies who visited her establishment on the walls of Jericho, of P.C. Edward Robertson's courageous arrest of multiple murderer Charles Peace, of the memorably gallant charge of the Light Brigade at

Balaclava, or of Edward VIII's choice of the lady he loved rather than the British Crown.

It would be as just as rational to argue that the *Titanic* never existed simply because Morgan Robertson had written a novel in 1898 in which a giant liner called the *SS Titan* hit an iceberg and sank in the Atlantic on her maiden voyage with terrible loss of life.

Another confusion arises because there are *two* Croglins. When we made our first research visit to the village in the early 1970s, it was clear that the Parish Church of St John the Baptist was not the church towards which the vampire had fled. The church we studied then had been built in 1878 on the site of an old Norman church, which had itself replaced a Saxon one. There were people living in and around Croglin in the Bronze Age — one of the moulds from which they cast their spear-heads was found in the 1880s. Opposite the church stands a house called *The Old Pele* which dates from 1400 and was once the Rectory.

On subsequent research visits we discovered that a mile or two further down the stream was the *second* Croglin, the tiny village of Croglin Parva. All that now remains of it are two large farmhouses known respectively as Croglin High Hall and Croglin Low Hall. It is to Croglin Low Hall in Croglin Parva, and to the old Church with its ancient vaults which once stood near it, that the historical episode of the vampire rightly belongs — and there is every indication that the attack occurred long before the 1870s. Croglin Low Hall is at least as old as Carlisle Castle, and — originally a fortified farm — must now be one of the oldest 'working farmhouses' in Cumbria.

The third problem attached to the Croglin vampire episode is the difficulty of pinpointing *which* Captain Fisher of Croglin gave the facts to Augustus Hare, and exactly who the three Cranswells were — if indeed their name *was* Cranswell — who took Croglin Low Hall from the Fishers on the seven year lease which plays an integral part in the story. It is also of major importance to try to ascertain *when* they lived there.

Croglin was originally part of the Barony of Gilsland. The Lordship passed to the de Vallibus family and from them to the de Hastings family. In 1214 it changed hands yet again and passed to the Whartons of Westmoreland. In later times it became the property of the Fishers, and the house which went by the name of Croglin Low Hall seems to have belonged to the Fisher family since at least 1730. The Captain Edward Fisher of the vampire story — whose full title was Edward Rowe Fisher-Rowe, Late Captain of the 4th Dragoon Guards — seems to have been the grandson of Edward and Deborah Fisher, whose graves are in Ainstable churchyard. He made the acquaintance of Augustus Hare in 1874 when he married Hare's cousin, Lady Victoria Liddel. The newly married Fishers then moved to Thorncombe near Guildford, where Edward eventually died on his seventy-seventh birthday, November 8th, 1909. Victoria survived him until 1935, and they now lie side by side in Holy Trinity Churchyard at Bramley.

The north-western English dialect name "crog-lin" can mean "the twisting river" or the "crooked river". This is the stream that flows close to Croglin Low Hall. Can vampires cross running water?

The dating difficulty in Augustus Hare's account may well have arisen because he had naturally assumed that Captain Fisher's narrative coincided with his own move from Croglin to Thorncombe. There is a substantial body of evidence, however, which seems to suggest that Fisher knew the story well as an old established tradition in Croglin — and the account of the vampire's attack on Amelia was considerably more than a century old when Fisher first heard it as a child.

The Fisher ancestors from the relevant period were wise in their choice of tenants for Croglin Low Hall. We shall continue to use the name Cranswell for convenience, as that name was associated with the vampire episode by local residents to whom we spoke in Croglin village. The family consisted of two brothers, Michael, stocky and muscular and Edward, rather slimmer and more athletic. The Cranswell brothers lived with their attractive younger sister Amelia, an intelligent and practical girl with conspicuous courage and resourcefulness.

The Cranswells were popular in the district. They had a reputation for being unfailingly generous and helpful to their less fortunate neighbours, and they were popular members of the local social circuit: always welcome as dinner guests, at house parties, concerts or card evenings. They were regarded as sociable, sensible and totally acceptable.

One summer evening, after a particularly sultry day — not the usual Cumberland weather — they had dined early and gone to bed early. Amelia was propped up on her pillows, looking out across the lawn towards the derelict ruined church beyond. Her casement window was secured, but she had not fastened the shutters. It was not the kind of area where that sort of security was necessary.

She became aware of what she described later as two points of light moving towards the house from the direction of the old, abandoned churchyard. They seemed to be glowing in the way that an animal's eyes sometimes glow when caught in the beam of a lantern. As the lights drew nearer Amelia could see that they were quite unmistakably eyes, and they were set in one of the most frightening faces she had ever seen.

There was nothing in the world she wanted more at that moment than the reassuring presence of her two loyal and protective brothers, but her bedroom door was locked on the inside, and before she could get it open the *thing* with the gleaming eyes was unpicking the lead of her ground floor bedroom window.

What she later described as a claw-like, skeletal hand came through the aperture left by the removal of the small diamond pane which the creature had unpicked, and undid the catch. Something like an animated scarecrow entered her room, gripped her hair and forced her head back. By the time Mike and Ed had been woken by her screams, she had been savagely bitten about the face and throat and was unconscious and bleeding profusely. Even as the brothers broke the door down and rushed to help Amelia, the *thing* was escaping across the lawn. Edward raced after it, surprised by the speed with which it covered the ground. As far as he could tell, it was heading for the churchyard, and he *thought* he saw it disappear over the wall with a surprisingly powerful bound. He did not pursue it further, but ran back to see how badly Amelia had been injured.

Although in considerable pain and shock, and bleeding profusely from the bites to her face and throat, Amelia's strength and courage pulled her through the crisis. In an era long before the discovery of antibiotics, infection from bites could sometimes prove life-threatening, but Amelia's strong mind and robust constitution saw her well on the road to recovery within a matter of weeks. There was, of course, the question of permanent scarring at a time when cosmetic surgery was either very basic or non-existent. A girl's appearance — and its effect on her marriage prospects — were highly significant.

In the days that followed, news of the attack on Amelia became the central talking point in the Croglin area. Two or three neighbours called to see the Cranswells with information about similar attacks which had occurred over the past two or three years.

The doctor advised a good long holiday for the family, so that Amelia could convalesce and recuperate fully. The Cranswells were comfortably off and decided on a few weeks in Switzerland. While they were there, it was Amelia who insisted that they return to Croglin Low Hall instead of wasting the rest of their seven year lease on it, and as far as is known it was also the quick minded and resourceful Amelia who devised a very successful contingency plan to be put into action if her attacker returned.

Another of the research problems connected with the Croglin adventure is that traditionally — and it is an important factor in the investigation — the house was said to be only a single storey building. Croglin Low Hall is *not* a single storey building today, as the photographs we took on a recent research visit clearly show. However, when writer and researcher F. Clive-Ross examined the building carefully in 1962, he observed a large corbel in the room with the bricked up window which is traditionally associated with the vampire. The most common architectural purpose of such a corbel is to support a roof. It is, therefore, highly likely that at some period well *before* the nineteenth century Croglin Low Hall had been only a one storey building, just as the legend maintains it was at the time when the vampire attacked Amelia.

Amelia's plan was that all three of them should arrange to sleep in adjacent downstair rooms so that both brothers would instantly hear her shout for help. The bedroom doors were also to be kept open so that they could reach her quickly if they were needed. While in Switzerland, the family had purchased a matching pair of boxed pistols complete with ammunition and cleaning equipment. The lead from which this ammunition was made had a distinctive greenish tinge — quite unlike standard British lead — and this made it readily identifiable. The guns were kept primed and loaded on the brothers' bedside tables.

Should Amelia's attacker return, the plan was that Mike would rush immediately to her side to protect her with one of the pistols, while Edward would race outside to cut off the monster's retreat with the other.

The Cranswells returned to Croglin — and in due time, Amelia did see the weird, gleaming eyes *again*, as they approached her window from across the lawn. Her contingency plan worked to perfection. The bulldog-like Mike was at her side in a matter of seconds with his gun grimly raised. Ed was away through the front door and racing after the intruder before the thing realised its danger. Aiming for its legs, Ed fired from close range. There was a scream of pain and the creature began limping away across the lawn in the direction of the derelict church which still stood near Croglin Low Grange at that time.

Ed pursued it doggedly, but his single shot pistol was now empty. He was no coward, but he was nowhere near as powerful as Mike, and he knew from what Amelia had said after the first attack that the *thing* — whatever it was — was both dangerous and abnormally strong. He watched it clear the wall of the derelict churchyard and vanish into a tomb. His understandable reaction at this point gives the whole account a clear ring of truth. Uncertain of what to do next, Ed stood in the darkness outside the door of that sinister old vault listening and watching. His dilemma was whether to go for help and so risk letting their quarry escape, to take his chance against it in a hand to hand fight and go straight in after it, or to wait and watch in the slender hope that someone would come that way so that he could send a message to Mike.

As time passed, he still felt undecided, but thought that the best course of action would be to go and get help. Perhaps the pistol ball had done the thing more damage than had first appeared? Was their opponent already dead or dying from loss of blood? Ed finally left the tomb unguarded and went in search of Mike and whatever other help he could find.

Not long after, a determined party consisting of the Cranswells and their more venturesome friends broke into the tomb, which Ed had seen the wounded creature enter an hour or so before. The interior was filled with old, broken coffins and their decaying contents — with one exception. According to the Croglin tradition, what the men saw was a sort of raised dais in the centre of the tomb, on which lay just one sturdy old open coffin containing a dried and wizened —- but otherwise remarkably well preserved — corpse. The light from their lanterns revealed fresh red blood on the lips and skeletal finger tips. Again, according to the Croglin tradition, the men carried this corpse to the crossroads, where they grimly dismembered and burned it. During this macabre destruction rite a pistol ball of greenish, Swiss lead was discovered in one of the creature's withered legs.

Too many factors make it difficult if not impossible for this to have been a late nineteenth century adventure. Single shot muzzle-loading pistols were far more common in the seventeenth and eighteenth centuries than in the late nineteenth. The Cranswell brothers would have been far more likely to buy a six-chambered revolver each if they had made their purchases in the 1870s.

There is strong historical evidence via Mrs Parkin, whose husband, Inglewood Parkin, owned the estate containing Croglin Low Hall in the 1930s, that the old church of Croglin Parva had been ruined by Ireton, Oliver Cromwell's brother-in-law, at the time of the civil war. She recalled that in her early days on the Parkin Estate, there were many stones from this church lying about in an area adjacent to Croglin Low Hall and known then as the Church Field. Local tradition asserted that there had been tombs and graves there — including a Fisher family vault.

After the dismembered corpse had been burned, no further vampire attacks were reported in or near the village.

If the Croglin Vampire is taken back to the seventeenth century, where he more than likely belongs historically, the whole story becomes far more comprehensible and believable. But what *was* the horrifying scarecrow-like creature that almost killed young Amelia Cranswell on that hot summer night?

When we were lecturing on the Croglin vampire phenomenon in the 1970s, an ingenious young medical practitioner in the audience put forward a fascinating — and totally rational —theory. He suggested that there was nothing paranormal about the case: Amelia was attacked by someone mentally ill, who had — as part of that mental illness — made himself a den or hiding place among the tombs surrounding the derelict church adjacent to Croglin

Low Hall. After Ed shot him in the leg, the psychopath retreated to the vault where he had been living for some time. His mental illness did not mean that he was stupid — far from it. He had no more idea what Ed was doing outside the vault than Ed had of what was going on inside the vault. It was a guessing game for them both. The 'vampire' gets a sudden bright idea. Having used the vault as a hide-out for weeks, he knows all about the one old but well preserved body: inspiration strikes. They want a vampire — they'll get a vampire! The psychopath extracts the green lead pistol ball from the wound in his leg. He smears fresh red blood from that same leg wound on to the mouth and hands of the long dead corpse. Then inspiration really strikes. He takes the Swiss lead pistol ball which he has prised from the deep flesh wound on his injured leg — and thrusts it into the dried parchment-like flesh of the long dead occupant of the coffin on the central dais. Then he peers very cautiously around the door of the vault . . . He's in luck! The dangerous young man with the gun has gone! The psychopath sneaks silently out and puts as much distance as he can between himself and Croglin. "And," said the Doctor, thoughtfully, " the gangrene which he had caught from handling an open wound with fingers that had just been touching a corpse killed him a few days later. A poor vagrant is found dead in a ditch. Apart from an acrimonious argument about which parish he belongs to — so that's the one with the responsibility for his funeral fees — no real notice is taken of him. Not surprisingly, no more vampire attacks occur in the Croglin district. Those who helped to dismember and burn the innocuous old corpse at the crossroads are delighted that their work has been so successful. No-one associates the nameless dead tramp found in a ditch forty miles away with the Croglin vampire."

As the old fairground stall proprietors used to say: "Yer pays yer money and yer takes yer choice!" So it is with the Croglin Low Hall vampire. The weight of evidence suggests that *something* odd and disturbing happened there three centuries ago and more, something involving an attack on a girl and her brothers, and their final vengeance on the thing. Whether it was paranormal, an extra-terrestrial, a pan-dimensional voyager, or just a traditional vampire on the lines of Dracula or Varney cannot be fairly decided on the evidence currently to hand. Open mindedness combined with sharp critical appraisal of *all* the known facts will usually take the honest researcher to the truth in the end.

GLOZEL AND OTHER STRANGE ALPHABETS

Near Vichy, France, in 1924, young Emile Fradin uncovered an ancient store of clay tablets engraved with an unknown alphabet.

T he farm belonging to the Fradin family is situated in the tiny hamlet of Glozel, near Vichy in central France. On March 1st, 1924, when Emile Fradin was only seventeen, he was helping his grandfather to rescue one of their cattle which had fallen through the apparently, smooth, safe, grassy surface of one of their meadows. A totally unsuspected, artificial cavity lay below.

It was lined with interlocking bricks and several of them were glazed as though by intense heat. The cavity could have been an ancient kiln or, perhaps, an old glass works.

Once Emile and his grandfather had succeeded in rescuing their cow, Emile went down to explore the cavity in more detail. In a matter of minutes he had made several very interesting discoveries. The cavity was lined with burnt brick and stone shelves, and there were also numerous storage niches. All of these were filled by unusual objects of great age. Emile found statuettes of primitive deities, carved antlers and bones, and clay tablets covered with an alphabet which no-one could read. Because a great many human remains were found in the vicinity as well, the area became known as *Champs des Morts:* the Field of the Dead.

Dr Albert Morlet was a medical man practising in Vichy at the time the Fradins made their discovery. He was also a very enthusiastic amateur archaeologist. Sir Arthur Conan Doyle's *Lost World* (1912) contains two wonderfully antithetic characters: Professor Challenger and a rival academic, who argue with great heat and animosity about their cherished, contradictory, archaeological theories. The great strength of Doyle's writing — whether it featured Sherlock Holmes himself or some of Doyle's romantic or historical characters instead — was that his fictional people behaved realistically. Sir

Co-author Lionel Fanthorpe with Emile Fradin, the Glozel farmer who actually discovered the ancient and mysterious objects inscribed with an unknown alphabet in a subterranean storage chamber.

Arthur filled his pages with men and women who would have been as much at home in history as in fiction. Challenger and his rival were perfect examples of the senior scholastic types who hurled acrimonious comments at each other when their theories were in conflict. Morlet and the Fradins lined up on one side of the bitter Glozel arguments and the majority of the French archaeological establishment lined up on the other. The battle lines, thus drawn, continued to bombard each other viciously for many years.

Morlet visited the Fradin farm on April 26th, 1925, and was positively impressed by what the family showed him. He examined the site and its artifacts carefully and pronounced them ancient, genuine and highly significant.

Morlet made a deal with the Fradins. They were to own all the artifacts which were extracted from their site, but he would have exclusive rights to the scientific study, reporting and publication of what was found there.

News of the amazing discoveries at Glozel — and particularly the tablets bearing the mysterious, unknown alphabet — reached Dr Capitan, widely

Co-author Patricia Fanthorpe on the actual discovery site at Glozel, near Vichy in Central France. It was from this field that the strange old artifacts were retrieved in 1924.

recognized professionally as one of France's leading archaeologists. He visited the site and was — *initially* — just as impressed as Dr Morlet had been. He wrote to Morlet accordingly: "You have a marvellous stratum here. Please write for me a detailed report of your findings which I can pass to the Commission for Historic Monuments." If Morlet had done just that, the whole history of the Glozel adventure would have been completely different. But he didn't. He and the Fradins ignored Capitan and produced an independent publication entitled: *Nouvelle Station Néolithique* — a New Neolithic Site.

Dr Capitan felt humiliated because he had been left out. He thought his authority and his professional reputation were being put on the line. He regarded Morlet as a mere amateur, and saw himself as the epitome of professional archaeology in 1920s France — and he was infuriated beyond measure because this mere amateur upstart had dared to challenge *him* — the man who regarded himself as the expert of experts — whom all other experts humbly and rightly followed and obeyed.

With that kind of ego, Capitan's retaliation was massive. He proclaimed that the Glozel site was not authentic and that the Fradins had made the 'finds' themselves.

Not all the French archaeologists of repute jumped obediently on to Capitan's bandwagon, however. The learned Professor from St. Germain-en-Laye, Saloman Reinach, was on the side of the Glozelians. Reinach believed that

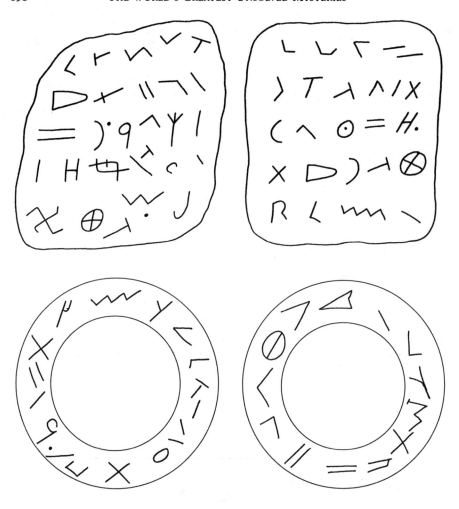

Samples of the unknown alphabet discovered on the artifacts retrieved from the ancient site at Glozel near Vichy, France.

the Mediterranean — rather than Babylonia or the Far East — was the true cradle of civilisation. If its artifacts were genuine, the Glozel site would be a powerful weapon in his armoury. The mysterious inscribed tablets also supported the theory of historian Camille Jullian, who had made a special study of the Roman occupation of Gaul. The Academy of France weighed in with Professor Loth, who studied one of the stone death masks and thought it bore a strong resemblance to Beethoven. Professor René Dussaud joined the ranks of Capitan's anti-Glozelian party, and declared that what Loth had failed to understand was that this particular Glozel mask resembled Beethoven because the Fradins had *copied* the death mask of Beethoven. As the real Beethoven had died in 1827, Dussaud argued that all the Glozel finds were fakes — rather a sweeping conclusion to make about carved bones and antlers, which bore an uncanny resemblance to all the accepted museum specimens that had been authenticated by acknowledged leaders in the archaeological field — men such as Capitan himself.

Battle was then joined by a forensic scientist named Edmond Bayle who thought that he could detect grass in some of the clay tablets. He said they were probably fakes. Hunter Charles Rogers — a notorious faker of relics, like Dawson and the Piltdown Skull fiasco in Britain — 'confessed' that he had made some of the Glozel artifacts, but Rogers was not noted for his strict adherence to the truth, and he would have welcomed the publicity associated with the Glozel controversy.

During the 1970s, while Lionel was lecturing for Cambridge University's E-M Board, our research work for that course took us to Glozel. We had a long session with Emile Fradin — who had rescued the cow and made the great discoveries almost half a century before we met him. We also had ample opportunity to study the site itself and the artifacts in the Glozel museum at first hand. In our considered opinion Emile Fradin was sincere and genuine, the site had been found by accident when the cow fell into it in 1924, and the

Glozellian	Cretan	Early Greek	Runic
↑ Γ	∀	↑	
日	B	⊐	♭
⅄	ℚ	⌐	⟨ λ ʎ
▷ ▽ △	△	△	Ⅱ ▷
✗ ∈	ϑ	⌡	₣
℘	ʃ	⅂	↑ ℓ
✗	✗	I	|
⊨	⋕	⊟	N И H
⊗ ⊕	⊕ ⊗	⊗ ⊕	Я
⋋	⅂	⟨ ⟨	✗
Ϝ ⱪ	Ψ	↑ ↑	Ψ
⌡ ⌐	(⌐	↑ ✓	⌐
⊣⊢ ✗	⧧	⊥	Π
⊙	⊙ ⊙	∘	

Table of alphabetic comparisons between the unknown Glozel Script and other ancient scripts.

artifacts discovered in it were ancient work not twentieth century forgeries. Whatever strange history lies behind the objects and the alphabet — all that Emile Fradin did was to bring the mystery to light: he had no hand in its manufacture.

It was the discovery of thermoluminescence that turned the tide overwhelmingly in favour of the Glozelians. The earliest work and the first experiments with thermoluminescent dating were carried out at the Universities of Edinburgh and Copenhagen, but the work is now being done by good laboratories everywhere. The TOSL Research Laboratory at Dalhousie University, for example, is among the field leaders who now offer thermoluminescent analytical services to private collectors, art galleries and museums.

Thermoluminescence — often abbreviated to TL — works on the principle that many crystals such as feldspar, quartz, calcite and diamond absorb energy from ionising radiation: cosmic rays, alpha, beta and gamma. This energy frees some of the electrons in the crystals and they move around its lattice. Because this lattice contains certain faults and imperfections, a number of electrons inevitably become trapped in them. Heating the crystal or directing powerful light towards it will release the trapped electrons and the crystal will start to glow. By measuring the light from the glowing crystal, TL scientists can estimate how many years have elapsed since energy was lost on some previous occasion — such as the kilning of the pottery of which the crystal now forms a tiny part.

Suppose that a beaker was fired 4000 years ago. All the energy its quartz crystals had ever contained would have been forced out by that original kilning. If the beaker then lay undisturbed in the ground for 4000 years, exposed neither to heat nor to light energy, it would gradually become recharged by natural background radiation.

Reheated in a TL laboratory today in a light-proof cylinder with a luminescence detector attached, the ceramic specimen would glow again when the appropriate temperature was reached. This data — together with the level of background radiation applicable to the site where it was found — would enable a reasonably accurate date to be assigned to its last firing. The TL results for the Glozel finds showed that the youngest were several centuries old, and the oldest went back for millennia.

Twenty seven ceramic objects were taken at random from more than 300 which had been found at Glozel over the years. Their dates averaged somewhere about 100 BC when tested by TL in several different and totally reputable laboratories. An ox tooth found inside one of the decorated urns at Glozel was subjected to independent radio-carbon dating and gave a similar result. One tablet containing the Glozel inscriptions was already coated with glass fired at some time during the 17th or 18th century when it was retrieved. There does not seem to be any method by which the Fradins could have carved the inscription on that one — even with help from Dr Morlet.

Morlet and his friends the Fradins were totally vindicated, whereas Capitan's learned disciples and successors were left with some embarrassingly conspicuous archaeological egg on their faces.

To be fair to the archaeological establishment, however, it needs to be made clear that one of their chief grounds for scepticism was the *age range* of the finds at Glozel. They did not all come from the same period: in some cases they were separated by centuries — and longer. The only explanation seems to be that it was some sort of a collection. But if it was, *who* had assembled it and *why?* To be fair to the archaeological establishment again, until scientific archaeology and palaeontology came on the scene and set up the ground rules, the weirdest and wildest speculation held sway about the origin of the puzzling ancient objects that were uncovered from time to time by ploughmen, well diggers and miners.

Stone age sites were attributed to angels, demons, giants, wizards and fairies. Huge bones of extinct dinosaurs and mammoths were said to prove the biblical record that "there were giants on the earth in those days." When flint arrow heads were found, elven and fairy armourers were given the credit for making them.

However, there is a case to be made for suggesting that medieval wizards, witches, shamans and sorcerers, thaumaturgists and necromancers collected these strange ancient things *in the belief that they had magical origins and so could convey magical power to the user.* Did some medieval magician have his headquarters and workshop at Glozel? Was it his spells and incantations that were written in the unknown alphabet? Were charms and talismans manufactured there and sold to clients? Was it not reasonable to assume in that pre-scientific day and age that carrying a fairy flint arrowhead wrapped with appropriate herbs gathered by moonlight would render the wearer immune to attacks from mortal archers, while enabling his own arrows to find their mark unerringly each time?

What about helping an undersized child to grow strong, sturdy and tall by feeding him a potion containing the ground up bones of giants? (Remnants of fossilised dinosaurs, mammoths and mastodons perhaps.)

An underground chamber well equipped with brick and stone shelves would make an ideal workshop, consulting room and living cell — like the one which Shakespeare's Prospero had on his island. Glozel is remote enough today. In the middle ages it would have seemed much more remote: an ideal hiding place for a magician's store-cave — a long way from the prying eyes of the civil authorities, and relatively safe from the Holy Inquisition.

Another strange mystery brushes the fringes of Glozel: the proximity of the ancient Château Montgilbert. Montgilbert, adjacent to Glozel, was built in the twelfth century when the Templars were approaching the height of their power. The Templars built almost as well as they fought. Their skill as masons matched their skill and courage in battle. Was the strange underground store which young Fradin found in 1924 in any way connected with the Montgilbert Château and the numerous codes and mysteries with which the Knights Templar were involved?

Glozel is barely two days ride from Rennes-le-Château, the tiny mountain top village associated with the mysterious wealth found by Father Bérenger Saunière, the Parish Priest in 1885. If there is a link between Glozel and the Rennes treasure, there may also be a link between Glozel and the equally mysterious treasure in the Oak Island Money Pit just off the coast of Nova Scotia. The Templars were almost certainly involved with Montgilbert and with Rennes-le-Château: if the theories about Henry Sinclair of Orkney and the Templar refugees whom he helped to cross the Atlantic are also true — and there is every reason to believe the evidence which supports them — then the Templars may well be involved in the Oak Island Mystery in addition to the mysteries of Rennes and Glozel. The Templars were masters of codes and cyphers. The enigmatic alphabet inscribed on the tablets from Glozel could, perhaps, contain Templar secrets.

Whatever the final truth about the mysterious Glozel writing may be, it is by no means an isolated case. The so-called Tartarian tablets of Bulgaria, which have been widely accepted as genuine by the international archaeological establishment, are thought to be at least 1000 years older than the Jemdet Nasr alphabet from ancient Sumer. If the Glozel inscriptions are both ancient and genuine — which they certainly seem to be — they challenge the previously understood history of the development of writing.

Another very curious form of writing was discovered on Easter Island — one of the most mysterious sites on Earth, located at 27 degrees, 8 minutes, 24 seconds south and 109 degrees, 20 minutes west. Easter Island is 2700 miles from Tahiti, and 2600 from Valparaiso. The Galapagos archipelago — where Darwin found so much remarkable data for the theory of evolution — is 2000 miles north east of Easter Island. Nothing but the Antarctic lies to the south. The island is so small that it fails to register an area of even fifty square miles, yet within its narrow limits three great mysteries still lurk.

Seen from the air, it has a triangular coastline with sides of approximately 10, 11 and 15 miles. Prevalent Antarctic winds fail to chill the island's climate — and it usually remains pleasantly temperate. December to May is dry: June to November is rainy and cold.

Easter Island is volcanic in origin, and possesses powerful magnetic variations. Such anchorages as there are, are dangerous, and there's no harbour to speak of. Facilities are limited. There is a radio transmitter, a small hospital and an airstrip that isn't really in the business of competing for regular Concorde landings.

Juan Fernández, the navigator, made a brief and rather cryptic statement about a visit to what must have been Easter Island in 1576. He reported meeting people there whose culture was more advanced than any of those he had yet encountered in Peru or Chile. Fernández vowed to return, but died before he could pay a second visit. Captain John Davis (a Dutch seafarer despite his British surname) saw what *may* have been Easter Island in 1680, noted that huge flocks of birds were circling around it, and sailed on. In keeping with seventeenth century custom, he named it Davis Land. When Dutch Admiral Ruggewein went looking for it in 1722, he couldn't find it at the chart co-ordinates Davis had given. He did, however, find land on Easter Day, and rather predictably decided to call it Easter Island. Navigational historians are still debating whether it was one and the same place as Davis Land. Later visitors included such famous explorers as Captain Cook, González and La Pérouse.

In addition to its unknown alphabet, Easter Island is famous for its magnificent stone statues. Well over 200 of these have been erected on various parts of the island, mainly along a ten kilometre road which leads to a sacred burial ground. Quarried in a particularly difficult manner — each cut from its own niche in the slopes of the volcanic Mount Rano Raraku, and topped with a crown or red hat of different stone — the statues all show the same distinctive, aristocratic features of a face with extraordinarily long ears.

The historical legends of Easter Island — preserved mainly by oral tradition — tell how, long ago, there was a kingdom called Maraerenga far to the west of Easter Island. When the King died, his sons fought for the throne, and the defeated brother Hotu Matua, sailed away with his family, friends, bodyguards and followers until they reached Easter Island. Planting the seeds they had brought with them, they named their new country Rapa Nui, and prospered there.

The legends describe Hotu Matua as ostentatiously aristocratic in appearance in his red-feathered cloak, and particular emphasis is also placed on his long ears — a characteristic of the elite class who then ruled on Rapa Nui. This educated minority had monopolised education, and were the only ones who could both inscribe and read the mysterious *Rongo-rongo*, the sixty seven engraved stone tablets which Hotu Matua had brought with him from Maraerenga. The legends say that the *Rongo-rongo* contained mostly hymns and history: the Maraerengian equivalent of the Biblical books of Samuel, Chronicles and Kings as well as the Psalms.

In the 1860s slavers took over 1000 men from Easter Island — including the last of the aristocratic Long-eared people who could read the *Rongo-rongo*. A pathetic handful of these captives were eventually repatriated — bringing a deadly smallpox epidemic with them. It is now highly unlikely that any of the original Easter Island *Rongo-rongo* scholarship has survived.

When questioned as to the location of the *Rongo-rongo* today, Easter Islanders answer: "They are here but not here" which would seem to indicate that they are carefully hidden somewhere on the island — most likely near the sacred burial places of those who could once read them. Over the years, various scholars and academics made a limited number of copies before the *Rongo-rongo* vanished.

Bishop Tepano Jaussen was among the first to try to decipher the mysterious script, and further in depth studies were carried out many years later by Professor Barthel at Hamburg University. The *Rongo-rongo* tablets stubbornly refuse to give up their secrets.

Another ancient and mysterious script — far better understood, however, than either the Glozelian writing or the *Rongo-rongo* inscriptions of Easter Island — is Ogham, or as it is occasionally spelt, Ogam. It is the earliest known form of Goidelic (an early Irish version of the ancient Celtic language). Besides Ireland, Ogham was also in use in Wales and Scotland. Over twenty Ogham inscriptions have been discovered north of Hadrian's Wall, thirty or so have been found in South Wales, and one or two have turned up in Devon and Cornwall. However, the great majority of the 300 inscriptions which have come to light so far have been found in Ireland — mainly in Kerry and Cork. Much of it occurs on early tombstones, and is regarded by several experts as a code or cypher rather than as a straightforward alphabet.

The basic principle of Ogham is a simple one. A line can be marked either vertically or horizontally, and from this foundation line a number of strokes are drawn, cut or scratched at right angles. The smaller strokes going away from the base line are usually at ninety degrees to it, although a few Ogham lines are at an angle, reminiscent of some modern shorthand systems.

A remarkable and linguistically important fifteenth century Irish volume — *The Book of Ballymote* — explains the Ogham system, and gives instructions on how to use it for ciphers. This unique volume is kept in the Royal Irish Academy in Dublin. There are only twenty letters in the oldest form of Ogham, although later variations and adaptations exist in which the entire English alphabet of twenty six letters can be represented.

An old Irish rhyme, apparently dating back several centuries, gives basic instructions for writing Ogham.

> *For B one stroke at your right hand,*
> *For L two strokes must always stand,*
> *For F draw three, for S make four,*
> *When you want N you add one more.*

Our friend George Young of Nova Scotia has made a lengthy and detailed study of Ogham inscriptions, and has concluded that the manual version of the Ogham alphabet was used by the esoteric seventeenth century painter Nicholas Poussin. Poussin was apparently involved with the mystery of Rennes-le-Château, and one of the coded parchments which were allegedly found in an old Visigothic altar pillar in the church there, stated that Poussin and another painter named Teniers " . . . guarded the key . . . "

By his careful and thorough examination of many of the Poussin canvases, George Young discovered that the way the painter had depicted the hands of his subjects enabled messages to be read in Ogham. By holding the hand either up or down, or pointing it to the left or right — and using the hand itself as the main stroke of the letter — the number of fingers displayed *could* be used to show the number of strokes forming an Ogham letter. For example, one finger pointing upwards or to the right would be the letter B, four plus the thumb would be N, and so on.

Some art historians specialising in the work of Poussin's period have noticed that his canvases tend to have complex geometrical designs governing their compositions. In the case of "The Shepherds of Arcadia" — the painting alleged to be involved with the Rennes-le-Château code — at least one analyst has observed a regular pentagon tied to the measurement of the shepherd's staff, a pentagon which appears to govern the composition of the painting from outside. There is, therefore, a strong possibility that the riddles allegedly concealed in Poussin's canvases are not only complicated by his Ogham hand signals but by the curious geometry which the painters of his period loved to employ.

Ancient unknown alphabets are among the most intriguing and challenging unsolved mysteries which confront the researcher. It can sometimes be tempting to assume that a perfectly natural piece of erosion which coincidentally forms what looks for all the world like an Ogham letter, or a Glozelian character, is part of a mysterious message from the past. When dealing with unknown alphabets, patience, caution, a readiness to admit the strong possibilities of error and misinterpretation — and a willingness to scrap five years' misdirected work and begin again on a completely new tack — are essential pre-requisites for ultimate success.

THE PROPHECIES OF MOTHER SHIPTON AND NOSTRADAMUS

Did the strange old Yorkshire Wise Woman and the gifted French Doctor really see into the future?

Mother Shipton, the Yorkshire Wise Woman of Knaresborough, was born circa 1488. Her mother, Agatha Sontheil, was orphaned as a teenager, and had to fend for herself. There are varying accounts of who made young Agatha pregnant with the child, Ursula, who grew up to become Mother Shipton. One version suggests that the mysterious father was a high-ranking clergyman, and certainly the Abbot of Beverley Minster went in person to baptise the baby, and kept a watchful eye on her for years afterwards. Some versions of Mother Shipton's conception and early childhood suggest that her father was a nobleman, an itinerant Knight — perhaps even one of the Troubadours — who had met Agatha while passing through Knaresborough.

In one account, Agatha handed two-year-old Ursula over to the care of a local nurse, and then went off to a convent. In another account, the nurse took pity on the toddler when Agatha died. One of the most persistent legends of Ursula's infancy while in this nurse's care is that she and her cradle somehow found their way into the cottage chimney, and hung there without visible means of support: episodes of this kind added to the dark rumours that her mysterious unknown father was a demon — perhaps even Lucifer himself.

What is particularly significant is the choice of the name *Ursula* — the Bear. The legendary King Arthur was connected with the ancient and mysterious Clan of the Bear — as were several other old British families. Was Ursula's father a member of that enigmatic Clan, and was it at his instigation that the Abbot of Beverley Minster assumed a distant but effective guardian's role to protect young Ursula? Was it, in fact, at the absent father's specific request that the Abbot not only travelled sixty miles to baptise the baby, but also told Agatha what the father's choice of name was for their new daughter? Might the Abbot also have been a Bear Clan member?

Notice board outside Mother Shipton's Cave in Knaresborough, Yorkshire, England.

Ursula was sent to a school in the Knaresborough area, where her arthritis — perhaps the result of spending her early childhood in a damp cave beside the River Nidd where Agatha had taken refuge — made her a laughing stock to the other children. Despite the unfriendly attitude of the pupils in her school, Ursula got on well with the teachers, and proved to be highly intelligent. She also had unusual gifts of communicating with birds and animals.

At the age of twenty-four, she met Toby Shipton, a good-hearted carpenter, who was happy to marry her in spite of the physical deformities which had prompted her peers to mock her at school. It was from the time of her marriage onwards that she was given the title of Mother Shipton.

One of the earliest accounts of her prophecies and aphorisms seems to have been compiled by Joanne Waller, who died at the age of 94 in 1561 — the same year that Mother Shipton herself died, having prophesied her own death well in advance, prepared for it with tranquillity, and then lain down quietly on her bed to await what she had prophesied.

Some of the earliest editions of Mother Shipton's Prophecies were published in 1641, 1684 and 1686 — an important factor for investigators into cases like hers. Research frequently reveals that the so-called "amazing prophecies" and "strange pieces of foreknowledge" were actually written by someone else long *after* the event, and are more accurately described as garbled anachronistic history than as divination.

Co-author Patricia Fanthorpe in Mother Shipton's Cave.

Shipton's prophecies usually appeared in rhyme — as did those of Nostradamus in his enigmatic quatrains, and the meanings of both were often coded and hidden. A typical example is the couplet:

When the Cow doth ride the Bull,
Then the Priest beware thy skull.

Interpreters ingeniously suggested that the Cow meant Henry VIII because of one of his armorial bearings, and the Bull was Anne Boleyne, alternatively spelt *Bull*oigne. Her father had a black bull's head in his armorial bearings, and shortly after their marriage Henry dissolved the monasteries and other religious houses, and instigated difficulties and persecution for many priests.

Far less obscure was Mother Shipton's forecast concerning the reign of Queen Elizabeth I:

A maiden queen full many a year
Shall England's war-like sceptre bear.

From the same era came her prophecy about Drake's destruction of the Spanish Armada:

The Western Monarch's wooden horses
Shall be destroyed by the Drake's forces.

Two of her most remarkable prophecies concerned the Great Plague and the Great Fire of London. She wrote:

Triumphant Death rides London through
And men on tops of houses go . . .

During the panic and chaos caused by the Great Fire men did scramble up on to the roof tops to see which way the flames were heading, and Samuel Pepys made an entry in his Diary for October 20th, 1666, about Sir Jeremy Smith. Pepys wrote:

> *He says he was on board the 'Prince' when the news came of the burning of London; and all the Prince said was that now Shipton's prophecy was out.*

While something as historically definite as an entry in Pepys' Diary silences the objection that Shipton's alleged prophecy was written after the event, it does not overcome the difficulty of the ambiguity — men might well have taken to the rooftops because of a great flood, and had the Thames overflowed dramatically, that too would have been regarded as a fulfilment of Shipton's enigmatic words. This characteristic ambiguity has been a feature of prophecies since earliest times. A classic example was the forecast given to Croesus of Lydda when he asked the Delphic Oracle what would happen if he attacked the Persians. Croesus was told that " a great empire would fall". Happily inferring that this meant victory for him, he launched an enthusiastic attack on the Persians. The great empire which fell, however, was his own.

The River Nidd which flows by Mother Shipton's Cave.

One of Mother Shipton's totally unambiguous prophecies related to the fate of Cardinal Wolsey, who had vowed to have her burnt at the stake when he reached York. She had referred to him contemptuously as "the butcher's boy" (Wolsey's father was a butcher from Ipswich) and "the mitred peacock". When told of Wolsey's intentions, she laughed and said that he would see York, but never enter it. Reaching Cawood Castle, he climbed the tower and surveyed the city. That night, during Wolsey's celebration banquet in Cawood, the Earl of Northumberland arrived to arrest him on King Henry VIII's orders and take him to London to stand trial for treason — an experience during Henry's reign which almost invariably ended in a brief meeting with the executioner on Tower Green! Wolsey was luckier than most of those who had angered the irascible King — he died of natural causes on the way to London.

Another of her tragic prophecies which came true was her warning to the Lord Mayor of York:

> *When there is a Lord Mayor living in Minster Yard in York,*
> *let him beware of a stab . . .*

A Lord Mayor of York who took up residence in Minster Yard, was fatally stabbed by thieves one night.

The Patagonian Welsh in Argentina have also managed to preserve a handful of Shipton's traditional sayings over the centuries. It has been suggested by some researchers, including David Toulson, that the following lines of one of her prophecies may refer to the Falklands War:

> *In time to come hereafter,*
> *Our land will be ruled by two women.*
> *A child of ours will be contested*
> *By a child of Spain . . .*
> *In this time, blood will be shed*
> *Yet shall the child stay.*

Britain was ruled at that time by Margaret Thatcher and Queen Elizabeth II. The British 'child' might be said to be the Falkland Islands. The Argentinean 'child of Spain' tried to take possession of it, and many lives were lost on both sides.

Although there is some dispute about the dates of some of her most interesting prophecies, which are suspected of being later interpolations written after the events had occurred, it is worth mentioning that she forecast cars, trains running through mountains, and thought flying around the world in the twinkling of an eye — a pretty good soundbite for the Internet, e-mail services and the World Wide Web, considering she wrote it nearly 500 years before the Internet came into being!

Knaresborough Castle overlooking Mother Shipton's Cave. Was a travelling Templar Knight who stayed at this castle Mother Shipton's unknown father?

Baby Michel de Nostredame, who grew up to become the semi-legendary Nostradamus, was born on December 14, 1503, in St Rémy, Provence, France. His father, Jacques, was comfortably off, and practised as a notary. His mother, Renée, was a great homemaker.

As a child, young Michel was surrounded by her love and good Provençal cooking, together with the stimulating conversation of the friends and relatives who were almost always present at meals in his parents' home. As he grew older he became the eager student of his grandparents, Jean St de Rémy and Pierre de Nostredame, who taught him Hebrew, Latin, Greek, mathematics and astrology. They also taught him a wide range of other things — including medicine, herbalism, history and literature. Most significantly of all they introduced him to the secrets of the Jewish Kabbalah, or Cabala, and alchemy.

Their families had accepted the compulsory Christianity of fifteenth and sixteenth century Europe only in order to escape persecution. In secret, in the privacy of their homes, they preserved and maintained the essence of their old Jewish learning, faith and culture.

It was through the friendship of Michel's good and wise grandfathers that his parents had met in the first place. The two men were the personal physicians to the liberal and tolerant old King René of Provence (known with some justification as René the Good) and to his son the Duke of Lorraine and Calabria. With this background it was hardly surprising that Jean's daughter married Pierre's son.

Unfortunately, on the death of good King René, the throne passed to Louis XII of France, who lacked the old King's tolerance and enlightenment.

At fourteen, Michel went to Avignon where he studied grammar, rhetoric and philosophy. But the College was run by very conventional priests, and the boy's interest in astrology and the occult were noted with considerable disfavour. Young Nostradamus also realised that Copernicus was right about the sun rather than the Earth being at the centre of things. He argued the point fearlessly, but this was not a propitious time to get involved in a scientific-religious controversy. Martin Luther (1483 – 1546) was busily nailing his Declaration to the church door in Wittenberg, and starting the Protestant Reformation. John Calvin (1509 – 1564) was also about to come on the scene with his gloomy and fatalistic doctrines. In later years, Nostradamus, who hated Calvin's narrow puritanism, was to refer to the famous Genevan theologian and his religious work as "*. . . that loathsome odour . . .* "

Grandfather Pierre called Michel home and gave him politically shrewd advice on when it was advisable *not* to speak out too boldly. One root of the problem was that fifteenth and sixteenth century Christianity had an irrational dislike of the Jews, whom it saw as the murderers of Christ — while conveniently forgetting that Jesus himself was Jewish. Torquemada (1420 – 1498) and the Holy Inquisition had tortured and killed thousands of Spanish Jews, and those who could had escaped to Provence to live under the benign rule of René the Good. When he was replaced by Louis XII, the situation for such refugees deteriorated, and Pierre had no difficulty in explaining the need to walk on eggshells to his sensitively intelligent grandson.

The strange petrifying well near Mother Shipton's Cave.

Petrified souvenirs of a Victorian Wedding trapped in the uncanny stone curtain outside Mother Shipton's Cave.

As a teenager, Michel expressed keen interest in becoming a professional astrologer, but the family persuaded him to study medicine first and retain his interest in astrology as an adjunct to it. Accordingly, in 1522 he began his medical studies at Montpelier University. His youthful dissatisfaction with the priestly teachers at Avignon was repeated on a larger scale at Montpelier. His grandfathers had already taught him more than the staff at the Medical College knew, and he had to remember Pierre's advice about keeping silent on many occasions when he was in sharp disagreement with the learned professors at Avignon.

Nostradamus did not share his teachers' enthusiasm for bleeding patients, and his concern for cleanliness was looked upon as the worst kind of medical heresy. Qualifying in 1525, Nostradamus left Avignon with alacrity and went off to practise his own brand of medicine in his own way. It was a difficult period in which to practise. Most European cities were overcrowded, insanitary breeding grounds for the plague. Southern France in particular suffered from *le Charbon*, a form of bubonic infection which produced hideous black pustules.

Nostradamus surprised many of the patients whom he cured by advocating fresh air, clean drinking water, and his own unusual herbal preparations, the ones he had learned from his grandparents.

Fearlessly tending the sick — from whom many physicians of the period fled — Nostradamus's travels took him through most of southern France, including Narbonne and Carcassonne, where he met Bishop Amenien de Fays and became his personal physician. Was it *possible* that Nostradamus knew about pathogenic micro-organisms as a result of seeing the future? He actually *named* Louis Pasteur, the great nineteenth century medical researcher, in the course of his curious prophecies: could he possibly have glimpsed him in action? Ironically, whatever paranormal futuristic medical skills he might have had failed to save his beloved wife and children from dying of the plague which he had been able to halt so effectively elsewhere.

Nostradamus was soon in trouble over a comment he made to a craftsman making a bronze statue of the Virgin Mary. The craftsman complained to the church authorities and Nostradamus had to leave quickly to avoid being summoned before the Inquisition at Toulouse. For the next six years he travelled frequently and extensively to keep ahead of the sinister forces of the Inquisition. During these journeys his powers as a prophet seemed to develop remarkably.

One of his most remarkably specific prophecies concerned his encounter with a group of Franciscan friars. He moved aside politely to let the holy men pass on the narrow, muddy road, and then suddenly fell to his knees in front of a young brother named Felice Peretti. He explained to the startled friars that he was paying homage to a future Pope. This seemed incredible to them: Felice had been a pig-keeper before joining the Franciscans. His chance of even modest promotion within the church seemed slight. Forty years later — almost twenty years after the death of Nostradamus — Peretti became Pope Sixtus V.

After these years of wandering, Nostradamus finally settled in Salon where he met and married a wealthy young widow: Anne Posart Gemelle. They shared a beautiful home in the Rue de la Poissonerie, where Nostradamus turned the top floor into a study. It was here that most of his famous prophecies were written.

His actual methods of attempting to study the future began with staring at a thin flame until he had emptied his mind as far as possible. Seated on a brass tripod, he then stared into a brass bowl filled with water. As he passed into a trance-like state, he saw and heard pictures and messages from the water in this brass bowl. Technically referred to as hydromancy, this predicting of the future by reflections in water, was very closely allied to catoptromancy, predicting the future by the use of mirrors. The two techniques are linked by J.R.R. Tolkien in *Lord of the Rings*, when he refers to "the Mirror of Galadriel" the Elven Queen who is able to show Sam Gamgee, the Hobbit, reflected visions of his beloved home in the Shire.

Nostradamus's moral dilemma was that although he felt duty bound to share his visions with others, he knew that to do so was to invite persecution and serious charges of heresy and witchcraft. In 1550, he published his first Almanac, a volume which contained twelve quatrains, one dealing with events for each month of the year. The Almanac was highly successful and became an annual publication for the rest of his life. The uncanny accuracy of his quatrains brought crowds of wealthy and distinguished visitors to seek his advice.

Tourists visiting Mother Shipton's Cave. Notice the symbolic witch's broomstick beside the antique chair!

Prior to this, however, Nostradamus had already had striking successes with some other earlier prophecies. If the account is true — and there is no good reason to doubt its authenticity — his black and white pig forecast was one of his most striking successes. It happened when he was a guest of the sceptical Seigneur de Florinville, who showed him two piglets, one black and one white, and invited him to forecast their fate. Nostradamus said that they, themselves, would eat the black one that night, but that the white one would be eaten by a wolf. In order to prove the prophet wrong, de Florinville ordered his cook to prepare the white piglet for dinner. As they were eating it, the Seigneur laughed at Nostradamus and said they were eating the white one — thus proving the prophecy false. Nostradamus assured him that they were eating the black one.

The cook was sent for to settle the matter. He arrived in terror, and confirmed that they were eating the black one. He explained that after he had killed and prepared the white one for the spit, a pet wolf belonging to one of the huntsmen had got into the kitchen, dragged it away and eaten it. In order that there should be a banquet at all, he had promptly killed and cooked the black pig.

Another of Nostradamus's extraordinarily detailed and accurate prophecies concerned the death of King Henry II of France. He had ordered a three day tournament to celebrate the double wedding of his daughter to Philip II of Spain, and his sister Margarite to the Duke of Savoy.

Four years previously, Nostradamus had published the following quatrain:

> *Le Lion jeune le vieux surmontera,*
> *En champ bellique par singulier duelle*
> *Dans caige d'or les yeaux lui crevera*
> *Deux classes une, puis mourir, mort cruelle.*

> The young lion will overcome the old one,
> In single combat, on a military field,
> Inside a golden cage his eyes will be pierced,
> Two wounds shall result from one blow, and afterwards he will
> die a painful death.

The whole horrific prophecy came true on June 28, 1559. Towards the end of the tournament, King Henry, who was proud of his prowess in the lists, and had been competing successfully until then, persuaded young Montgomery, his Scotts Captain of the Guards, to ride against him. The light was fading, and Montgomery was very reluctant to joust with the King in case there was an accident. During their third clash, Montgomery's lance splintered: one shard entered the King's eye, another pierced his throat. It took Henry — who was in agony — a full ten days to die of his wounds. His helmet had had a visor in the form of a golden cage.

Nostradamus also forecast what would become of Montgomery. Centuries 3, quatrain 3 translates as:

> The man who on the military field
> Has won a victory over a man who is greater than he is,
> Six enemies shall take him by surprise at night,
> He will be naked and without his harness.

Although the dying Henry had stated clearly that Montgomery was not to blame for the fatal accident, the young Scotts Captain of Guards had left France. Back in Britain he had joined the Huguenots, and had consequently become involved in a failed Protestant invasion of Normandy. Catherine sent six members of her Royal Guard to abduct him in the night. In accordance with the prophecy, the hapless Montgomery was dragged from his bed naked. It was May 27th, 1574 — nearly twenty years after Nostradamus had predicted it.

One of his strangest predictions was the manner of his own death:

> He will be able to do no more.
> He will have gone to God.
> His family, friends and brothers will find him
> Dead between his bed and his bench.

And so he was found, having apparently fallen and died there during the night of July 2nd, 1566, a special feast day for Notre Dame, Nostradamus, Our Lady Mary. Was that, perhaps, rather more than coincidence?

He left explicit instructions that he was to be buried standing up, inside the wall of the church of St. Laurent in Salon, and there he remained until his tomb was disturbed during the French Revolution. These wall burials have interesting associations. Frequently, a request for a wall burial came from a wealthy benefactor of the church concerned who was not too sure how he stood over the matter of salvation. A wall was believed to be technically *nowhere*: it was neither within the church, nor in the land outside. It was, therefore, hoped by the people so buried that their wall burial would prevent both God and the devil from finding them. Was Nostradamus implying that he had performed his miracles of prophecy as a result of some sort of demonic pact, and that he did not wish to be found and made to pay his dues on Judgement Day?

That the prophecies contained in *The Centuries* were not to be easily understood, is made clear by Nostradamus's son, César. He maintained that "only those with the key could unlock the prophecies". So what might this key have been? An interesting study *Le secret de Nostradamus* by P.V.Piobb was published in 1927: it argues that the dedication to King Henry II in the second edition of *The Centuries* is full of hidden Biblical references. Piobb suggested that by getting these into chronological order and then performing a series of additions, it would be possible to establish links with the quatrains in *The Centuries*, and so discover their true, clear meaning.

Was Nostradamus talking about the South Sea Bubble or the great Wall Street Stock Market Crash of 1929 when he wrote:

> The copies of gold and silver lose their value . . .
> . . . All is exhausted and wasted by debt.
> All notes and bonds will be annihilated.

Or is it possible that the verse (*The Centuries* 8, quatrain 28) refers to the hyper-inflation which destroyed the Weimar Republic and brought Hitler and the Nazis to power? Certainly Nostradamus refers more than once to a character called Hister, which has led some researchers to wonder whether he was clairaudient rather than clairvoyant.

Century 4, quatrain 80, refers to:

> . . . a vast trench (or fortification)
> from which the earth has been dug
> . . . divided into fifteen parts by water
> . . . the city captured . . . blood, fire, cries and battle . . .

Might this possibly be the ill-fated French Maginot Line, built during the 1930s to make France impregnable? Fifteen rivers interrupted it, and Hitler's troops simply avoided it by going through Belgium in any case.

In *The Centuries* I, quatrain 26, there are references to three brothers, the greatest of whom "will be struck down in the day by a thunderbolt". Some students of Nostradamus's work have suggested that this refers to the Kennedy assassination. *The Centuries* dates these three brothers at a time when the Pope's name is Paul, and the Montini Pope, Paul VI, was in the Vatican at the time.

Another of Nostradamus's prophecies which seems to have referred to events in the twentieth century was centred on the great French hero, General Charles de Gaulle. Nostradamus said:

> . . . three times one who is named de Gaulle
> Will be the leader of France . . .

De Gaulle led armoured units in the Battle for France with great skill and courage during World War II. His second period of leadership was when he was in charge of the Free French Forces which played such an important role in overthrowing Hitler. His third occasion to lead was during his memorable presidency from 1958 to 1970.

Mother Shipton's prophecies and those of Nostradamus raise questions that are of major importance not only to academic theologians, metaphysicians and philosophers but to all of us. In the first place, if prophets are able to glimpse the future, does that mean that the future already exists in an unalterable state? If that is the case, then there is no free will and no autonomy. What we fondly imagine to be our own personal choice and decision making is as far beyond our control as the movements of planets or electrons. If we cannot make choices, then morality and ethics are as dead as free will. Jack the Ripper cannot be reproached for being Jack the Ripper, if his grisly performances in Whitechapel were all fore-ordained before he was born. Multi-millionaires, winners of Oscars and Nobel Prizes deserve no thanks and no congratulations because some force beyond their control gave them their talents and opened the path for their inevitable success. Presidents and Prime Ministers have never won an election since the world began — it was all done for them — *if* the future is already fixed. The world's greatest and most dedicated lovers never felt any free, genuine, spontaneous affection for each other — it was all planned out for them before they were born . . . and so on, and so on . . .

This makes a hopeless, fatalistic mockery of all human endeavour, and robs life of the last shred of its meaning . . . So there has to be another scenario . . .

Charles Dickens gets close to it in *A Christmas Carol*. Seeing all sorts of unwelcome sights in Christmas-yet-to-be, he asks desperately whether they can be averted, and the spirit assures him that they can: nothing is inevitable. What Scrooge saw were the shadows of what might very probably happen *if nothing was done about it.* In other words, Scrooge was being shown the likeliest of the probability tracks, the most reasonable forecast of the future based on extrapolations of current data. That would seem to be what Nostradamus and Mother Shipton saw. It raises, of course, another fascinating possibility: *that those alternative realities do exist elsewhere . . . it's just that we're not travelling along that particular experiential track.* When prophets see and hear that which has not yet come to pass, they may be looking at alternatives which are actually being experienced *elsewhere . . .* or they may be looking at the hazy blueprints of futures that will never leave the drawing board.

Like Ebenezer Scrooge, our 'prophetic' glimpses of unpleasant future *possibilities* should make us not fatalistic nor pessimistic but dynamically deterministic. The best response to a paranormal vision of an unwelcome futurescape is to work like fury to prevent its coming to pass. As Shakespeare says in *Julius Caesar:* "The fault's not in our stars but in ourselves . . ."

THE RIDDLE OF WROXHAM BROAD AND OTHER TIME SLIPS

Does an ancient Roman procession still cross Wroxham Broad today?

The origins of the Norfolk Broads are still the subject of much controversy among historians, archaeologists and historical geographers. The most widely accepted traditional theory follows the line that when the Ice Age ended, the sea level rose and flooded the flat East Anglian land where the rivers Bure, Waveney and Yare wend their slow ways to the North Sea. The water level fell and alluvium began to collect in large quantities. The wide estuary formed by the flooding of the three rivers became a marsh. The alders and other vegetation that grew there turned into a deep stratum of brushwood peat.

In Roman times this whole area was flooded again, and the large estuary reformed. In medieval times Norfolk was relatively densely populated. Forests had been cleared. Agricultural land grew excellent crops there instead. Peat was the next best fuel after the forest had gone.

With the long-handled wooden spades of their day, the fuel seekers cut through the poor quality, recent reed-peat, then on down through the clay layer into the brushwood peat that burnt well. It was cut into rectangular blocks and stacked up to dry before being used as fuel. Baulks were left between the digging, partly as paths for the diggers, partly to act as demarcation lines between one digging site and the next.

By the twelfth and thirteenth centuries, most of the work was completed, and the land was slowly subsiding. Severe storms caused flooding. There were none of the famous Norfolk wind-pumps there in those days, and very few coastal defences. The diggings filled with water. It was now far too difficult and expensive to get the peat out from under the flood water, and so the work was more or less abandoned. Once they were no longer maintained, the old boundary baulks collapsed of their own accord. Some were deliberately

View across Wroxham Broad, Norfolk, England.

demolished to aid navigation. The resulting scenery has more or less survived to the present day, although the reeds have spread and many new layers of reed-peat have formed over the intervening centuries.

Aerial photographs tend to support this idea that the Norfolk Broads were originally excavated to extract peat. Medieval records from Norwich Cathedral Priory show that substantial quantities of peat were, in fact, extracted. One bill of sale shows that £19 was paid for 400 000 blocks of peat in the early part of the fourteenth century. Later records show that serious production difficulties were being encountered and that the peat was having to be dredged up in nets.

The significant point is that there is substantial academic support for the view that the Broads were man-made: whether they were all innocuous peat cuttings or whether some had other purposes is open to further debate and discussion.

If the strange reports centering on Wroxham Broad are accurate and reliable, then that one at least was a Roman amphitheatre — not a peat cutting. It also seems to have been the focal point of what can only be described as a series of *possible* time slips, persisting over several centuries. Reports of the Wroxham Broad phenomena go back a long way and are well authenticated and documented.

In outline, what appears to happen is that a Roman procession passes through, or close by, the present broad. Eye-witness accounts maintain that the event is audible as well as visible, and, on some occasions, meaningful conversations seem to have taken place with a mysterious *Custos*, or Roman Guardian, who somehow belonged both to the time of the human witnesses *and* to the long-vanished Roman spectacle.

The river at Wroxham, which connects with the mysterious Broad where witnesses have reported time-slip experiences.

Benjamin Curtiss described the strange events at Wroxham in his *Archives of the Northfolk for 1603:*

> ". . . in the great Broad of Wroxham, near unto Hoveton St John. Two friends and myself were swimming across the lake from the Bure side to that opposite, when strangely enough we felt our feet touch the bottom. Now at this part there is much water, as much as twelve and in other places some fourteen feet. We kept together and presently found ourselves standing in the middle of a large arena with much seats one above the other all round us. The water was gone and we were standing there dressed as Roman Officers. What is more astonishing still, we were not surprised, neither we were incommoded by this piece of enchantment, but rather we were quite accustomed to it, so that we forget (sic) that we had been bathing. The top of the amphitheatre was all open to the sky, and many flags of divers colours floated in the wind from the top of the walls . . . "

Then followed a lengthy and detailed account of the Roman pageant which Benjamin and his two friends witnessed. The story is repeated with one or two interesting variations in an account given by the Rev. Thomas Josiah Penston in *The Gentleman's Gazette* dated April 16th, 1709:

" . . . We were holding a picnic on the banks of a beautiful lake in Norfolk about eleven miles from the ancient city of Norwich, when we were suddenly and very peremptorily ordered away by a very undesirable looking person, whose appearance and clothes belied his refinements of natural good breeding.

"As we were somewhat enangered by this unpleasant person's persistence, we made to go away, when suddenly we had to quickly stand aside to make passage for a long procession of regal splendour, the outstanding characters of which were a golden chariot containing a hideous looking man dressed as a Roman General, and drawn by ten white prancing stallions, about a dozen lions led in chains by stalwart Roman soldiers, a band of trumpeters making a great noise, and another band of drummers, followed by several hundreds of long-haired, partly armoured sea-faring men, or sea-soldiers, all chained together.

"They passed quite close to us, but no-one apparently saw us. There must have been seven or eight hundred horsemen in this long procession of archers, pikemen and ballistic machines. Whither they went or from whence they came I know not, yet they vanished at the lake side. The noise of their passing was very loud and unmistakable."

There is another reference to the Wroxham Broad phenomenon to be found in a poem by Calvert, published in 1741, and entitled *Legend of the Lake*.

Swans on the river near Wroxham Broad.

While through the trees of yonder lake
There comes a cavalcade of horsemen near.
Gaze not upon these Romans, friends,
For fear their eyes may meet with thine.
Stand back, well back, and let them pass,
These denizens of death, and close thine orbs,
Lest out upon a scene of death they fall,
In hapless misery for those who play
Their parts for nigh a thousand years.
Doomed for a term to re-enact
The life they led, the parts they played;
Go not with them, look not at them, but
Pray for them, dear friend, for they. . .
Are dead.

Day's *Chronicles of East Anglia* for 1825 contains a curiously cryptic reference to this Wroxham Broad phenomenon.

"The Royal progress of Carausius . . . has passed through . . . the village of Wroxham . . . on its way from Brancaster."

The next item comes from the private letters of Lord Percival Durand, and gives an account of some experiences which he and some friends shared on 21st July, 1829. On that date, Lord Durand and his party were on board his yacht

Wroxham village sign.

Pyrford Church, Surrey, England, where Mrs Turrell-Clarke experienced a time-slip.

Amaryllis, anchored about 200 yards from the eastern entrance to Wroxham Broad. They went ashore and sat looking out across the broad. It is recorded that the day was a particularly hot one. According to Durand's account, an old man appeared who seemed " . . . very shrivelled and worn, leaning on a tall stick . . . " No one in Durand's party saw the old man arrive, and no-one saw where he went afterwards. They asked him who he was and he claimed to be Flavius Mantus, the Custos Rotulorum for that part of Roman occupied Britain.

He warned Durand and his guests that they were trespassing on land belonging to the Western Emperor Marcus Aurelius Carausius. It seemed obvious to Durand's group that the old man was mentally ill, but they still asked him for further explanations. He told them that there was a sense in which Rome had never relinquished her claim on Britain, and that he was still the Custos, and that today there was to be a great parade and celebration of the Emperor's birthday.

Lord Percival then went on to describe how to his amazement the waters of the broad seemed to roll back, and the strange old man was transformed into a splendidly dressed Roman Officer. Durand records that he and his friends then saw a vast Roman amphitheatre complete with a procession such as the one earlier witnesses had described. At last the pageant faded again, their strange old visitor drifted into the woods and walked away slowly through the trees until he was beyond their line of vision. Valentine Dyall's *Unsolved Mysteries* contains a very well written, balanced and thoroughly researched account of the Wroxham

Broad phenomenon, and Charles Sampson's *Ghosts of the Broads* gives details of the dates on which the phenomenon is most likely to be visible: 13th and 16th April, 7th and 21st May, 1st, 4th and 11th June, 5th, 13th and 19th of August, and again on various dates in September and October — that is between the Ides of March (which Shakespeare made famous in *Julius Caesar*) and the Nones of October. According to the old Roman method of dating, the Nones were reckoned to fall on the 5th of some months and the 7th of others. The Ides were always eight days after the Nones.

A strange experience, which could well have ben a similar time-slip to the ones reported from Wroxham concerned John and Christine Swain and their sons, from Ilminster in Somerset. Near Beaulieu Abbey in the New Forest in Hampshire, they were driving down some quiet lanes in search of a picnic spot when they saw a strange, mist enshrouded lake with a large boulder in the centre. In this boulder was a sword — almost exactly like the one in the Arthurian legends, and their first thought, naturally, was that it was some sort of Arthurian memorial. *Despite many years of searching they have never found that lake again.*

Pyrford Church in Surrey is another site where what seems to have been a time slip took place. The witness concerned was Mrs Turrell-Clarke, who was on her way to evensong one Sunday night when the modern road seemed to change into a footpath in a field. She distinctly recalls that a man in what looked liked medieval peasant clothes moved aside politely to let her pass. She then found that she seemed to be dressed as a nun. The experience ended, and she was back in her own 'normal' time as though nothing had happened at all.

The little church at Pyrford had once been associated with a nearby Abbey, and had somehow managed to survive Henry VIII's depredations better than most.

A few weeks after her strange experience with the road that became a footpath, Mrs Turrell-Clarke was in Pyrford Church where the choir were singing some monastic plainsong. As they sang it felt to her as if the church itself seemed to be going through the same weird process as the road had done. Lancet windows, an earthen floor and stone altar gave it an early medieval look. She saw a procession of brown robed monks chanting the same piece of plainsong that the modern choir had been singing only seconds before. It also seemed to her that she was now somehow at the back of the church, and no longer taking part in the singing. The strange experience faded — as the Wroxham phenomenon had done for its witnesses — and everything was back to twentieth century normality.

Intrigued by these uncanny events, Mrs Turrell-Clarke began to investigate the history of her village church. So far as she knew, the neighbouring Newark monks would have worn black, not brown. However, records showed that in 1293, brown robed monks from Westminster Abbey were granted use of the Pyrford Chapel.

Colin Ayling and John England are enthusiastic and experienced metal detector users, whose very strange time slip experience was featured in my "Fortean TV" show on Channel 4 in the UK in 1997. They were working over 2000 acres of a country estate on a quiet autumn evening, which began with tea and a snack, before they set out to explore. Colin took a diagonal route across the field while John went around the edge. It was a night of worthwhile finds. Colin turned up a Republican silver denarius from the time of Julius Caesar, several Roman bronzes and then another denarius dating from the period of Rutilius Flaccus. They found several more ancient artifacts, whose exact nature they were unsure of, and the tip of a Roman javelin with the name 'NIGEL' punched into it.

Next moment both men heard the sound of galloping horses coming straight for them. They ran for safety in opposite directions, and heard the horses pass right over the spot where they had been standing. Neither Colin nor John had seen anything of the horses making those unmistakable galloping sounds.

They were strangely disorientated by the experience and wondered whether they were still in the same field where their search had begun — the place they called Boulder Field because of a heap of boulders which stood in one corner.

Carving outside the ancient Church at Pyrford in Surrey, England, which was built in the Norman style in 1150.

What really puzzled them was the sudden and unaccountable appearance of what seemed to be a tightly packed and impenetrable hedge about ten feet high some forty metres ahead of them. They approached it cautiously and walked along beside it for nearly 100 metres before finding their way back to their car.

When morning light came they went to search for hoofprints and the strange barrier hedge. *There were no hoofprints. There was no barrier hedge.* Yet both men could clearly make out their own footprints, and they saw where they had had to make a detour to get around the obstacle that had now vanished.

Mike Stokes, the archaeologist at the Rowley House Museum in Shrewsbury, later identified some of the artifacts Colin and John had found near the javelin tip as parts of Roman cavalry tackle. Had John and Colin heard a Roman cavalry patrol leaving their stockade-fortress? And had the mysterious obstacle in Boulder Field been part of that old Roman stockade? Was the name 'Nigel' on the javelin tip short for Nigelus? Had he been one of the invisible Roman riders, galloping across time?

Mrs Anne May, a school teacher from Norwich, was on holiday in Inverness with her husband, where they were studying the Bronze Age Clava Cairns — a small group of three burial mounds. At the end of their tour, Mrs May rested momentarily on one of the stones — where she apparently experienced a time slip of the Wroxham and Pyrford type. She saw a group of men with long dark hair, wearing rough tunics and cross-gartered trousers. They were dragging one of the massive stones. At that moment a party of tourists entered the site, and everything returned to normal.

Joan Forman, author of the interesting time slip study *The Mask of Time*, actually had a time-slip experience herself while visiting Haddon Hall in Derbyshire. She saw four children playing happily on the stone steps of the Hall's big courtyard. The oldest was a girl of nine or ten with shoulder length fair hair. She was wearing a greenish-grey silk dress with an attractive lace collar, and a white Dutch-styled hat. Joan could see only her back view at first, but before the time slip experience ended the girl had turned so that her face was clearly visible. She had broad distinctive features, a wide jaw and an upturned nose. As the researcher moved towards the group, they vanished — it was almost as if by moving slightly Joan had inadvertently turned off whatever strange telechronic current had been making the children visible.

Inside the Hall, Joan searched everywhere for a portrait of the children she had seen — especially a picture of the eldest, the girl with the unmistakably strong and distinctive face. She found one. The greenish-grey dress was the same, so was the hat, so was the lace collar. The girl was identified as Lady Grace Manners, who had been connected with Haddon Hall centuries ago.

Some so-called time slip and similar 'out-of-the-body' experiences are so dramatic that they almost acquire the dubious characteristics of anecdotal urban myths, but when one of these episodes has documentation, names and places firmly attached to it, its impact is powerful. We were delivering a course of

The ruins of Newark Abbey just a few hundred yards from Pyrford Church.

lectures on Unexplained Phenomena for the Lowestoft Scientific and Literary Society, in Suffolk in the UK, when A.M. Turner, a member of the audience, gave us the following information about his great-grandfather.

Documentation exists in the form of *The Mercurian*, the Lowestoft College Magazine, Number 11, Midsummer Term, 1910, printed by Flood and Son, Ltd., The Borough Press, Lowestoft. The article contributed by our Mr Turner's grandfather begins on page 29, and is entitled "*Curious Coincidences*":

> "Nearly everyone has doubtless at some time experienced a sensation of having been in some particular spot in exactly the same position, with the same company and speaking the same words, before, and yet perhaps the person in question has never before been within 100 miles of the place . . . This lady was visiting a Scotch house for the first time, and as she drove up to it the surroundings seemed familiar. When she got to the house, it seemed more familiar still, and she could even tell exactly what was inside the hall door, and exactly how the furniture was situated, and then she suddenly realised it was a place about which she had dreamt. The butler opened the door, and when he saw the lady he was so terrified that for a few moments he appeared almost paralysed. The lady, seeing his fright, asked what was the matter.

'Nothing,' replied the man, 'only you are the lady who
haunts this house.' "

The lady referred to in the magazine article was Mrs Emma Turner, the
great-grandmother of our friend, A.M.Turner. She lived from 1840 until 1917,
and her grave can still be seen in St Margaret's Church Cemetery in Lowestoft.
But her strange *deja vu* experiences with the house in Scotland, were by no
means her only contacts with the paranormal. She woke up one night to see her
father, who was the skipper of a trawler, standing in dripping oilskins at the foot
of her bed.

"My God, Emma, we're done!" he said in a sepulchral voice, then faded and
vanished. She woke her husband who tried to comfort her by suggesting that it
was only a bad dream. A day or so later, however, he came home looking very
grave. Before he could speak, Emma said, " I know what you're going to say —
my father's been drowned, hasn't he?" Her husband nodded and took her
comfortingly into his arms.

"They were run down in the channel by a much larger craft just at the time
you woke me," he said gently.

On another occasion, Emma dreamed that she was standing on some tall
and rather unusual cliffs. A thick mist rolled below them, and just above the
mist she could see the mast-tops of a large sailing ship, heading straight towards
the cliffs, and the jagged rocks below. She screamed loudly and saw the ship
veering away, back towards the open sea, just before she woke up. She told her
husband about it, and described the island and its peculiar cliffs in detail. "I
think I know where that might be," he said, and together they looked at some
of his marine maps and charts. He did a few quick navigational calculations and
realised that Jack Hellings, her brother in law, would have been in the area at
about that time. In view of her previous experiences, he made a careful note of
the time of her 'dream' and the probable position of Jack's ship.

They were very pleased and relieved to welcome Jack safely home again in
due course. His first words were: "I didn't think I'd ever see you again . . . "
Before letting him tell his story, they handed him the account of Emma's weird,
dream-like experience on the strange cliff top.

"We were a bit off course because of the fog," explained Jack, "and heading
for the rocks below the cliffs. We had no idea that we were so close until we
heard a woman screaming. We pulled the ship round just in time, and headed
back for open water."

The psychic gift in the Turner family was not restricted to Emma. Mr
Turner himself had a strange dream in which he found himself dressed in Naval
uniform and standing in a bus queue. Asked if he was waiting to go to his
submarine, he replied that he was, and was told that it was too late, as she had
already sailed without him. The dream was so powerful and vivid that he
remembers being worried about being court-martialled, and pacing the dark

streets wondering what to do to clear his name. During these wanderings, he met the same mysterious informant, who now told him that he was very fortunate as his sub had gone down and all on board had been lost. The following day a sub *was* lost with all hands in the Thames Estuary.

What sort of *connection* is there between experiences like those that Mr Turner and his great-grandmother had, and the events which happened to the Wroxham Broad witnesses, the ladies at Clava Cairns, Haddon Hall and Pyrford? If it is possible for some non-physical part of personal consciousness to travel practically instantaneously over large *spatial* distances, can it also travel through *time?* The problem, of course, about its travelling into the future, is that the future is almost certainly infinitely unresolved and flexible: at best, all that could be visited would be some of the amorphous future *alternatives*, parallel universes, or probability tracks. Perhaps that accounts for *some* visions of the future being fulfilled, whereas others are not.

Or is there a totally different solution — at least as far as revisiting *past* scenes is concerned? Do stone, metal, wood, soil and rock somehow absorb and record the dynamic vibrations of everything that happens around them — and within them — and then replay it to certain sensitive people, when external conditions are right?

Perhaps the most famous and puzzling time slip of all is the Versailles visit of "Miss Lamont and Miss Morison" as they called themselves in *An Adventure*, although their real names were Anne Moberley and Eleanor Jourdain. Anne was the Principal of St Hugh's College in Oxford; Eleanor was Head of a girls' school in Watford. In August, 1901, they were touring the Palace of Versailles, and had gone to have a short rest in the Galerie des Glaces. The windows were open, and the scent of the summer flowers induced them to venture out again and stroll towards the Petit Trianon. This was a small château, originally built on the orders of Louis the XV and given by Louis XVI to his Queen, Marie Antoinette.

In Anne and Eleanor's own account they walked for some distance down a wooded avenue and then reached the Grand Trianon, built by the illustrious Louis XIV, the "Sun King". Leaving this building to their left, they reached a wide, grassy drive. Not knowing their way, they crossed this drive and went down another lane to the side of it. Had they stayed on the grass drive, it would have led them straight to the Petit Trianon that they were looking for.

The first really strange anomaly that they encountered was a woman shaking a white cloth out of a window. Anne saw this woman quite clearly, and was a little surprised that Eleanor did not stop to ask her for directions to the Petit Trianon. It was only afterwards that Anne learnt from her friend that she had not seen the woman shaking the white cloth. More disturbingly, she had not even seen the *building* which contained the woman's window.

Up until this point, neither of the two English visitors realised that anything was at all odd or extraordinary. Turning right as they went past some buildings, they caught a brief glimpse of a carved staircase through a door which had been left open. Choosing the central path of the three which now lay in front of them, they met up with two men whom they described as working with a wheelbarrow and spade. Anne and Eleanor thought that they were gardeners, but were mildly puzzled by their unusual clothes — long, grey-green coats, and tricorn hats. The supposed gardeners pointed out the route straight ahead, and the two friends continued their walk.

It was from here onwards that they both began to feel inexplicably depressed — although neither told the other about it at the time. Another very odd factor was a subtle shift in the landscape itself. They described it as looking somehow *two* dimensional — as if they were walking on a stage with painted scenery all around them, instead of the normal, solid, three dimensional world.

These feelings grew steadily worse, and reached their nadir when Eleanor and Anne arrived at a circular garden kiosk, where a strange-looking man was resting. They both felt an instinctive fear and dislike of him, and refrained from passing the kiosk simply because that route would have taken them closer to him.

When running footsteps sounded behind them, they turned eagerly to welcome whoever the newcomer might turn out to be — only to discover that there was no one there. Anne, however, now saw someone else close to them, who had not been there before. They described him as looking refined: a tall man with big dark eyes, and curly black hair. He directed them to the house, but seemed to smile in an unusual way. When they looked back to call out their thanks for the directions he had given them, he was nowhere to be seen.

Once again, they heard the inexplicable running footsteps quite close to them, but look as they would for the runner, they could not see anyone.

Eventually reaching the Petit Trianon, Anne saw a woman sitting on the grass, apparently busily sketching. She seemed to look directly at the two English visitors as they walked by. Anne later described her in detail: she had a low-cut dress with a fichu neckline, luxuriant fair hair and a shady white hat. As she and Eleanor walked up on to the terrace, Anne felt as though she was walking in her sleep, or moving in a dazed, disconnected dreamlike state. When she saw the woman again it was from behind, and she felt glad that her companion had not paused to ask her the way. Once again, however, it was Anne alone who had seen the woman with the shady white hat: Eleanor had simply not observed her.

The next person they met — and both of them saw and heard him clearly — was a young footman, who asked if they would like him to show them the way round. A boisterous group of wedding guests came on the scene very soon afterwards, and Eleanor and Anne felt their inexplicable depression lifting.

Each wrote a separate and carefully detailed account of what they had seen and heard that day: and their experiences were by no means identical.

Eleanor was so intrigued by the whole affair that she made a second visit in

January of 1902, when several things in the area again seemed to have strange, unreal, almost haunting qualities — but the *details* were weird in slightly different ways.

Prolonged research into the strange experiences that Anne and Eleanor shared — and the acrimonious controversies that followed the publication of *An Adventure* — have never finally settled the question of what happened to them at Versailles. On balance, it is certainly possible that they experienced a genuine time-slip which enabled them to see and hear events from over a century in the past.

From Wroxham Broad, Lowestoft, Surrey, Derbyshire, Inverness, the outskirts of Paris — and hundreds of other sites — the evidence for time slips mounts steadily. The case may not yet be proven, but the strange nature of time and the possibility of irregularity — even *reversal* — in its behaviour would seem to suggest that it's as vulnerable to warps, rifts and unpredictable movements as is the seemingly stable earth's crust. By the end of the next millennium, timequakes may be as thoroughly understood as earthquakes are today.

It scarcely seems possible that the brilliantly imaginative and fearlessly controversial Sir James Jeans wrote *The Mysterious Universe* as long ago as 1930. Ranking alongside Einstein and Hawking, Jeans approaches the enigma of time as something central to our understanding of the universe as a whole — and humanity's place in it. If, as Jeans rightly argues, determinism and causation, are *not* as unalterable as the much vaunted "Laws of the Medes and the Persians", if they are not handed down to us like gold letters set into tablets of stone, then *why do things happen at all?*

In his own words:

> "If we, and nature in general, do not respond in a unique way to external stimuli, what determines the course of events? . . . we are unlikely to reach any definite conclusions on these questions until we have a better understanding of the true nature of time . . . It is the puzzle of the nature of time that brings our thoughts to a standstill."

WHERE DID
BEN BATHURST GO?
*He simply walked around the horses
and was never seen again.*

Young Benjamin Bathurst, born in 1784, was the third son of the then Bishop of Norwich, and an up and coming member of the British Diplomatic Service, when a mysterious tragedy overtook him on November 25th, 1809. He disappeared as suddenly and inexplicably as if he had been abducted by aliens, or taken like some medieval knight in a ballad into an enchanted faerie ring.

While still in his twenties, Bathurst was appointed as Envoy Extraordinary by the British Government with a special mission to the Court of Vienna. The main purpose of his trip was to try to persuade the Austrians to attack Napoleon from their side, while the British launched an attack through the Spanish Peninsula. This would have involved Napoleon in an unwelcome war on two fronts simultaneously, so that if French spies had discovered who Bathurst was and what he was up to they would have done everything possible to prevent it — including removing him.

In the Europe of 1809 transport systems were slow, chaotic and hazardous. Roads were atrocious. Bandits and spies abounded. Pack horses and ungainly carriages lumbered and lurched slowly and uncertainly towards their destinations.

Despite the problems, Bathurst reached Vienna safely, relayed his message, and started for home. All that the Austrians actually achieved on their front was an ineffectual skirmish or two with the French, followed by a heavy defeat at the Battle of Wagram — after which they didn't have too much interest in the British proposals which Bathurst had laid before them.

Ben's next problem was to select a safe route home which would avoid direct contact with the French. He decided to take the Berlin-Hamburg option and disguised himself as a travelling merchant using the assumed name of Koch. With a brace of pistols in his pockets, and a miniature arsenal hidden in the back of the coach, he set out with his valet and secretary.

They reported later that he had seemed nervous, stressed and depressed during the journey. He was evidently very frightened and anxious about something, and was behaving with unusual caution, like a trapped animal that senses the approach of a dangerous predator.

On November 25, 1809, Bathurst and his companions reached the little town of Perleberg, which lay on their direct route from Berlin to Hamburg. They stopped at the Post House to change horses, and explored the area for somewhere which could supply a meal. Two minutes walk from the Post House, along their road to Hamburg, and close to the town gates, stood the White Swan Inn. There were also a few small, run down houses and cottages nearby. The district had an unsavoury reputation. There were desperate criminals in the area who would have considered murdering a passer-by for the value of his coat.

Bathurst decided to eat at the White Swan, and ordered a meal for himself and his companions. Their later evidence showed that he seemed morose and quiet at this time. When he had finished eating, he asked the landlord who the local Police or Military Commander was in Perleberg and where he could be located. The landlord sent him to the home of Captain Klitzing, near the Town Hall.

When Bathurst arrived he told Klitzing that he had decided to stay overnight in Perleberg, at the White Swan, but that he felt himself to be in grave danger. He asked for a

Silhouette portrait of Bishop Henry Bathurst of Norwich, Norfolk, England, drawn in 1826. Bishop Bathurst was the father of Benjamin Bathurst, who vanished mysteriously in Perleberg.

(Kindly provided by Mr Neal Wood of St German's Church, Cardiff, Wales, UK.)

bodyguard of two troopers, which Klitzing — although rather sceptical — agreed to supply. The nearest French soldiers were in Magdeburg, and Klitzing did not really feel that a guard was necessary. Bathurst's agitation was such, however, that the Captain felt it best to humour him.

Back at the inn, Bathurst went to his room and locked himself in. He seems to have spent a long time there, writing letters and burning documents in the grate. His valet and secretary felt that he was working himself up into a mental illness of some kind. They were well aware at this time that he was terrified of *something*, but they could not discern what it was.

Bathurst suddenly changed his mind and decided during the early evening that it would be better to set out for Hamburg again that night after all — travelling through the relative obscurity and anonymity of darkness. It was a two-way argument: night held advantages for both hunters and their prey, but Bathurst felt that the balance lay just in favour of the prey. He gave the necessary orders and dismissed his two bodyguards. Fresh horses were supplied and Bathurst's luggage was taken out to the carriage. He himself waited impatiently, fidgeting nervously as the luggage was loaded, and the carriage prepared for the journey. The ostler held a horn lantern. A few lights shone out from the windows of the inn. There was a dim oil street lamp across the way. The total effect was gloomy and shadowy, even when eyes grew accustomed to it.

As soon as everything was ready, the valet stood by the door of the coach, waiting to help Bathurst inside. The secretary was just inside the open inn door, chatting convivially to the landlord, whose account he had just settled. Everyone was waiting for Bathurst to enter the carriage — *but he never did*. As far as the witnesses could tell, Bathurst simply walked around the horses *and was never seen again*.

They waited for a reasonable time and then went to see whether he had gone back to his room. He hadn't. Their next idea was that he had gone back to Captain Klitzing to request an armed escort all the way to Hamburg — or even that he'd changed his mind yet again and wanted the troopers back. But there was no sign of him at the Captain's house.

Klitzing himself went into action with great effectiveness. He impounded the carriage and luggage for safe-keeping until matters could be sorted out, then he transferred the valet and secretary to another inn, the Golden Crown, which was on the opposite side of the town. He placed a guard on their door — partly to protect them and partly to ensure that they didn't leave town without his express permission. Klitzing also posted a guard over the White Swan Inn.

At first light, he ordered a very thorough search, participating in it vigorously himself. In an age when unconcern, idleness, bribery, corruption and *laissez faire* were rife among people in authority, Captain Klitzing was a model of commitment, energy and efficiency. He and his men went through Perleberg like hungry ferrets in a rabbit warren. They searched everywhere they could think of, even dragging the river bed.

Because of some local political resentment from the civilian police chief and the Bürgomeister, Klitzing went directly to higher authority in Berlin for permission to take full charge of the case. His dynamic energy gave him the time to investigate the affairs of the police chief and the Bürgomeister as well as hunting for the missing British Diplomat. In due course both his opponents lost their offices: Klitzing was one of those characters who had a cutting edge as sharp as his sabre.

One of the theories relating to Bathurst's disappearance was that he had been targeted by a Napoleonic espionage agent, the Count d'Entraigues. If there had been such a plot, it would have seemed logical for the plotters to try to dispose of Klitzing as well because his exhaustive investigations would eventually have flushed them out. It is, therefore, significant that no record of any such attempt on the Captain's life exists. The word was undoubtedly out among the criminal fraternity that attempting to attack Klitzing would not be a good idea.

Questions to the landlord of the White Swan revealed that the only other guests on the night in question had been two Jewish merchants. Klitzing sent out orders that they were to be detained and questioned. This was done. Enquiries soon established that they were totally respectable citizens and beyond reproach. They were dropped from the case.

At one point, as well as dragging the River Stepnitz repeatedly, Klitzing pre-empted Sherlock Holmes and brought in bloodhounds — but they failed to trace the missing Englishman. However a rigorous house to house search produced Bathurst's expensive fur coat in the home of a dubious character named Augustus Schmidt. His mother was a servant at the White Swan, and Augustus himself had something of a reputation as a local hard man and petty criminal. Mrs Schmidt explained that she had found the coat and thought that it had probably belonged to one of the Jewish merchants. She had, she said, been keeping it in the hope that they would offer a reward for its return. According to the evidence of the valet and secretary, however, Bathurst had either left the coat accidentally at the Post House, or had been wearing it when they saw him for the last time before he disappeared. Klitzing saw to it that the Schmidts spent a few months in jail for their involvement with the hidden coat, but although Augustus could not give a satisfactory account of his whereabouts at the time when Bathurst had gone missing, there was not enough evidence to convict him of Bathurst's murder — especially as there was no body.

Clothing continued to feature prominently in the investigation: Ben's trousers were found in the forest by two women who were out gathering firewood. The trousers had bullet holes in them, but no bloodstains, and from the position of the holes it looked as if the trousers had been hung up on a line or tree branch and deliberately used as a target. The intriguing question is *why?* Was someone setting up the trousers as a red herring? The poverty which some sections of the community endured in Perleberg at that time would have made

Bathurst's good quality clothing relatively valuable, either to wear or sell. There was also a letter in Bathurst's writing in the pocket. This said that if anything happened to him the person responsible was the Count d'Entraigues, who was known to be a French secret agent. D'Entraigues himself was murdered not long afterwards, but not before he vehemently denied any knowledge of the Bathurst affair.

The official German line was that the French were almost certainly responsible. Almost all the Francophiles in or near Perleberg were duly interviewed, but no significant progress was made from those investigations. The generally accepted theory in Vienna was that Napoleon's agents were responsible, but as Bathurst was on his way home after a more or less failed diplomatic enterprise, they didn't have any motive except spite and revenge.

A press war between Britain and France was fought with a fury that rivalled the cavalry charges at Waterloo. The British press accused the French of murdering Bathurst for the lowest and meanest of reasons. The French press made scathing remarks about the lack of intelligence of the foppish young aristocrats who drifted into the British Diplomatic Service. Bathurst, they said, had a wholly erroneous concept of his own significance in the present European conflict, and was probably foolish enough to have committed suicide without realising what he was doing. In their opinion his exaggerated fears were a symptom of mental illness. This acrimonious battle of public words went on for some time.

The British Government offered £1000 reward — an immense sum in those days, and one which would have tempted almost any criminal or espionage agent to come forward with information. Bathurst's family added another £1000 — but still no information surfaced. Prince Frederick of Prussia was keenly interested in the Bathurst case, and he added yet another reward: but if anyone knew what had happened to Bathurst and who had been responsible they were either too terrified or too far above financial temptation to respond to the colossal sum now being offered.

Throughout the excitement aroused by these vast reward offers and all the furious Anglo-French press propaganda, Klitzing stuck resolutely to his theory that some local criminal, or criminals, were responsible. Possibly the Captain was so proud of his own efficiency and thoroughness that he could not bring himself to believe that the French would have contemplated pulling off such an abduction or murder within his territory. Klitzing went on chewing away remorselessly at Schmidt — and Klitzing had formidable investigative jaws. The Captain was very suspicious because Schmidt knew that Bathurst had possessed two pistols. Augustus explained this incriminating knowledge by saying that his mother had been sent out to buy powder for them while Bathurst and his party were at the White Swan.

More damning was the witness who testified that he had seen Bathurst walking up the alleyway in which the Schmidts' house stood. It was an odd piece of evidence. Bathurst would have had absolutely no reason to go anywhere as dangerous as that, and in his overwrought and anxious state of mind, the last thing he would have been likely to want was additional risk. Unless of course, Schmidt's mother had said in the White Swan that her son was a particularly tough character and might be available for hire as a minder on the journey to Hamburg.

Another line of investigation which Klitzing pursued vigorously concerned a local cobbler named Hacker, who was known to be a criminal associate of Schmidt's. This Hacker had left Perleberg almost immediately after Bathurst vanished, and had turned up in Altona shortly afterwards with more spending power than usual. It looked extremely suspicious — except that Bathurst was not in the habit of carrying money: his secretary attended to all that kind of work.

Klitzing weighed the available evidence — and lack of it — carefully, and reluctantly decided that however strong his hunch that Augustus Schmidt had murdered Bathurst, there wasn't enough to ensure a conviction. There were too many problems which a good defence lawyer would present to the Court on Schmidt's behalf. Firstly, how could Schmidt — or any other kidnapper or assassin — have taken Bathurst away so silently, and completely unobserved, when the area around the coach was full of witnesses? Secondly, what could the criminal have done with Bathurst as a live prisoner, or as a corpse? Every available hiding place that Klitzing and his men could think of had been thoroughly searched, and searched more than once. The river had been dragged repeatedly. If comparatively small items like Bathurst's coat and trousers had been located, how on earth could the criminals have hidden the Englishman's body so successfully?

When Hacker was interrogated, his wife made a statement saying that a man called Goldberger was the killer, but that 'evidence' led nowhere.

The Emperor Napoleon himself was approached by Bathurst's family but denied on his honour that he knew anything at all about the missing diplomat except what he had read in the papers.

Time passed.

On April 15, 1852 a house in Hamburg Road, scarcely 300 metres from the White Swan inn, was demolished. A skeleton was found in the rubble. It was male, and of approximately the right age and height for Bathurst. Whoever the skeleton belonged to had died from a fractured skull. Bathurst's sister, Mrs Thistlethwaite, bravely visited Perleberg to try to identify it but after lying concealed in the house for over forty years the remains were completely unrecognisable.

When the building was demolished it belonged to a stone-mason named Kiesewetter, who had bought it in 1834 from Christian Mertens Junior. He had inherited it from his father, Christian Mertens Senior, *who had once been a servant at the White Swan.*

Klitzing had not sent a search party to this particular house because Mertens had always enjoyed a blameless reputation and had not been under the slightest suspicion.

However, there had been considerable surprise in Perleberg when he endowed both his daughters with more money than any of their friends and neighbours thought possible out of his modest wages from the White Swan.

When Mrs Thistlethwaite came to write her book *Memoirs of Bishop Bathurst* she noted that Mertens had left his job at the inn not long after her brother vanished. She thought that he had been an ostler there, but other evidence suggests that he was once the 'boots'. As such, with necessary access to the guests and their rooms, his opportunity to commit the crime would have been greater than if he had been one of the outside staff looking after the horses.

In fact, if Bathurst's stolen coat had been inadvertently left in his room in the White Swan, rather than at the Post House, a whole new hypothesis opens up. We were lecturing on Bathurst's disappearance as part of a week-end seminar on Unsolved Mysteries at Holt Hall in Norfolk, UK , when one of the most ingenious theories we've yet heard about the Perleberg tragedy was put forward by our good friend, Peter Grehan, who was attending the seminar. Peter was particularly interested in the details of Bathurst's highly significant coat. His suggestion was that Bathurst was able to vanish so suddenly, silently and inexplicably *because the figure in the coat who 'walked around the horses' was not Bathurst.* If it can be assumed that whatever tragedy overtook young Benjamin happened to him while he was still in his room, and that he was killed or overpowered there by a combination of Mertens, Schmidt and Hacker, then two of the killers took him out the back way, unobserved, while the third man — most likely Mertens, strolled nonchalantly around the horses in the gloom — *and walked away into the night.* A few hours afterwards, the coat was given to Mrs Schmidt to conceal and sell later when the furore had died down. The dead man's trousers were taken into the woods, and his pistols discharged through them as they hung over a branch. The killers had read the letter in the pocket accusing the Count d'Entraigues — if Bathurst's bullet-riddled clothing was found along with that letter, it would, they hoped, divert the search away from their own criminal fraternity of Perleberg.

We are left with four basic theories about Bathurst's disappearance. He was so mentally disturbed that he committed suicide somewhere and his body was never discovered. He was robbed and murdered by Schmidt, Hacker or Mertens — or a combination of all three. The Count d'Entraigues or some other French agents killed or abducted him. The British Secret Service gave him a new identity and a new mission elsewhere, for reasons known only to themselves.

The Bathurst tragedy needs to be considered in conjunction with other unexplained disappearances, if it is to be seen in perspective. There are *thousands* of disappearances every year. There is a frequently used Internet site today: *http://www.unsolved.com/oconnell.html.* It helps to trace missing persons. It has a fair degree of success in finding some of them, but even today, in a world of high speed electronic communications such as Klitzing's Perleberg team never dreamed of, a great many people vanish as mysteriously and completely as Benjamin Bathurst did.

In 1880 a strange hoax centred on the alleged disappearance of David Lang of Sumner County, Tennessee, who was said to have vanished in full view of his wife and some other witnesses. A mysterious circle on the ground was alleged to have marked the place where he disappeared, and his children were supposed to have said that when they stood within it they *thought* they could hear their father's distressed voice calling for help. However, the brilliant and experienced investigator, Colin Wilson, carried out some detailed research via a colleague on site and discovered that although the Lang story was false, it was based on a historical account of a similar and genuine disappearance which took place in 1854 and was recorded by Robert Jay Nash. This one took place in Selma, Alabama. The victim was a farmer named Orion Williamson, who literally vanished into the air while two of his friends were riding towards him in a buggy. Professor George A. Simcox, who was a Senior Fellow of Queen's College, Oxford, went for a walk in County Antrim and was never seen again. In 1913 Ambrose Bierce, the author, vanished. Persistent rumours suggested that it had happened in Mexico, but the mystery was never satisfactorily cleared up. Victor Grayson, the MP, apparently walked out of existence in 1920. Reginald Arthur Lee, a Diplomat like Bathurst, was serving in Marseilles in 1930 when he also disappeared. Another tragic disappearance episode centred on seven-year-old Denis Martin. He vanished in full view of his father and other adult witnesses in the summer of 1969 while they were walking together in the Great Smoky Mountains.

That diligent collector of bizarre tales, Charles Fort, also amassed a huge collection of unexplained disappearances.

Wherever Benjamin Bathurst went it is safe to assume that he is not alone there!

BIBLIOGRAPHY

Andere, Mary. *Arthurian Links with Herefordshire.* Great Britain. Logaston Press. 1995

Ashe, Geoffrey. Editor. *The Quest for Authur's Britain.* London. Granada Publishing. 1972

Bord, Janet & Colin. *Alien Animals.* London. Granada Publishing. 1980

Bord, Janet & Colin. *Mysterious Britain.* Great Britain. Paladin. 1974

Bradley, Michael. *Holy Grail Across the Atlantic.* Toronto. Hounslow Press. 1988

Briggs, Katharine M. *British Folk Tales and Legends: A Sampler.* London. Granada Publishing in Paladin. 1977

Brown, Michael. Editor. *A Book of Sea Legends.* England. Puffin Books. 1975

Brown, Theo. *Devon Ghosts.* Great Britain. Jarrold Publishing. 1982

Canning, John, Editor. *50 Great Ghost Stories.* London. Chancellor Press. 1994

Carrington, Richard. *Mermaids and Mastodons.* London. Arrow Books Ltd. 1960

Carter, MA George, *Outlines of English History.* London & Melbourne. Ward Lock Educational Company Ltd. 1962

Cavendish, Richard. Editor. *Encyclopedia of The Unexplained.* London. Routledge & Kegan Paul. 1974

Clark, Jerome, *Unexplained.* USA. Gale Research Inc. 1993

Dunford, Barry. *The Holy Land of Scotland.* Scotland. Brigadoon Books. 1996

Dyall, Valentine. *Unsolved Mysteries.* London. Hutchinson & Co Ltd. 1954

Ehrlich, Eugene, *A Dictionary of Latin Tags and Phrases.* London. Robert Hale Ltd. 1986

Enterline, James Robert. *Viking America.* Great Britain. New English Library 1973

Fanthorpe, Lionel & Patricia. *The Oak Island Mystery.* Toronto. Hounslow Press. 1995

Fanthorpe, Lionel & Patricia. *Secrets of Rennes le Château.* USA. Samuel Weiser Inc. 1992

Fanthorpe, Lionel & Patricia. *Rennes-Le-Château.* England. Bellevue Books. 1991

Fortean Times. London. John Brown Publishing Ltd.

Fowke, Edith. *Canadian Folklore.* Toronto. Oxford University Press Ontario. 1988

Gant, T.H. & Copley, W.L. *More Dartmoor Legends and Customs.* Plymouth. Baron Jay Ltd. Publishers.

Gettings, Fred. *Encyclopedia of the Occult.* London. Guild Publishing. 1986

Godwin, John, *This Baffling World.* New York City. Hart Publishing Company, 1968

Goldsmith, Oliver. *A History of the Earth and Animated Nature.* Edinburgh. Thomas Nelson. 1842

Graves, Robert. Introduction By. *Larousse Encyclopedia of Mythology.* London. Paul Hamlyn. 1959

Green, John. *On the Track of the Sasquatch.* New York. Ballantine Books. 1973

Green, John Richard. *A Short History of the English People.* London. MacMillan & Co. 1878

Gribble, Leonard. *Famous Historical Mysteries.* London. Target Books. 1974

Harmon, J.F. (Ed.) *Concerning the Carvings on the Braxton and Yarmouth Stones.* West Virginia History. USA Vol. XXXVII Jan. 1976

Hancock, Graham. *The Sign and the Seal.* London. Mandarin. 1993

Hancock, Graham. *Fingerprints of the Gods.* New York. Crown Publishers. 1995

Hapgood, Charles, *Maps of the Ancient Sea Kings.* USA. Adventure Unlimited Press. 1996

Heywood, Abel. *Mother Shipton's Prophecies.* U.K. George Mann. 1978

Hitching, Francis. *The World Atlas of Mysteries.* London. Pan Books. 1979

Hogarth, Peter & Clery, Val. *Dragons.*
London. Penguin Books Ltd. 1979
Hogue, John. *Nostradamvs & The Millennivm.*
New York. Doubleday Dolphin. 1987

Knight, Gareth. *The Secret Tradition in
Arthurian Legend.* Great Britain. The
Aquarian Press. 1983

Lacy, N. J. *The Arthurian Encyclopedia.*
Woodbridge, Suffolk, U.K. Boydell Press.
1986
Lampitt, L.F. Editor. *The World's Strangest
Stories.* London. Published by Associated
Newspapers Group Ltd. 1955

MacDougall, Curtis D. *Hoaxes.* New York.
Dover Publications, Inc. 1958
Mahan, Joseph B. *North American Sun Kings.*
USA. ISAC Press 1992
Maziére, Francis. *Mysteries of Easter Island.*
New York. Tower Publications Inc. 1968
Metcalfe, Leon. *Discovering Ghosts.* U.K. Shire
Publications Ltd. 1974
Michell, John. & Rickard, Robert J.M.
Phenomena A Book of Wonders. London.
Thames & Hudson 1977
Morison, Elizabeth & Lamont, Frances. *An
Adventure.* London. MacMillan & Co.,
Ltd. 1913
Moss, Peter, *Ghosts Over Britain.* Great
Britain. Sphere Books Ltd. 1979

Newton, Brian. *Monsters and Men.* England.
Dunestone Printers Ltd. 1979

Pohl, Frederick J. *Prince Henry Sinclair.*
Halifax. Nimbus Publishing Ltd. 1967
Poole, Keith B. *Ghosts of Wessex.* England.
David & Charles Ltd. 1976
Porter, Enid. *The Folklore of East Anglia.*
London. B.T. Batsford Ltd. 1974

Rawcliffe, D.H. *Illusions and Delusions of the
Supernatural and the Occult.* New York.
1959
Reader's Digest Book. *Strange Stories, Amazing
Facts.* London. The Reader's Digest Ass.
Ltd. 1975
Reader's Digest Book. *Folklore, Myths and
Legends of Britain.* London. The Reader's
Digest Ass. Ltd. 1973

Saltzman, Pauline. *The Strange and the
Supernormal.* New York. Paperback Library,
Inc. 1968
Sampson, Chas. *Ghosts of the Broads.*
Norwich. Jarrold & Sons Ltd. 1973
Sinclair, Andrew. *The Sword and the Grail.*
New York. Crown Publishers Inc. 1992
Snow, Edward Rowe. *Strange Tales from
Nova Scotia to Cape Hatteras.* New York. Dodd,
Mead & Company. 1946
Spicer, Stanley, T. *The Saga of the Mary
Celeste.* Nova Scotia. Lancelot Press Ltd.
1993
Strong, Roy. *Lost Treasures of Britain.* USA.
Viking Penguin. 1990

Toulson, H. David. *Knaresborough. It's Murder,
Mystery & Magic.* Leeds. Yorkshire Press
Agency. 1991
Trevelyan, George Macaulay. *History of
England.* London. Longmans, Green and
Co. Ltd. 1926
Turner, Dr. Maurice. *A Brief History of
Knaresborough.* North Yorkshire. The
Bookshop 14, High St.. 1990

Underwood, Peter. *The Ghost Hunter's Guide.*
U.K. Blandford Press. 1987

Whitehead, Ruth Holmes. *Stories From The
Six Worlds.* Halifax. Nimbus Publishing
Ltd. 1988
Wilson, Colin & Damon. *Unsolved Mysteries.*
London. Headline Book Publishing plc.
1993
Wilson, Colin, Damon & Rowan. *World
Famous True Ghost Stories.* London.
Robinson Publishing. 1996
Wilson, Colin & Dr. Evans, Christopher,
(Editors). *The Book of Great Mysteries.*
London. Robinson Publishing. 1986
Wilson, Derek. *The World Atlas of Treasure.*
London. Pan Books 1982
Wise, Leonard F. *World Rulers.* England.
Sterling Pub. Co. Inc. 1967

X Factor. London Marshall Cavendish
Partworks Ltd.

INDEX